DATE DUE

DE 20 '96			
JY 2 '97			
AP 8 '99			

IRA GERSHWIN

IRA GERSHWIN

The Art of the Lyricist

Philip Furia

OXFORD UNIVERSITY PRESS
New York   Oxford
1996

Oxford University Press

Oxford   New York
Athens   Auckland   Bangkok   Bombay
Calcutta   Cape Town   Dar es Salaam   Delhi
Florence   Hong Kong   Istanbul   Karachi
Kuala Lumpur   Madras   Madrid   Melbourne
Mexico City   Nairobi   Paris   Singapore
Taipei   Tokyo   Toronto
and associated companies in
Berlin   Ibadan

Copyright © 1996 by Philip Furia

Published by Oxford University Press, Inc.
198 Madison Avenue, New York, New York 10016

Library of Congress Cataloging-in-Publication Data
Furia, Philip, 1943–
Ira Gershwin: the art of the lyricist/Philip Furia.
p.   cm.   Includes bibliographical references and index.
ISBN 0-19-508299-0
1. Gershwin, Ira, 1896–1983.
2. Lyricists—United States—Biography.
I. Title.
ML423.G334F87   1995
782.1'4'092—dc20
[B]   94-45715

Since this page cannot legibly accommodate the acknowledgments,
pages 259–268 constitute an extension of the copyright page.

9 8 7 6 5 4 3 2 1

Printed in the United States of America
on acid-free paper

Preface

This book developed quite naturally from *The Poets of Tin Pan Alley: A History of America's Great Lyricists* (Oxford, 1990). In that book I surveyed the lyricists of what has been called the "golden age" of American songwriting—Irving Berlin, Lorenz Hart, Cole Porter, Ira Gershwin, Dorothy Fields, and many others—concentrating on the poetic qualities of their greatest songs, the "standards" that seem as fresh today as when they were first popular. Even as I worked on that book, I realized that another approach to this great era would be to focus on a single lyricist, taking all of his songs from classic standards to the least known gems, and trace the growth of his art against the historical background of developments in the American musical theater, Hollywood musicals, and the commercial song industry then known as Tin Pan Alley.

As I considered such an approach, the lyricist who so obviously came to mind was Ira Gershwin. Unlike Irving Berlin and Cole Porter, who wrote both words and music for their songs, Ira Gershwin was exclusively devoted to the art of the lyricist. That art, as I try to show in this book, is a poetic art, but unlike poetry in that words must be intimately wedded to music. That intricate connection makes it impossible to discuss the art of the lyricist apart from that of the composer, particularly in the songs that Ira Gershwin wrote with his brother George. The Gershwin brothers not only worked but lived side by side, and, while songs usually started with George's musical ideas, it is evident that they were written in a give-and-take of accent and rhythm, phrase and cadence, syllable and note. Over the years, their collaboration grew as intertwined as the brothers' lives and produced a body of work in which words and music coalesce into a seamless artistic whole. George Gershwin has long had and continues to receive his rightful acclaim for his contribution to that work; this book, I hope, will add to the recognition that is equally his brother's due.

Although we most often associate him with George Gershwin's music, Ira Gershwin also collaborated with virtually every other great composer of his time—Vincent Youmans, Harold Arlen, Jerome Kern, Kurt Weill, Burton Lane, Aaron Copland, and Arthur Schwartz. Where other great lyricists, such as Lorenz Hart, worked almost exclusively with one composer, Ira Gershwin's versatility in adjusting to the demands of a variety of musical styles gives the fullest perspective on the craft of the lyricist. Ira Gershwin was also one of the few lyricists of his time to write with equal success on Broadway and in Hollywood. Whether writing for the stage or for film, moreover, he increasingly sought to integrate his lyrics into characters and dramatic context, making him a central figure in the major transformation of the musical during his lifetime. In this book, accordingly, I concentrate not only on the poetic quality of his lyrics but on their relation to the dramatic moment out of which they emerge in a musical show or film. Of all the lyricists of his age, finally, Ira Gershwin left the fullest record of manuscripts, commentary, and other materials germane to the art of lyric-writing, as well as to that art's relation to poetry.

Through the kind assistance of the Ira and Leonore Gershwin Trusts I have been able to examine that body of material. I want to thank Mark Trent Goldberg, Executive Director of the Trusts, and those who helped me at various Gershwin archives: Raymond White at the Library of Congress; Marty Jacobs at the Museum of the City of New York; and Cathy Henderson at the Harry Ransom Research Center of the University of Texas. Robert Kimball, Edward Jablonski, and Lawrence D. Stewart shared their knowledge of the Gershwins with me, including their personal reminiscences of Ira; their generosity, sensitivity, and astuteness gave me some sense of what Ira Gershwin himself must have been like among friends.

My own friends and colleagues, Marty Roth, George T. Wright, and Michael Hancher, read versions of this book and responded with the same kind of insight, criticism, and enthusiasm that stamps their own books. Other friends read the manuscript and offered their own special insights—Brian Kent, a former student who, together with Marsha Hunter, performs the songs of the Gershwins and others with unparalleled excellence; Tony Hill, an aficionado of Irving Berlin, who is indefatigable in promoting my research on American song; Les Block, my favorite pianist, who included me in his show on the Gershwins and helped me prepare a script that became the germ for this book. Karen Johnson Furia read the original manuscript and offered excellent editorial suggestions, as well as the support and encouragement she has given to my work for many years.

In the earliest stages of my research I was ably assisted by Marianne Ahokas, a graduate student at the University of Minnesota, who painstakingly surveyed critical reviews of all Gershwin shows. Another graduate student, Michael Eldridge, ferreted out new and obscure recordings of shows and songs. Laurie Patterson assisted me with archival research and gave an astute editorial reading of the final version of the manuscript before it went to press. Others who love these songs kindly offered recordings, sheet music, research material, and relevant information: Arthur Geffen, Louis Aborn, Ken Carley, Dick Carson, Ted Roberts, Rosemary Hanes, Sally Leach, and Jack Rosner. My research was also supported by the Bush Foundation, the McKnight Foundation, and the Graduate School, the College of Liberal Arts, and the Department of English at the University of Minnesota. I also want to thank Dennis Cass, of the Lazear Literary Agency, for his work in seeing this book through to publication, and Leona Capeless and Joellyn Ausanka for their thorough editing of the manuscript. Sheldon Meyer, Vice President of Oxford University Press, has supported this book from its inception; I hope that it furthers his longstanding celebration of American popular song. A final acknowledgment goes to a great lyricist of more recent years, Sammy Cahn, who took an interest in my research, corresponded with me, and discussed his special art with me over the phone. Although we never managed to meet before he died, he taught me a great deal about his—and Ira Gershwin's—craft.

CONTENTS

IRA GERSHWIN

1

BidiN' My TiME
1896–1917

Ira was the shyest, most diffident boy we had ever known.
In a class of lower east side rapscallions, his soft-spoken
gentleness and low-keyed personality made him a lovable
incongruity. He spoke in murmurs, hiding behind a pair of
steel-rimmed spectacles . . . Ira had a kid brother who wore
high stiff collars, shirts with cuffs and went out with girls.
—E. Y. "Yip" Harburg

ONE day in 1910 a second-hand piano was delivered to the Gershvin residence—evidently to their Second Avenue apartment in Manhattan, but it is difficult to be sure, since the Gershvins were a peripatetic family, changing homes some twenty times before their children had grown up. What kept the family on the move was Morris Gershvin, who kept changing his business—from a bakery to a restaurant to a cigar store, then a pool hall, a Turkish bath, even a bookmaking parlor. Since he liked to walk to work, the family residence changed with each new enterprise. A whimsical family, the Gershvins also liked to change their names. Upon arriving in America from Russia, Morris Gershvin changed his name from Moishe Gershovitz, and when his wife Rose (born Rosa Bruskin) bore a son on December 6, 1896, they named him Israel—but always called him Izzy. By the time he was old enough to ask what his real name was, Rose and Morris had forgotten. Years later, when he applied for a passport, "Izzy" found out his name was not "Isidore," as he had assumed, but "Israel." By then, however, he had long since gone by the name "Ira."

The piano was for Ira, the Gershvins' bookish and quiet son, who in 1910 earned a place in Townsend Harris Hall, a high school open to the brightest offspring of the teeming Lower East Side. Not content to rely on Ira's academic promise, the Gershvins, like many immigrant families, saw musical training as another step that would make the ladder of success one rung easier. With what trepidation the fourteen-year-old must have watched as the piano was hoisted up alongside the apartment building then eased through the second-story window into the Gershvins' "front room." Before Ira could be escorted to it, however, his younger brother, George (whose birth name was Jacob), rushed to the keyboard and, miraculously it seemed, banged out a popular song of the day. The miracle was soon explained by the fact that George had secretly learned to play on a friend's player piano. Miracle enough for Rose and Morris, since George's only other accomplishments had been in roller-skating and street-fighting. The trick worked—George got the lessons and Ira got to go back to his books.

If the piano tale marks George as his mother's son—aggressive, impulsive, flamboyant—it also reveals that Ira inherited something of his father's reticence and taciturnity. As S. N. Behrman, a lifelong friend, recalled, "the difference in the personalities of the two brothers was striking":

> If George was streamlined and propulsive, Ira was reserved and scholarly. He was gently humorous. One sensed in Ira even at the very center of involvement, a well of detachment. George gave you everything at once; he was boyish, with an extraordinarily sweet character. He wanted his listeners to participate in the excitement of his own development.[1]

The brothers' contrasting personalities would later prove perfectly suited to the craft of songwriting, where, to answer that perennial question, the musical idea usually came first. "I hit on a new tune," George once explained with characteristic gusto, and "play it for Ira and he hums it all over the place for a while till he gets an idea for a lyric. Then we work the thing out together."[2] Their sister, Frances, the last surviving member of the family, painted their work habits in more detail. George, she recalled, would

> write a song sometimes in just a few minutes. There were very few things he would have to struggle over . . . he had no routine. He'd go to the piano after breakfast and a few songs would happen. He'd suddenly play something and say, "This is a nice phrase," and he would develop it. It all came so easily to him. Ira, on the other hand, was a perfectionist. He would work all night on one word sometimes.

Ira's tortoise-like pace was not just a reflection of his personality but an indication of how difficult it was to find syllables, words, and phrases to match George's music. Where composers such as Jerome Kern and Richard Rodgers gave their lyricists long and flowing melodic lines that provided ample space for lyrical development, George Gershwin strove for what he termed "*staccato* effects" and a "stencilled style."[3] His melodies consisted of abrupt, angular phrases that gave a lyricist, as Ira himself put it, little room to "turn around." In "Embraceable You," for example (a song frequently cited as the perfect match of words to music), George rattled off a percussive string of repeated notes that so daunted Ira he checked into a hotel room for three days to find words to fit them. What he finally came up with, "Come to papa, come to papa do!," gave "Embraceable You" the rhythmic kick that is the "hallmark"[4] of a Gershwin song. Ira's phrase also delighted Morris Gershvin, who regularly demanded that his sons "play the song about me," proudly thumping his chest and beaming at what he took to be the paternal allusion.

Ira, understandably, compared the art of lyric writing to that of creating a mosaic, carefully choosing the precise verbal shard to fit into each jagged musical space his brother provided. The meticulous artistry with which he selected and polished those vernacular facets would soon earn Ira Gershwin the nickname, among songwriters, of "The Jeweller." Yet it was not only Ira's skill at matching syllables to notes that produced the Gershwins' exquisite songs. Song, as Ira was fond of saying, quoting the *Encyclopedia Britannica*, is a "joint art of words and music, two arts, under emotional pressure, coalescing into a third."[5] If the secret to a Rodgers and Hart song is the sweet-sour blend of sumptuous melody and unsentimental, even acerbic lyrics, then in a Gershwin song it is the way George's sensuous, driving energy is tempered (but never blunted) by Ira's urbanely innocent wit. Ira might at first give free rein to George's ardent insistence—fitting the abrupt notes that open a melody with

—Em-brace me!

However, when George aggressively reworks that phrase, Ira turns wryly playful:

My sweet embrace-
-able you!

With their fusion of passionate energy and laconic wit, the songs of George and Ira Gershwin are distinctively individual creations, standing out in a popular medium whose products are often indistinguishable one from the other.

In achieving that distinction, the Gershwins joined Richard Rodgers and Lorenz Hart, E. Y. "Yip" Harburg and Harold Arlen, Cole Porter, and other composers and lyricists of what has been called the "golden age" of American song. In that era between World Wars I and II, American popular song radiated the casual elegance, literate wit, and stylish verve that distinguish the literature of the period as a whole. Like the novels of F. Scott Fitzgerald or the poetry of e.e. cummings, the songs of the Gershwin brothers embody the style of the "Jazz Age." Just as George Gershwin surpassed all other composers in wedding European classical traditions to the African-American strains of blues and jazz, Ira Gershwin was attuned to the tradition of English lyric poetry but also sought to capture the way Americans "spoke to each other—their slang, their clichés, their catchphrases."[6] "Embraceable You," for example, reflects the 1920s penchant for suffixes among the new breed of "ad men" as well as Fitzgerald's teenagers, who swoon over each other's "kissable" mouths. With his brother's idiomatic music to inspire him, Ira Gershwin, more than any of his contemporaries, took the American vernacular and made it sing.

Not only was he the perfect artistic complement to his brother, Ira's personality was ideally suited to the subordinate role of the lyricist in American songwriting. Although critics may affirm that, in song, words and music must join "in a true marriage of equal partners,"[7] the lyricist has always had to assume the traditional role of the self-effacing wife. The frustration many lyricists felt is reflected in a famous comment by a real-life wife, Mrs. Oscar Hammerstein. After years of hearing people refer to "Ol' Man River" as a great "Kern" song, Mrs. Hammerstein finally snapped, "Jerome Kern did not write 'Ol' Man River.' Mr. Kern wrote, *dum, dum, dum, da*. My husband wrote *Ol' Man River*."

Yet Ira Gershwin, who sometimes had to endure references to "George and his lovely wife, Ira," was perfectly content to be "the other Gershwin." S. N. Behrman recalled how

> at the Gershwin parties, with everyone spellbound around the piano, while George was playing and singing Ira's lyrics, I would steal a look at Ira, standing on the outskirts of the crowd, a small, benignant smile on his face, stirred to happiness by the effect his brother was creating. That they were his lyrics George was singing was, to him, peripheral. He was under the spell of his brother's overwhelming personality, as the rest of us were.[8]

Never ceasing to admire the ease with which George could sit down at the piano, seemingly to amuse himself, then produce brilliant compositions, Ira Gershwin always regarded George as the consummate genius, himself as the loyal helpmate. When Behrman once told him, " 'You know, Ira, you are every bit as good as George,' Ira shook his head. 'No,' he said, 'George was more original.' "

While Ira marvelled at George's fecundity and originality, he also helped harness and direct it. During their collaboration "many little musical figures, and ideas, which in passing George might have tossed aside, were held onto because Ira caught them and pinned them down with words that could sing well and have meaning."[9] From their earliest days, Ira's success in school and his facility with language prompted his immigrant parents to designate him as the family representative who conferred with teachers and principals about George's behavior problems. George Gershwin always spoke, with some awe, of "my brother Ira, the scholar." According to lyricist Yip Harburg, a friend since childhood, George "looked to Ira for guidance, for critical evaluation, for taste." His respect for Ira was "lifelong, profound and of the greatest significance . . . When Ira failed to nod, George would attack the keyboard with renewed dynamic vigor, until he met Ira's intransigent demands."[10]

Before their contrasting personalities coalesced into percussive chords and whimsical words, George and Ira moved to different rhythms. George, with his usual fervor, plunged directly into a career in music. After a few years of studying classical piano and composition, he was confident enough of his future in popular song to quit high school and, at age fifteen, go to work on Tin Pan Alley, the sheet-music publishing industry centered on West 28th Street. Starting as a lowly plugger at the Jerome Remick Company, he demonstrated the firm's latest wares all day long for vaudeville performers in search of new material. Even then, however, his sights were set on songwriting, and, in 1916, he sold his first song to an Alley publisher. Its catchy bugle-call melody was reminiscent of "Alexander's Ragtime Band," the 1911 hit by his idol Irving Berlin. Unfortunately, George's lyricist, Murray Roth, violated the Alley maxim that, for a song to sell, it needed a short, memorable title—one that could be repeated frequently throughout the refrain (so listeners would remember it when they went to buy the sheet-music). "When You Want 'Em, You Can't Get 'Em, When You Got 'Em, You Don't Want 'Em" earned George no royalties, but did establish him as a composer; he rechristened himself George "Gershwin," and the entire Gershvin family followed suit.

Ira's course, typically, was as aimless as George's was direct. In what he called his "peregrinatory Manhattan boyhood," his wanderings enabled him to absorb the sights, smells, and, above all, the language of the polyglot city.

> The horse-drawn street cars on Delancey Street, their stoves hot in winter; the trips with other kids to Chinatown to buy sugar cane at about a cent a foot; learning to swim in the mucky Harlem River; picking up some Italian phrases to serve as passwords in case you were ganged up on around Mulberry Street (a ploy which sometimes worked—if it didn't you got at least a sock on the jaw and ran like hell).[11]

Proudly he recalled how at twelve he was deemed not the "smartest boy" in his class but "the best informed about New York" and was therefore chosen to lead a class expedition through lower Manhattan. "No question," he told himself late in life, "you were—first and last—a New Yorker."

New York, particularly in those early years of the century, was a city of words, and Ira not only absorbed the language of the streets, he read avidly. By his own admission, however, he read "without plan or purpose."[12] He first discovered books at

> the laundry with a two-cent lending library side-line (in the back a wooden bench with three or four piles of nickel novels to exchange: the *Young Wild West*, *Pluck and Luck*, *Fred Fearnot*, and *Liberty Boys of '76* series); then the discovery of the public library, and the first book you took out was one on Thackeray's contributions to *Punch*.[13]

That first library loan is significant, since what William Makepeace Thackeray contributed to *Punch*, along with satirical sketches and cartoons, was light or "society" verse. Thackeray may have sparked Ira's lifelong interest in light verse with such elegant irreverence as

> Spitting is a nasty thing,
> Which French people do.
> Little Lordling, don't begin
> Expectorating too.

By the time Ira was in high school, light verse had become his passion as much as music was George's. The high school curriculum in those days stressed a "rigorous training in classical poetic forms." "We were well-versed," a classmate recalled, "in the ballad, the triolet, the rondo, the villanelle, the sonnet. We were highly disciplined. We were never permitted to use an oricular rhyme or a tonal rhyme like *home* and *tone*."[14]

"In my late teens," Ira recalled, "I fooled around with French verse forms, such as the triolet, villanelle, and especially the rondeau—with its opening phrase taking on new meanings when repeated."[15] Writing poems such as "Rondeau to Rosie," as he himself observed, later helped him in writing song lyrics:

> My Rosie knows the places where
> One goes to lose all trace of care:
>   The ultra swagger cabaret . . .
>   The crystal chandeliered cafe . . .
> And oh, she knows the waiters there.
> Her wink will fetch from magic lair
> A bottle of a vintage rare . . .
>   And potent beer? Hot dog! I'll say
>   My Rosie knows!
>
> Without my Rosie, I declare
> I'd plumb the depths of dark despair.
>   To her I dedicate this lay;
>   To her I owe my spirits gay,
> My smiling mien, my cheerful air,
>   My rosy nose.

Just as he turned the title phrase "my Rosie knows" on its head in a rondeau, he could conclude a song lyric such as "But Not for Me" with an even cleverer twist:

> The climax of a plot
> should be the marriage knot—
> but there's no knot for me.

As a lyricist, he found that the hardest part of his task was to find a title phrase; once he got his title—often "from thin air, figuratively and literally . . . by listening to the argot in everyday conversation,"[16] he usually jumped "to the last line" of the melody and tried "to work the title in again; with a twist, if possible"—the kind of witty turnaround characteristic of light verse.

Ira's apprenticeship in light verse extended well beyond the schoolroom, however. Poetry, in those years, was everywhere, it seemed—even in the daily newspaper. All the big New York papers carried regular columns devoted to light verse; F. P. A.'s (Franklin Pierce Adams) "The Conning Tower" in *The New York World* was the most famous, but there was also Don Marquis's "Sun Dial" in the *Sun* and C. L. Edson's "Always In Good Humor" in *The Daily Mail*. In such columns, amateur

as well as professional versifiers, usually employing a clever pseudonym, could flaunt their mastery of the intricacies of meter and rhyme
while skewering some contemporary topic or burlesquing a traditional
poetic theme. Writing under the name of "Dotty," Dorothy Parker could
deftly (and daftly) sing:

> Oh, life is a glorious cycle of song,
>   A medley of extemporanea;
> And love is a thing that can never go wrong;
>   And I am Marie of Roumania.[17]

Light verse wasn't confined to these columns, however; from front
page to back one could encounter a theater review done completely in
quatrains or, turning to the sports page, find Grantland Rice writing
up baseball scores and prognostications in couplets.

Beginning in 1908, Ira would cut out his favorite poems and paste
them in scrapbooks, and he even put out his own one-page weekly,
The Leaf. In high school, he met Yip Harburg, who shared his love of
light verse and would go on to craft witty lyrics for such musicals as
Finian's Rainbow. "We were living," Harburg recalled, "in a time of
literate revelry in the New York daily press—F.P.A., Russel Crouse,
Don Marquis, Alexander Woollcott, Dorothy Parker, Bob Benchley. We
wanted to be part of it."[18] Seated near each other alphabetically, the
two boys discovered they shared not only a love for light verse but a
distaste for algebra. In what Yip termed an "antidote to the boredom
of mathematics," they started their own column, "The Daily Pass-It."
Printing the column on Townsend Harris Hall toilet paper ("to make
it real establishment stuff"), they would circulate poems and cartoons
surreptitiously around the room. Soon they had a more official column,
"Much Ado," in the school newspaper, where they satirized their teachers and classmates in quatrains.

In 1914, when "Gersh" and "Yip" went on to the City College of
New York, they continued the column as "Gargoyle Gargles" in the
campus newspaper. While most of their verse was topical humor, one
of Ira's poems from 1915 conjures up the way the Gershwin apartment
must have sounded ever since the day George first sat down at the piano:

> I remember, I remember
>   Those peaceful happy times
> When we heard no music other
>   Than distant church-bell chimes.
> That picture cannot now be drawn;

> The flat wherein we dwell
> Alas! Of late it has become
> A throbbing torture cell.
>
> I remember, I remember
>   The time when peace prevailed;
> When no budding prima donna
>   Above "Lucia" wailed;
> When the tenants living near us
>   No phonograph did own,
> To drive me to insanity
>   With its metallic tone.
>
> I remember, I remember
>   When no infernal chump
> On a pianola, down below
>   Both day and night would pump.
> Someone next door the bugle flares
>   He's blowing himself pink . . .
> They're all to music taken, Woe!
>   I think I'll take to drink.

Beneath the comic despair, one can hear a note here of Ira's real frustration in a world where everyone but he, it seems, is caught up, in music.

As an apprentice effort, the lines of "I Remember, I Remember" are heavily padded with unnecessary words ("No phonograph *did* own") and awkward inversions ("Above 'Lucia' wailed") as Ira struggles to fit words to the fixed poetic rhythm. In only one line, the last, do the metrical requirements accord with a perfectly colloquial phrase: "I *think* I'll *take* to *drink.*" In the other lines, the clash between meter and language robs the poem of that most essential quality of "light" verse—the ease, the spontaneity, the seeming absence of effort that gives light verse its "lightness of touch."[19] For poets such as F.P.A. and Dorothy Parker, such lightness came only after years of struggle to master poetic meters. For others, particularly Ezra Pound, Carl Sandburg, and Amy Lowell, the constraints of regular meter and rhyme had to be abandoned for "free verse" that could better register American speech. For Ira Gershwin, the lightness would come when he turned from poetry to song, where the accentual patterns created by varied sequences of musical notes gave his words the colloquial ease they lacked when he had to adhere to strict metrical versification.

Another of his early poems, from 1916, offers a striking instance
of how cramped and stilted his language could be when it conformed
to a regular meter:

> A desperate deed to do I crave,
>   Beyond all reason and rhyme;
> Someday when I'm feeling especially brave,
>   I'm going to bide my time.

Years later, after he shifted from poetry to song lyrics, Ira would find
wit and ease by setting his syllables to a more flexible musical pattern:

> I'm bidin' my ti-me
> 'cause that's the kinda guy I'-m.
> While other folks grow dizzy,
> I keep busy—
> bidin' my time.

Where the metrical regularity of light verse forces Ira into awkward
inversions and padding ("deed to do I crave"), the sequence of musical notes for "Bidin' My Time" frees him to play with the clipped
and elongated syllables of American speech. Here the "bidin' "s and
" 'cause"s register a laziness that shortens some words, while "ti-me"
and "I'-m" sluggishly drag themselves out over two notes. It was their
apprenticeship in the rigors of light verse, its "metrical discipline and
rhyming virtuosity"[20] that later enabled Ira, Yip, and other lyricists to
match words to music with such apparent ease.

Their love of light verse soon carried Ira and Yip beyond New York
newspapers to anthologies of poetry. Ira began collecting anthologies
in high school, purchasing them out of his forty-cent-a-week allowance,
and eventually had more than two hundred volumes of verse. One
of their favorite books, Yip Harburg recalled, was *A Vers de Société
Anthology*, edited by Carolyn Wells, herself one of the most prolific
of newspaper versifiers. There they found their literary anteced-
ents—Lewis Carroll and Austin Dobson, James Russell Lowell and
Thomas Hood, as well as a distinguished poetic lineage that reached
back through Dryden and Lovelace, Suckling and Herrick, to Jonson,
Raleigh, and even Shakespeare. From such anthologies, Ira learned
his poetic craft just as George honed his skills by studying piano
exercise books. Reading poems that ranged across the full literary
tradition, Ira and Yip learned that light verse is an art, not of origi-

nal poetic expression, but of giving a witty turn to a formulaic sentiment.

In one of their joint compositions, a 1915 poem called "Shackled," "Yip" and "Gersh" reflected upon their "blasé conscious funning":

> Sometimes to us so queerly,
> There comes this feeling clearly,
> "We do not write sincerely!"
> And then mayhap we pause.
>
> And accuse ourselves of playing
> On words, great Nothings saying,
> When we might be a-haying—
> And so we rage and rant—
>
> Our comedy decrying
> Alas! It sets us sighing.
> But give up versifying?
> Good gracious! We just CAN'T!

While poets strive for "high seriousness," "originality," and "sincerity," the light-verse writer repeats the clichéd "great Nothings" with a playful twist. If successful, the versifier calls attention less to his ostensible subject than to his own deft treatment of it. We praise not so much what he says but his clever way of saying it, delighting in his "conscious funning"—his open display of poetic devices, artifices, and contrivances.

Skimming through the poems in Wells's anthology, Ira Gershwin saw how poet after poet took up a well-worn romantic formula—a catalogue of a mistress's beauties, a plea for her favors, a lament over her scorn—and refreshed it with some trenchant turn. One such formula is that of celebrating a woman by rhyming her name, which light-verse poets enliven by choosing a name that challenges their skill at rhyme. They thus invite us to marvel not only at the glory of the lady but at the ardent struggles of the poet to capture her in words. Richard Watson Gilder, for example, sets himself the task of finding a rhyme for "Janet," then slyly wonders "how *do* they plan it?," while Eugene Field manages to rhyme his "Mistress Pyrrha" but only with a desperate "posie-dizened sirrah." Frank Dempster Sherman begins with the same problem in "A Rhyme for Priscilla" but sidesteps it to display his skill at rhyming virtually any other name, from "dilettante"/"Dante" to "Il Penseroso"/"only so-so." Only after he has strained his imagination

in a tour de force that continues for more than fifty rhymes, does he
finally find one for his beloved—literally at hand—in the cigar he holds:

> O Priscilla, sweet Priscilla,
>   Writing of you makes me think,
> As I burn my brown Manila
> And immortalize my ink

As is typical in light verse, we are concerned less with Priscilla herself
than the witty inventiveness she occasions in the poet.

In another of Ira's apprentice efforts of 1916, "To Sophonisba," he
tried his hand, somewhat awkwardly, at this girl's-name formula,
pleading,

> Oh! Lady, if you still want me to
> Write you in lilting,
> Pulsating rhythm, in prancing swinging
> Meter, with smooth silv'ry rhyme,
> Oh, Sophonisba—
> DEAR Sophonisba—
> Change
> Your unrhymable name!

Years later, however, Ira gave a much better twist to the formula in a
song lyric, "A Rhyme for Angela," where he strikes Sherman's pose of
the rhymester able to come up with a rhyme for any other girl in
the world:

> I can find a rhyme for Lucy—
> for instance, her kiss is juicy,
> but I must confess
> I'm lost, more or less,
> with Angela, Angela.

Like Sherman, Ira evinces his pyrotechnic skill by rhyming other
names:

> Takes no time to rhyme, say, Chloe—
> For instance, her breast is snowy . . .
> I can find a rhyme for Irma:
> She's Heaven on Terra Firma . . .
> I can find a rhyme for Margot:
> On her favors there's no embargo . . .
> I can find a rhyme for Edith:
> She possesses what Everyman needeth . . .

But where Sherman ultimately triumphs in rhyming Priscilla, Angela remains unrhymed to the last—literally (and linguistically) beyond compare.

By bringing these techniques of society verse to bear upon the formulas of popular song, Ira Gershwin, along with Yip Harburg, Lorenz Hart, Cole Porter, and other lyricists of the golden age transformed the lowly genre of song into a vehicle of urbane wit. Before these lyricists performed their alchemy, the job of a Tin Pan Alley lyricist was simple: "You gotta say 'I love you' in thirty-two bars." While most of these wordsmiths were content to repeat the same formulaic expressions for love longed for, first sighted, lost, or unrequited, lyricists nurtured on light verse delighted in tackling the problem with witty variations upon the most hackneyed of formulas. Thus Cole Porter could have a lover confess his thralldom with "I've got you—under my skin," as though romance were a dermal irritation. Lorenz Hart, similarly, could praise his beloved as a "Funny Valentine" whose "looks are laughable—unphotographable." Ira Gershwin's mastery of such light-verse inversions is evident when he takes the formula of lovers experiencing their first truly passionate kiss and has them ask a question usually posed when one finds one's mate in bed with someone else: "How Long Has This Been Going On?" Speaking for all such lyricists, Yip Harburg averred, "I doubt that I can ever say 'I love you' head on—it's not the way I think. For me the task is never to say the thing directly, and yet to say it—to think in a curve, so to speak."[21]

The light-verse principle of refreshing stale romantic clichés was so fundamental to Ira Gershwin's lyrical art that when he collected his lyrics in a book, *Lyrics on Several Occasions*, he organized them not by chronology but by the standard formulas upon which each lyric formed its particular "curve." Thus one group of songs is labelled "The Not Impossible He" and includes songs like "The Man I Love," "Looking For a Boy," and other lyrics where a woman longs for the man of her dreams. Another formula, where a man pleads for his beloved's favors, Ira dubbed "The Importunate Male"; he included in that category such variations as "Put Me to the Test" and "I Can't Get Started." Still another category, "A Quintet of Findings," includes five songs of love at first sight, such as "Love Walked In" and "This Is New," while torch songs such as "But Not for Me" and "The Man That Got Away" fall in the category Ira dubbed "Ladies in Lament." By studying the various lyrics in each category, one can see how, in song after song, Ira Gershwin gave a subtly different turn to the same basic formula.

But while his organization of *Lyrics on Several Occasions* was based upon light verse, Ira prefaced his collection with a notice that clearly distinguished the art of lyric-writing from that of poetry. Since lyrics consisted of words wedded intricately to music, Ira insisted, any "resemblance to actual poetry, living or dead, is highly improbable."[22] Before a lyric could bristle with the witty variations and deft rhymes of light verse, the lyricist, unlike the poet, had to begin with a composer's musical idea and then craft words "mosaically" with music, fusing syllable with note, accent with rhythm, and phrase with cadence, in the give-and-take of collaboration. Equally important, as Ira insists throughout the book, is that the words must "sing"—with precisely the right syllable wedded to the proper note and with plenty of open vowels to enable a vocalist to sustain and project the longer notes. Only after the lyricist had mastered those tasks could he strive for poetic effects. Little wonder that the great light-verse writers of the day seldom were successful at songwriting. Dorothy Parker and Ogden Nash only rarely managed to wed their wit to music, and when the dean of light verse, Franklin Pierce Adams, tried fusing singable syllables with musical notes, he confessed to finding the "method of the lyrist," as he termed it, "infinitely harder."[23]

Thus when Ira Gershwin traced the genealogy of his mosaic art back to the Elizabethan age, he excluded the "great art-song writers," such as John Dowland and Thomas Campion, because for them "the words always came first." He found his true lyrical forebears in the Renaissance "satirists and parodists" who put new lyrics to traditional airs. Even Martin Luther, by this measure, was Ira's literary ancestor, for he crafted new lyrics to secular tunes, throwing out "the worldly lyric to substitute one of spiritual quality." For Ira Gershwin, this "practice of putting new words to pre-existent song" culminated in the eighteenth century, his favorite literary period, when John Gay took "sixty-eight short 'airs' " from "the great store of English, Irish, and Scottish melodies" and set new words to them for *The Beggar's Opera*.[24]

So insistent was Ira Gershwin upon the distinction between poetry and song that he excluded even the songs of Gilbert and Sullivan from this lyrical canon because "practically all the lyrics were written first." Ira had known W. S. Gilbert as a light-verse poet, prominently featured in anthologies such as Carolyn Wells's, but he discovered the Gilbert and Sullivan operettas one day when Morris Gershvin, an opera lover, brought home a recording of *H.M.S. Pinafore*. That knowledge gave him a bit of one-upmanship on his friend Yip. When Harburg confessed that his favorite book of poetry was Gilbert's *Bab Ballads*, Ira coolly inquired, "You know, of course, those 'poems' are song lyrics?" "There's music to them?" asked a flabbergasted Harburg. "Sure is," Ira told him and then invited Yip home to listen to the Gershwin family Victrola. "There were all the lines I knew by heart," Harburg recalled, "I was dumbfounded, staggered!"[25]

Harburg's astonishment is certainly understandable, given the enormous gap in quality between the songs of Gilbert and Sullivan and the tepid fare of Tin Pan Alley—a gap partly attributable to the fact that on Tin Pan Alley the "tunesmith" cranked out the music first, then the "wordsmith" tacked on the lyric (sometimes called merely "the words"). With Gilbert and Sullivan, however, Gilbert's words came first, so their "songs" are essentially light verse set to music. Under the pseudonym of "Bab," Gilbert had written light verse for *Fun* (a rival of *Punch*). When he and Sullivan first began collaborating on the Savoy operas, Gilbert simply asked Sullivan to set his "Bab Ballads" to music. *Trial by Jury*, their first successful work (which Ira recalled reading in 1911, the year of Gilbert's death), consisted primarily of musical settings for poems that had already appeared in *Fun*. Similarly, *H.M.S. Pinafore* contained more than half a dozen of the earlier poems.

By setting light verse to music, Gilbert and Sullivan revolutionized European operetta. In both Viennese operetta and French opéra bouffe, the audience is swept up in the romantic plot, dashing characters and sheer spectacle; far from trying to call attention to their own wittiness, lyrics in such operettas efface themselves to bring out the sumptuousness of the music. In the satirical operettas of Gilbert and Sullivan, however, characters are "constantly playing on the conventionality of their activity, on the unreality of theatrical illusion," keeping the audience aware of, rather than immersed in, "the fabricated nature of the plot and dialogue." Lyrics that bristle with outrageous puns and pyrotechnical rhymes thus contribute to this awareness of the "text's fictitiousness and fabricated nature."[26] When the lovers in traditional operetta pour out their hearts, we soar with their song; when the hero of *H.M.S. Pinafore* laments, "I love—and love, alas, above my station" and the chorus punningly responds, "He loves—and loves a lass above his station," we laugh with our lyrical feet on the ground.

The problem with setting light verse to music, however, is that while Gilbert's poems were "eminently recitable, with their carefully selected words all neatly clipped and set in rows, their spirited dactyls and anapests hurrying one along, their tempting but tongue-twisting alliterations and consonances, and their pompously reverberating syllabics, . . . they are not singable."[27] Where singability was practically the only requirement for lyrics in traditional operetta, Gilbert, admittedly "tone-deaf and unable to carry a tune," had to learn to make his wit more euphonious, to loosen his rattling rhythms, soften his thumping rhymes, and replace his gutturals and fricatives with liquid consonants and long open vowels. In *Pirates of Penzance*, for example, "nice associates" became the less s-laden "nice companions" and an "e'en" was inserted into the line, "Thou gildest—e'en—the pirate's trade" to give Sullivan an additional note for his melody and the singer a long vowel to sustain it.

In some cases a total lyrical overhaul was necessary to achieve "singability." Gilbert originally had his pirate hero confess, in a clever light-verse reversal of formulaic longings, that he wished to abandon his romantic roguery and settle into middle-class English life. As usual, Gilbert couched that desire in crunching consonants—the hero wants "to doff his pirate gear and turn tall-hatty and broad-clothy," for he "loathes his rude and draughty cave and sighs for brick relieved with stucco." In making this lyric more singable, however, Gilbert totally recast the sentiment, having the disaffected pirate long not just for the accouterments of middle-class respectability, but the love of a maiden, even one "whose homely face and bad complexion / Have caused all hopes to disappear / Of ever winning man's affection":

> To such a one, if such there be,
> I swear by Heaven's arch above you,
> If you will cast your eyes on me,
> However plain you be, I'll love you!

With more singable vowels and softer consonants, clearly, came a much less witty, more romantic sentiment, one that veers perilously in the direction of love songs in traditional operetta. When joined to Sullivan's "powerful, swelling melody," moreover, even such comic lines as "whose homely face and bad complexion" strike a "note of extreme pathos."[28]

By making his lyric more singable, Gilbert knew, the lyricist ran the risk of seeing his words lose not only their witty lustre but even their meaning. Keenly aware of music's power to transcend words, he always insisted that his lyric take precedence over Sullivan's music in order of composition. Otherwise, as he suggested in one of his songs, the words need not make any sense at all:

> "His gentle spirit rolls
> In the melody of souls—"
> Which is pretty,
> but I don't know what it means.

Precisely the same could be said of many lyrics written by the word-smiths of Tin Pan Alley, whose task was to fit a singable syllable to each note of music. Even Oscar Hammerstein, hardly an Alley wordsmith, confessed his difficulties in making sense of some of his own lyrics. "Tote dat barge—lift dat bale," Hammerstein pointed out, is rousingly euphonious, but while one can lift a bale no one, no matter how strong, can "tote"—that is, pick up and carry off—a barge. Similarly, "When I grow too old to dream" has an exquisite progression of vowels, but when, Hammerstein asked, is one ever too old to dream?

Hammerstein always regarded himself as a writer of what he called more "primitive" lyrics, where singability (or, as he termed it, "phonet-ics") was the paramount consideration, as opposed to Gilbert, whom he regarded as working in the very different "field of brilliant light verse."[29] It is between the wit of Gilbert and the "primitive" art of Hammerstein, between the clever variations of light verse and the mosaic art of wedding syllables with musical notes, that Ira Gershwin, along with such contemporaries as Lorenz Hart, Dorothy Fields, and Yip Harburg, would forge a new kind of lyric. Striving for a union of words and music, they gave a witty, but still singable and colloquial, curve to the most formulaic of romantic sentiments. Writing their songs primarily for sophisticated musical comedies, they struck a delicate balance between the flippancy of Gilbert and Sullivan and the strident sentimentality of traditional operetta.

By 1925, Ira Gershwin had mastered that balance, and he could reflect upon its rigors:

> It all comes down to this: in the old days they would write their lyrics first and then get musical settings, whereas today the worry of songwriters is the melody of the song. The song is the important thing, the combina-tion of words and music, rather than the words and music as separate entities. The reason that some of our songwriters are unsuccessful is that they regard lyrics the same way Gilbert did. They don't strive for union of the composer and the lyricist. They are not willing to sacrifice them-selves to the demands or limitations of the tune, the movement, and syncopation.[30]

By letting the emotional range of the music establish their themes and by plying their wit within the constraints of rhythm and cadence, these lyricists created an extraordinary hybrid, between light verse and popular song.

The catalyst for the emergence of this new kind of song was Jerome Kern's entry onto the American musical stage. Kern showed that the Broadway theater could produce popular songs of a distinctly higher order than those that came off the assembly lines of Tin Pan Alley. Taking the Alley's musical formulas, Kern handled them with a sophistication born of his extensive classical training. His songs were published by the T. B. Harms Company, headed by the great Max Dreyfus, which specialized in "theater songs" rather than run-of-the-mill Alley fare. Hearing an orchestra play Kern's first big hit, "They Didn't Believe Me," George Gershwin was inspired to quit his job on Tin Pan Alley and go to work on Broadway as a rehearsal pianist.

Just as George and other young composers took their inspiration from Kern, Ira, along with other nascent lyricists, looked to one of Kern's collaborators, the English writer P. G. Wodehouse, who demonstrated that song lyrics, even when the music came first, could sparkle with as much wit as light verse. In 1915, Wodehouse attended a Kern musical for which his friend Guy Bolton had written the libretto. After the show, Wodehouse commented to Bolton that he thought everything was superb—except the lyrics. Pressed by Bolton and Kern, Wodehouse agreed to join them in their next venture and supply lyrics while Bolton concentrated on the book. That arrangement led to a brief but historic series of musicals at the Princess Theatre, a small, intimate theater where the emphasis was upon wit and sophistication rather than spectacular sets, costumes, and production numbers. While the Princess Theatre musicals lasted only until 1917, they proved to be the most important development yet to have occurred in American musical theater.

When he first tried writing lyrics, Wodehouse was skeptical, for he knew that in Gilbert and Sullivan operettas words were written first and that Gilbert himself had affirmed it was impossible to write good lyrics if the music came first. Nonetheless Wodehouse found that, far from restricting him, the music actually led him to create effects that he couldn't have achieved on his own. Citing one instance of how Kern's sequence of "twiddly little notes" inspired him to come up with a subtle rhyme in the phrase "If every day you *bring* her diamonds and pearls on a *string*," Wodehouse said, "I couldn't have thought of that, if I had done the lyric first, in a million years. Why, dash it, it doesn't *scan*."[31]

Following the music, Wodehouse could rhyme with literate yet slangy sophistication, as in "Cleopatterer," whose "slim and svelte" figure "gave those poor Egyptian ginks something else to watch beside the Sphinx." At other times he rhymed so subtly one could barely detect it in the progression of thoroughly vernacular phrases:

> What bad luck! It's
> coming down in buckets.

When Kern's music presented him with problems, such as an unexpected triplet in the final phrase of "Bill," Wodehouse used the three-note interruption for a casual interjection that debunks sentimentality: "I love him because he's—*I-don't-know*—because he's just my Bill." Ironically, it took the Englishman Wodehouse to show that by following the music, a lyricist came out sounding much less "poetic" and "British," and much more colloquially "American."

The Princess Theatre shows also demonstrated that song lyrics could strive for what came to be called "integration" and "particularity." While most musicals of the time simply strung together a series of songs that were utterly unrelated to the plot or characters of the "book," Bolton, Wodehouse, and Kern tried to make songs emerge integrally out of dramatic situations. By tying a song lyric to a particular character, moreover, Wodehouse could refresh the tiredest of romantic formulas. Given a jaded ingenue, Wodehouse had her confess that—"at the age of five"—she let herself be kissed at parties "by small boys excited by tea." But, she coyly reassures her current lover,

> Had I known that you existed,
> I'd have scratched them and resisted

Witty lyrics were well suited to such characters; while hardly as openly artificial and theatrical as Gilbert and Sullivan, the Princess Shows were self-consciously, as it was then termed, "slick" and "smart."

Wodehouse never achieved anything like the full integration and particularity of Oscar Hammerstein, Frank Loesser, and other later lyricists, whose songs, such as "I Cain't Say No" or "Adelaide's Lament," are inseparable from their dramatic context and the character who sings them. Still, the Princess Shows were an important first step toward creating musicals where dialogue, lyrics, and music merged into an organic whole. As Ira Gershwin, along with his contemporaries, moved the American musical further toward that goal, he came to conceive of his lyrics as "lodgments" for specific dramatic occasions, always integrally related to some situation in the plot or to the personality of a particular character.

In a diary he began keeping in 1916, Ira recorded his enthusiastic responses to all forms of theater, from vaudeville to the movies. His greatest admiration was for the musicals of Bolton, Wodehouse, and Kern, particularly the shows *Leave It to Jane* and *Miss 1917*. After he enjoyed these in the theater, he would listen to recordings of them again and again on his father's Victrola. The Princess Shows thus were as vital to the Gershwins' development as they were for the young songwriting team of Rodgers and Hart, who, on their first meeting, discovered their common admiration for the Princess Shows and instantly agreed to become collaborators. Coming at precisely the time that George and Ira Gershwin, Richard Rodgers and Lorenz Hart, Cole Porter, and other aspiring lyricists and composers were beginning their careers, the example of Kern and Wodehouse sparked a creative outburst that would mark the songs of an entire generation.

Ira Gershwin's return to the family piano (this time with pen in hand) came at a particularly propitious moment in literary history. With the publication of T. S. Eliot's "The Love Song of J. Alfred Prufrock" in 1917 the "new" poetry movement firmly established itself in opposition to the adherents of metrical verse. While Franklin Pierce Adams could rail against "free verse" upstarts and use his column to ridicule e. e. cummings and *The Waste Land*, such "avant-garde" poets soon dominated the landscape of modern American letters.[32] Although Don Marquis, Phyllis McGinley, Witter Bynner, and Adams himself would fade into literary history, young writers like Ira Gershwin, who grew up under their sway but followed Wodehouse's lead in wedding light verse to music, produced a body of song that has become as "classic" as the work of the great modernist American poets.

2

Boy Wanted
1918–1924

Given a fondness for music, a feeling for rhyme, a sense of whimsy and humor, an eye for the balanced sentence, an ear for the current phrase, and the ability to imagine a performer trying to put over the number in progress—given all this, I would still say it takes four or five years collaborating with knowledgeable composers to become a well-rounded lyricist.
—Ira Gershwin

THE first indication that Ira Gershwin was moving from light verse to song lyrics came in May of 1917, when he submitted a poem, "You May Throw All the Rice You Desire," to Don Marquis for his "Sun Dial" column in the New York *Evening Sun*, claiming it was actually a song lyric:

> Mr. Marquis, *Dear Sir*: I have sent the following lyric to six different publishers and they all sent it back. Maybe you or some of your readers can tell me what is the matter with it as I am a young fellow and want to give the public what it wants . . . Maybe it is a little old-fashioned, but I don't know, the old songs are the best, they say, and it points a moral.

Marquis published the poem under the heading "There Is Nothing the Matter, It's Perfect," but despite that reassurance, "You May Throw All the Rice You Desire" is as padded and convoluted as Ira's collegiate poetry. In the verse, he describes a wedding ceremony where a "blushing bride and her lover to the steps did wend their way" while "their young friends them had proceeded." In the chorus, the lan-

guage becomes somewhat more colloquial but is still laden with
poeticisms:

> You may throw all the rice you desire,
>   But please, friends, throw no shoes.
> For 'twill surely arouse my ire,
>   If you cause my wife one bruise.

In a concluding note, Ira said, "If any reader likes it and can write
music to it I will go fifty-fifty with him." While the letter and poem
were tongue-in-cheek, Ira was clearly thinking about turning poetry
into song, albeit imagining that the process began with the words
rather than the music.

He was also beginning to think in commercial terms. The year
before he had dropped out of CCNY, daunted by "finding that in my
second year I was still taking first-year mathematics and when I heard
that calculus was in the offing, I decided to call it an education."[1] He
had gone to work as a cashier in his father's newest enterprise, a
bathhouse, but was flailing about in search of a career. While he, like
Harburg, toyed with the prospect of becoming a light-verse poet, it "was
evident you couldn't make a living this way."[2] Although he managed to
place an occasional poem in the newspaper columns, his acceptances
were far outnumbered by rejections—the crowning blow coming when
a poem he mailed to F.P.A.'s "The Conning Tower" at 5:00 p.m. on
Monday, May 5, was returned at 7:45 a.m. the next day. "That certainly
beats all records," he glumly confided to his diary.

Even his crowning achievement as a writer was a commercial
disappointment. On May 17 he wrote this satirical sketch, entitled
"The Shrine":

> Fascinated, he would sit before it, glorying. At such times a sublime,
> shivery sensation . . . an incomprehensive wonder at the beauty of it all.
> Reverent before it, he felt invigorated with the spirit of eternal youth
> and happiness. Such soul-absorbing devotion to the embodiment of an
> ideal was unprecedented . . .
>
> And one day it fell and lay shattered in a thousand sharp, jagged
> fragments.
>
> Panic-stricken, ashen-hued, he was scarcely able to mutter, "Gawd!
> Seven years' bad luck."

Overcoming his characteristic reticence, Ira showed "The Shrine" to
one of the residents who lived above the bathhouse—Paul M. Potter,
the English playwright who had dramatized George du Maurier's best-
selling novel *Trilby*. Potter gave Ira three brief but valuable suggestions.

The first was "Learn especially your American slang." Englishman that he was, Potter recognized that the American vernacular was a far richer instrument than the stilted idiom Ira was using.

Potter's second offering implied that Ira's shyness and reticence might actually prove to be assets in a literary life:

> Seemed to think that a writer doesn't necessarily have to experience everything he writes about, but by being an attentive listener and observer, can gain a good deal by second hand experience.[3]

Ira by this time was convinced that his younger brother "could do anything," but Potter's words promised that his own natural inclination to listen and watch—rather than *do*—could reap its own rewards in words.

Potter's last piece of advice was that he should send "The Shrine" to H. L. Mencken and George Jean Nathan's *Smart Set*, the premier magazine of the day. In his diary, Ira recorded the momentous day of November 14, 1917:

> Evening: opened the door, fresh, stale, rather, from the subway. Entered the flat into the dining room. "Izzy, I got good news for you," said Mamma. "Yes," I asked easily. "What is it?" "This letter," and I was given a letter from the "Smart Set" saying they liked my little filler, would send me a cheque and wanted to read more of my stuff. I read it and felt quite elated but nothing of the supreme delight I had always coupled in imagination with the realization of my "fondest dreams"—a real acceptance.[4]

Mencken promptly sent Ira a check—for one dollar. Buddy DeSylva, a young lyricist on Tin Pan Alley who was already collaborating successfully with George Gershwin, told Ira that he would "have preferred getting a dollar check from Mencken and Nathan than several thousands from Remick's." "This was very charming," Ira recalled, "but the fact remains" that DeSylva, who went on to write such hits as "April Showers" and "Button Up Your Overcoat," died leaving "several millions."[5]

The irony of "Ira, the Scholar," out of school and adrift, while his younger brother, who once seemed destined for nothing but trouble, rose to success on Tin Pan Alley and Broadway was undoubtedly not lost upon either boy. "I now belong, I see," he wrote to a friend, thanking him for clippings about George's success, "to the rank of Brothers of the Great."[6] George's dinner-table stories about the glittering world of the theater fired Ira's longings for the "bright lights and glamour of the Mazda chasms,"[7] as did the many performers and songwriters his

younger brother brought to the Gershwin household. (Morris Gershwin, always a believer in the talents of his oldest son, would listen
patiently as these guests praised the genius of George, then ask, "Have
you met my son Izzy?") Through George's help, Ira got a part-time job
with a trade paper, the New York *Clipper*, writing occasional vaudeville
reviews. Soon he was emboldened to try his own hand at songwriting.
His diary indicates that on December 18 he "wrote a chorus for a
melody of Geo.s 'You Are Not the Girl.'" Although that song does not
survive, Ira continued writing an occasional lyric.Two weeks later he
noted that "Geo. is writing songs at present with Lou Paley [an English
teacher who was a family friend], Irving Caesar + myself (a couple [of
songs])."[8] One of their efforts was a song called "Beautiful Bird," which
Ira confessed to his diary, "Hope it turns out to be a 2nd 'Poor Butterfly.'" The poetic aspirations of Ira and Lou Paley, however, resulted in
such tremulous paeans as "Beautiful bird, your plaintive piping I've
heard . . . 'Will' Oo? Will' Oo.'" Their fledgling lyric went nowhere.

George's career, by contrast, continued to surge ahead. His gamble
of giving up his job on Tin Pan Alley to follow in Jerome Kern's footsteps
on Broadway began to pay off. In February of 1918, Max Dreyfus gave
the young composer a job at Harms, an event Ira's diary entry records
with pride but also some understandable envy:

> George has been placed on the staff of T. B. Harms Co. He gets $35 a
> week for this connection, then $50 advance and a 3 cents royalty on each
> song of his they accept. This entails no other effort on his part than the
> composing, they not requiring any of his leisure for plugging nor for
> piano-playing. Some snap.[9]

Ira continued to work on lyrics in between handing out towels at the
St. Nicholas Baths. On bathhouse letterhead he would jot down ideas
for song titles—"It's Such a Lovely Day for Love," "You're the Treasure
I Treasure," "If You Only Knew What I Thought of You, You'd Think
a Little More of Me"—titles that showed his penchant for deft turnarounds of word and phrase. While he would later complain that the
hardest job for a lyricist was coming up with a title, these early forays
provided him with plenty of titles, but little more.

Finally, on one of those pieces of stationery, under the imprint
"ST. NICHOLAS BATHS, Russian and Turkish," we can find the begin-
nings of Ira Gershwin's first full-scale effort, "The Great American Folk
Song (Is a Rag)." Perhaps it was the European heritage emblazoned
on the stationery that inspired Ira to write a verse which advises new
immigrants to abandon their native folk songs—the "Neapolitan Street

Song" and "traditional Spanish tunes"—and adjust to the new, looser rhythms of American life:

> They may be songs that you can't forget
> they may be distinctive, yet—
> they lack a something—a certain snap
> the tempo ticklish that makes you tap.

Ira, too, was trying to adapt his light-verse skills to the new world of songwriting, but he was still working, poetic fashion, by writing words first, albeit words that he hoped "might be suitably developed to be classed in the category we'll call m.c."—musical comedy—"songs." The novelty of the exercise elicited his wry complaint that writing songs "gives me remarkable practice in applied penmanship." Starting on the chorus, he "wrote one. Discarded it. Wrote another. Started a third. Waste-basketed all." Finally, "after several sporadic starts," he "came to some agreement with myself" on a final version that was "not good, not bad."

When he showed the results of his long labors to his brother, he was pleased to report that "Geo. liked it," and George then, with his usual flair, proceeded to dash off some music:

> So we sat down on, (at, rather) the piano & Geo. started something. Something sounded good so we kept it. It was a strain for the first two lines. That in our possession we went along and George developed the strain along legitimate or illegitimate (if you prefer) rag lines and with a little editing here & there the chorus, musical, stood forth in all its glory.

At that point, however, Ira's lyrical apprenticeship began in earnest, for he realized that his words did not fit George's music:

> . . . unhappily the musical lines were of different lengths from the lyric, so after having sweated & toiled & moiled over 20 or so different versions, it now devolves upon me to start an entirely new one.[10]

Although George's ragtime melody had come second in the order of composition, music once again had assumed its primacy in the creation of song. Ira's new lyric was a lyric in earnest—not a piece of light verse to be set to music, but words, syllables, and phrases that had to be fitted, mosaically, to George's notes.

Some of the lyrical revisions were subtle ones, such as substituting the more singable (and vernacular) "The *Real* American Folk Song" for "The *Great* American Folk Song." Other changes, however, involved massive revision. Out went the clipped consonants and literate poly-syllables of

> Concert singers say that they despise it,
> hoary critics never eulogize it,

Instead Ira had to come up with simple, truncated phrases to match George's ragged musical accents:

> sweeter—
> than a classic strain
> Boy! you can't remain
> still and quiet
> for it's a riot!

By following the music he was creating not only a more singable but a more colloquial lyric. By the time he got to the end of the chorus, however, the frustrated lyricist dug in his heels and refused to change the last lines of his original lyric. George finally relented and set "A master stroke song—is a rag!" to music. Ira was pleased to salvage those "last two lines as a memento of a tussle strenuous and an intimation of a struggle heroic to materialize." His battlefield metaphor provides an apt description of his first real lesson in the difference between writing light verse and writing *lyrics*—words fitted to music and fit for singing.

He soon learned that it was not only the composer who called the tune. To accommodate the "public" taste, Max Dreyfus, the publisher, insisted that the word "aboriginal" be deleted for the more readily graspable (if redundant) "Old traditional." Next came a lesson in how a performer could make—or break—a song. Nora Bayes, who had made her name with "Shine On, Harvest Moon" in the original Ziegfeld *Follies* of 1907, had hired George Gershwin to be her accompanist for the tryout tour of *Ladies First*. When he played "The Real American Folk Song" for her, Bayes had it included in the show as an "interpolation" (a song by another composer—or a song not originally intended to be included—added to a score after a show's opening). When *Ladies First* reached Trenton on its out-of-town run, Ira took the day off from his job in the bathhouse. Dressed in sartorial spiffiness—purple shirt, blue tie, green suit—he took the train to Trenton, got off at the wrong stop, but still made it to the theater in time to hear his lyric performed.

While Ira was delighted by his debut in the musical theater, he soon received the first of many lessons in "doctoring," the euphemistic term for the extensive cutting and revising of a show during its out-of-town run. When "The Real American Folk Song" failed to catch on with audiences, Bayes insisted that the ending of the song be rewritten. George, perhaps recalling the recent struggle that had left his brother with nothing but that ending as a memento of his original lyric, staunchly refused to alter a note. Despite her haughty insistence that such luminaries as Jerome Kern and Irving Berlin would change songs for her, George still refused, so Bayes simply dropped the song from the show before it reached New York.

The hard lesson may have soured Ira on songwriting for a while, for in the summer of 1919 he took a job as treasurer for a traveling carnival, Colonel Lagg's Greater Empire Show. A relative who had an interest in the show turned to the reliable Ira after the former treasurer had run off with the weekly receipts (as well as with Princess Fatima). "With nothing better in sight," Ira took the job and discovered how little he loved to travel, as the carnival played one-week stands from Pittsburgh, across Ohio, and into Illinois. After five months of "stuck-in-the-mud" weeks, Ira, whose favorite spot, even then, was the couch, returned home to face his career crisis:

> I'm afraid I was pretty much of a floating soul. I couldn't concentrate on anything . . . To tell the truth, I was at a complete loss and I didn't care. It was at this moment, back from the carnival, that I first thought of becoming a writer of what they call "lyrics."[11]

As a sign of his determination he purchased his first rhyming dictionary and a *Roget's Thesaurus*.

Still, the way he described his aspiration—"to be a writer of what they call 'lyrics'"—holds the prospect at arm's length. At age twenty-three, he would be apprenticing himself in a business where his younger brother was already enjoying considerable success. By the end of 1919, George had written his first full score for a Broadway show, *La-La-Lucille!*, and already had what would prove to be the biggest hit of his entire career when Al Jolson took up "Swanee," which George had written with lyricist Irving Caesar.

It was George who approached his "sadder but wiser" older brother early in 1920 with the news that Edward MacGregor, the producer of *The Sweetheart Shop*, a show that was playing successfully in Chicago, wanted to add a new song for his star, Helen Ford, before the show reached New York. George had written a tune and, as Ira put it, "elder brother was promptly besought to devise a suitable lyric for the new-born work."[12] Since the song would be an interpolation, the lyric had to be tailor-made to fit into one of the generic moments of the musical comedies of the day—a "lady-in-waiting" song for the ingenue dreaming of her ideal man; a "euphoria" song celebrating love at first sight; a "gotta dance" number for the lead hoofer and chorus. Reflecting that "the musical-comedy cycle called for at least one Pollyanna song in a show,"[13] Ira suggested an interpolation that would give the heroine the formulaic opportunity to look for the silver lining, wait till the clouds roll by, or envision May flowers beyond April showers. The title he came up with, "Waiting For the Sun To Come Out," went all the way back to the meteorological optimism of the first song Ira recalled hearing as a child—"Wait Till the Sun Shines, Nellie."

Setting George's irregular musical phrases to words, however, had Ira reaching for verbal filler, inverted wording, and clichéd imagery:

> When the clouds the skies are filling,
> and the songbirds stop their trilling,
> don't take it to heart;
> let worry depart.
> Soon the sunshine will say, "Howdy!"
> Skies are not forever cloudy;
> just learn to sing and never mope;
> there is a thing that's known as hope.

While bereft of even the modicum of poetic wit that characterized "The Real American Folk Song," "Waiting For the Sun To Come Out" did, as Ira often put it, "sing well."

Once the song was completed, however, the brothers faced another problem: MacGregor had agreed to listen to George demonstrate the song, but the brothers feared that "if MacGregor learned the song was a sibling collaboration he might listen to it skeptically." Ira, drawing on his experience with pseudonyms in light verse, proposed a solution:

> I suggested that the lyricist be called Arthur Francis—a combination of the prenames of our younger brother, Arthur, and our sister, Frances.[14]

Ira's suggestion was motivated as well by a firm determination to succeed in show business without the aid of his brother's already considerable name. Even with the pseudonym, MacGregor was skeptical; he offered George $250 for the song but wondered about the credentials of his collaborator, the mysterious Arthur Francis. George dodged the question by saying Arthur Francis was "just a college kid with loads of talent."[15] MacGregor interpolated "Waiting For the Sun To Come Out" into *The Sweetheart Shop* and also had it published. Even though the show closed after only two weeks, Ira's royalties from sheet-music sales came to $723.40, and another $445.02 came from sales of phonograph recordings—a sure sign to the budding lyricist that even this beclouded novice effort at songwriting had more silver lining than his more enlightened light verse.

To recoup his losses from *The Sweetheart Shop*, MacGregor invited George and "the college kid" to supply all of the songs for a new musical. Such an invitation, it would seem, might have enabled Ira and George to work with a playwright to have songs grow integrally out of the dramatic context of the book for the show and to tailor them closely to particular characters. Despite the example Bolton, Wodehouse, and Kern had set with the Princess Shows, however, Broadway musicals of this period showed little concern for integration and particularity. The book was little more than a boy-meets-girl clothesline for songs, dances, gags, and "special material" to show off the talents of the stars. Characters were dimensionless stereotypes who warbled the same for-mulaic sentiments in show after show after show. Ira's task, therefore, was merely to write a set of generic numbers, from the standard polly-anna weather song, "Some Rain Must Fall" (with its hackneyed follow-up, "for one and all") to the euphoric "Just To Know You Are Mine" (with the clichéd rhyme on "divine," which Ira would later come to disparage).

While they lacked integration and particularity, some of Ira's lyrics nevertheless evinced a light-verse flair. In the obligatory rhythmic number, "Dancing Shoes," he rhymed "frolic," "diabolic," and "melan-cholic"; in "The Sirens" he concocted several triple rhymes, such as "beautiful" with "tutti-fruiti-ful" and "perpetual" with "get you all"; and in "Anything for You," he imbedded a subtle internal rhyme— "do the darndest *all he* could to be your Walter R*aleigh*." In "The Simple Life," a standard pastoral "let's-escape-from-the-city" song, he crafted a witty image of laziness that foreshadows "Bidin' My Time":

> I love to chase the butterflies,
> and watch them flutter;
> I think the greatest exercise
> is churning butter.

Ira himself dismissed even this bit of cleverness, years later, with the kind of self-criticism that earned him the sobriquet of "The Jeweller": he "had used the word 'butter' twice in the same stanza."[16]

By far the most ambitious lyric in *A Dangerous Maid* was "Boy Wanted," a catalogue song in the mold of Gilbert and Sullivan patter numbers, where four girls "list" the qualities they are looking for in a boy, as if each were placing a newspaper ad. Ira's development as a lyricist is clear from the very opening of the verse, where he concocts a triple rhyme on "ad*vertisement*": "no half-hearted Romeo or fl*irt is meant*." No sooner does he display his journeyman skills, however, than he lapses into an apprentice's error with a false rhyme between "ply" and "fy":

> Though anybody interested can ap*ply*,
> he must know a thing to quali*fy*

Years later, Ira would maintain that a lyricist must always use "exact" rhyme, which "is based solely on the pronunciation and harmonization of accented syllables":

> Most modern poets find "perfect" or "full" or "exact" rhyme too limiting, and favor sound devices called "visual rhyme," "suspended rhyme," "historical rhyme," "dissonance-consonance," and other literary and intellectual varieties. These are not, I feel, for the lyricist, whose output in the field of entertainment must be easily assimilable and whose work depends a good deal on perfect rhyme's jingle.[17]

Another lyrical peccadillo—one that, curiously, would mar some of his finest songs[18]—is his inversion of normal word order. In "Boy Wanted" Ira disrupted the conversational flow of his lyric in order to bring off a rhyme on Freud (the first mention of the psychiatrist in an American song lyric):

> The movies he must avoid.
> He'll know his Nietzsche and Freud.

The learned allusions suited the dramatic context of the song; one of the girls who sings "Boy Wanted" longs for an intellectual, rather than the stereotypically handsome, and wealthy, lover conjured up by her partners:

> I don't care if his bankroll totals naught,
> for we can live on love—and food for thought.

Given that bit of lyrical "particularization," Ira has this character dream of a boy, like himself, "who knows books" and thus "needn't have looks."

Although *A Dangerous Maid* closed out of town (in Pittsburgh) in the spring of 1921, Ira and George salvaged "Boy Wanted," kept it in their "trunk" (songwriters' slang for their unused material), and in 1924 retailored it for a British musical, *Primrose*. By comparing the revised with the original lyric, one can trace Ira's development from apprentice to journeyman lyricist. In the 1921 version of "Boy Wanted," Ira follows George's abrupt musical phrases with two brief verbal parallels:

> He must be able to dance;
> he must make life a romance.

Three years later, however, Ira revised these lines to create a more colloquial lyric, in which the syntax of a current catchphrase stretches across the musical phrases, stitching them together:

> To have a ghost of a chance
> he must be able to dance.

Similarly, in the 1921 version Ira continued to rely on repetitive padding, even enclosing words in parentheses to indicate their role as mere verbal filler:

> (I said a) boy wanted,
> one who can smile.

But in 1924 he made every word count:

> The sort of boy wanted
> must have a smile.

The strong "must" is deftly placed on the most heavily accented note in George's musical phrase. Along with more vernacular language came fresher sentiments. In the earlier lyric one of the girls expresses her longing in demure phrases:

> The kind of boy wanted
> needn't have gold;
> boy wanted,
> mustn't be cold.

Three years later she sounds more down to earth, in both phrasing and temperament:

> He must be quite reckless
> buying me things:
> pearl necklace,
> diamond rings.

Here the sharp syntactic breaks accent the abrupt turns of George Gershwin's angular melody, and the clipped, telegraphic phrasing of "pearl necklace—diamond rings" (like "Boy wanted—lovable style") echoes the language of newspaper ads. Such detailed revisions reflect Ira's growing mastery of the fine points of his mosaic art of fusing words with music.[19]

Such mastery, as he himself indicated, resulted, in part, from the fact that between 1921 and 1924, he worked primarily with composers other than his brother.[20] George's music, during this period, was in volatile flux. On the one hand, he continued to follow Jerome Kern's lead in recasting European classical traditions into the idiom of the American musical. At the same time, however, he was also making frequent treks to Harlem night clubs, where he listened to blues and jazz and emulated the "stride style" of black piano players such as James P. Johnson, Willie (The Lion) Smith, and Luckey Roberts. George's primary laboratory for fusing these disparate musical vocabularies was not musical comedy but George White's *Scandals*, an annual sequence of lavish revues that rivalled Ziegfeld's *Follies* for gorgeous girls and extravagant sets. Beginning in 1920, White commissioned George to write all of the songs for these revues, giving him a freer hand for musical experiments—including a miniature "blues" opera—than he would have had in straight musical theater.

While George worked on these annual editions of the *Scandals* with lyricists such as Arthur Jackson and Buddy DeSylva, Ira turned to other collaborators, most notably Vincent Youmans. George had introduced his brother to the young composer in 1921, then touted the pair to producer Abe Erlanger, who signed them to provide songs for *Two Little Girls in Blue*. While he sang the praises of Youmans and his older brother, however, George Gershwin kept the neophytes hidden from the producer:

> George thought I was such a young punk I'd better not show my face in the theatre. He always made good contracts for me, but he wouldn't even let me go to our first opening night. He said if Erlanger saw how young I was he'd throw us both out.[21]

Whether or not Erlanger found out how young his songwriters were, he brought in a more experienced composer, Paul Lannin, along with some co-lyricists, Schuyler Greene and Fred Jackson, to assist Youmans and "Arthur Francis." The team worked well; four days after *A Dangerous Maid* closed in Pittsburgh, *Two Little Girls in Blue* opened in New York, had a run of well over a hundred performances, and produced several modest hits. "I was scared stiff when tackling my first Broadway show," Ira recalled, adding, "(not that I ever learned to relax any time later on a job, whether a complete score or single interpolation). However, I managed to survive and turn out a passable set of lyrics."[22] More than passable, one could say, for, while a modest success measured by what was to come, *Two Little Girls in Blue* gave latecomer Ira a longer-running Broadway show than any George had had to date.

Once more, Ira faced problems with the book of a musical, which, in the case of *Two Little Girls in Blue*, was mere fluff designed to

> ev'ry hope hides a fear;
> ev'ry smile knows a tear.

Even as he penned such sentiments, Ira cast a cynical eye on them in "Questionnaire for Lyric Song Writers," an article he wrote for the New York *Sun* in 1923. Hinting that he himself was "one of Tin Pan Alley's skilled pome builders, heart wallopers, and word painters and grainers," he posed such mock exercises for would-be lyricists as:

> Complete the following with rhymes from the earl family:
> I had a g—
> She was a p——
> She put my head in a w——.

"If you know what rimes with 'home' besides 'alone,'" he averred with a straight face, "Tin Pan Alley wants you."[28]

In some of these journeyman efforts, however, one finds an increasing fascination with language itself. At times that love of language overshadows the romantic theme of the song, resulting in a lyric calling more attention to its own syntactic tangles than to the lovers who warble them:

> Imagine me
> without my you
> and you
> without your me!

Soon he would achieve a balance between witty wordplay and genuinely moving—but never sentimental—sentiment.

In 1924, Ira found his greatest opportunity yet to indulge his verbal playfulness when he worked with George S. Kaufman and Marc Connelly, two frequenters of the Algonquin Round Table, on the musical *Be Yourself*. Collaborating with such masters of light verse, Ira confected a set of lyrics that bristled with clever rhymes like "oil can" and "goil can," "Mrs. Potiphar" and "what if her," and "you skip the wayes-es of legal phrases." By far the most verbally playful of the songs, however, grew out of Ira's fascination with American speech—the very "slang" that the British playwright Paul Potter had exhorted him to study:

> When I was travelling with a carnival show in the Midwest some years before, I had heard for the first time the sound *Uh-uh* for *No*. In the East, I'd always known and used *mm-hmmm* for yes or agreement, but hadn't known the antonymic sound, which naturally intrigued me. The result was a song for Jack Donahue and Queenie Smith, where he protested that she was always "uh-uhing" him and wherein he wondered

when the miraculous day would occur that he'd hear *mm-hmmm* from her.[29]

In "Uh-Uh," however, Ira's linguistic playfulness upstages the romantic plea of the boy:

It's always "Uh-uh! uh-uh! uh-uh! uh-uh!" when I come closer
It's always "Uh-uh! uh-uh! uh-uh!" at the least caress.
All that I can ever get from you is "How dare you!" or "No, Sir!"
It makes me wonder if you've ever heard of the word "yes."

The girl responds with a cluck of the tongue, but again we take more note of her language than her feelings:

It's just too tch-tch, tch-tch, tch-tch, tch-tch,
    too bad about you.
I may have carried that "Uh-uh! uh-uh!" a bit too far.

In trying to wed light verse to song, Ira's lyric fell short of a true marriage of words and music—not just in sentiment but in singability. In his review of the show, Alexander Woollcott, another Algonquinite, found the lyrics "ornate and sometimes idly witty," but concluded, "with one or two exceptions they are not particularly singable, which is the meanest thing that can be said about a lyric."

Be Yourself did at least induce Ira Gershwin to be himself by dropping the "Arthur Francis" pseudonym and allowing "Ira Gershwin" to appear in the program and on the sheet music of published songs. The emergence from behind that mask signals Ira's sense of himself as an accomplished lyricist in his own right, an important step before reuniting with his brother. While they had continued sporadic collaborations since 1921, in 1924 they settled into virtually permanent union. By that time, both had reached major plateaus in their artistic development. George had finally assimilated his experiments in blues and jazz to the standard musical formulas of Broadway and Tin Pan Alley. Within the simple thirty-two-bar AABA structure of popular song (where the same eight-bar melody, the "A" phrase, is repeated three times, varied only by the different eight-bar "B" melody or "release"), he managed to weave shifting harmonies, rhythmic innovations, and chromatic surprises that give his melodies what Alec Wilder has dubbed their characteristic "aggressiveness" and "drive."[30] Ira, on the other hand, had learned to meld wit, vernacular ease, and "singability" into the same popular formulas, mastering that fundamental problem of the lyricist—"You gotta say 'I love you' in thirty-two bars"—with light-verse flourishes.

If one song demonstrates each brother's full mastery of his art, and their ability to fuse them together, it is "The Man I Love"—the first of their classic standards. The superb coalescence of words and music began with Ira's ability to discern what the melodic idea was "about"—to find words that would make articulate the emotional meanings in George's moving, but abstract, patterns of sound. Musicologist Wilfrid Mellers has characterized those tremulous, harmonic patterns as expressive of "all yearning,"[31] and indeed the evolution of the song is testimony to that musical meaning, for the melody expressed precisely such "yearning" to the Gershwin brothers as they worked on the song. It had originally been part of a verse George had written for another song, but as Ira tried to put words to this verse, both brothers felt that "It was a definite and insistent melody—so much so that we soon felt it wasn't light and introductory enough, as it tended to overshadow the refrain and to demand individual attention."[32] What the music seemed to call for, in other words, was its own expression, and Ira took that musical yearning and translated it into words that gave voice to a young woman's romantic longing for "The Man I Love."

As he put it, "I gave it a simple set of words,"[33] a remark that registers not only his characteristic modesty but his classification of "The Man I Love" as the kind of lyric that does not call attention to itself but instead lends itself unobtrusively to the articulation of the musical meanings. Nothing, apparently, could be simpler than the words that open the chorus:

> Some day he'll come along,
> the man I love.

Yet these opening phrases perfectly match the musical phrases, each of which begins, hesitantly, with a rest on the initial downbeat that quietly undercuts the singer's apparent assurance. That tension is strengthened by the clash of verb tenses—the tentative future of "he'll" set against the firm present of "I love" (instead of the grammatically parallel "I'll love").[34] With that and other subtle matches—or, better still, mismatches—between music and words, and words and words, Ira manages to weave witty sentiments out of the simplest of vernacular phrases.

These opening phrases also demonstrate Ira's mastery of another trick of the lyricist's trade, one which, as his friend Yip Harburg observed, "most laymen probably would never know about":

> When you're writing a song, where the rhyme falls makes it either hard or easy to remember. There are certain tricks that the skilled lyric writer

has to make a song memorable, provided it doesn't become mechanical and the hinges don't stick out. In other words, you want to rhyme as many places as you can without the average ear spotting it as purely mechanical.[35]

Ira deftly places such hidden rhymes at the very opening of the refrain, on *some* and *come*, then laces the next section with more insistently "memorable" rhymes that underscore the singer's rising hopes:

> He'll look at me and *smile*
> *I'll*
> underst*and*
> *and*
> in a little *while*
> he'll take my *hand*.

Throughout these first two sections, Ira has woven long singable vowels, from "*I'll* d*o* m*y* best t*o* m*a*ke him st*ay*" at the end of the first section to the long *o* sounds in the grammatically skewed negations that close the second:

> And *though* it seems absurd,
> I *know* we *both won't* say a word.

Ira also shows his mastery of the AABA musical structure. Here at the end of the second A-section he plants, in "say," an echo of the long *a* from the "m*a*ke him st*ay*" that closed the first A-section; then that same vowel recurs in the release with its renewed emotional urgency:

> M*ay*be I shall meet him Sun*day*
> M*ay*be Mon*day*. . . .

Then, just as those resonating vowels threaten to register too much confidence, George inserts what Alec Wilder has termed an "ingenious"[36] downward cadence and Ira matches it with another skewed parallel that sounds a note of clipped resignation:

> M*ay*be not.

When the singer's hopes again surge forward with the driving music, Ira constructs a powerful roll call of open and closed vowels, *i*s and *a*s and *e*s and *oo*s, plunging the release powerfully and irresistibly back into the final eight-bar A-section:

> Still—*I*'m sure to m*ee*t him one d*ay*.
> M*ay*be T*ue*sd*ay*
> will
> b*e* m*y* g*oo*d n*ew*s d*ay*.

With the reprise of the main melodic theme, Ira deepens those yearningly long *o* and *oo* vowels (even as he subtly weaves assonantal short vowels between "will" and "he'll," as well as among "build," "little," and "which"):

> He'll build a little *home*
> just meant for *two*
> from which I'll never *roam*
> *Who* would?
> Would *you*?

These phrases subtly but richly rework a much simpler passage from the 1921 version of "Boy Wanted":

> If he fits in my picture of a home,
> I'll be so nice, he'll never have to roam.

The revision, replete with the witty intrusion of the singer's vernacular rhetorical questions—"who would? would you?"—marks the maturation of the journeyman lyricist of "Boy Wanted" into the master of "The Man I Love."

That awareness carried over into the verse Ira had to write once this refrain was completed. While the introductory verse was regarded by many lyricists as the "throwaway" portion of a song (since singers frequently omitted it in performances), Ira Gershwin devoted as much care to verses as he did to refrains. George Gershwin devoted similar attention to verses, giving the brothers' songs yet another distinction— of all the great songwriters of their era the Gershwins were the masters of the verse. In the verse for "The Man I Love" Ira has the singer take the same wry cognizance of her listener as she does at the end of the refrain. Although she confesses "ev'ry night I dream a little dream," with a colloquial aside to the listener—"and, *of course*, Prince Charming is the theme"—she acknowledges the stereotypical character of her desire. Ira then follows that acknowledgment with a bit of pronoun by-play that further stresses her awareness that her longings are thoroughly generic:

> the he
> for me.

With such simple—and singable—phrases, Ira gave a light-verse curve to "the not-impossible he" formula. Balancing passion and wit, he sidestepped sentimental yearning by having the singer shrewdly reflect upon her emotions even as she expresses them.

With its near-perfect fusion of words and music (tarnished only by an awkwardly inverted "and so all else above I'm waiting for the man I love"), "The Man I Love" has become one of the great "standards" of American popular music—a song that sounds as fresh today as it did in 1924. Wilfrid Mellers, in fact, goes so far as to say it "can stake a claim to being the most moving pop song of our time."[37] If so, "The Man I Love" also exemplifies the unpredictable fate of "pop" songs. After the Gershwins completed the song in April of 1924, George played it at a party, whereupon financier and art patron Otto Kahn exclaimed, "This is the music of America. It will live as long as a Schubert lieder." Little could Kahn foresee that it would not even survive the "doctoring" that pulled a Broadway show together during its out-of-town run. Slated for the first act of *Lady, Be Good!*, "The Man I Love" was first moved to Act II because its languorous longing was "too quiet" for an otherwise fast-paced musical. Then, however, it was cut altogether, because the show was running long and audiences weren't applauding the song as energetically as they did the dance and novelty numbers.

Over the next few years "The Man I Love" was slated for other musicals—the original version of *Strike Up the Band* (1927) and *Rosalie* (1928)—but either the song did not survive the cuts or, in the case of *Strike Up the Band*, the show itself closed, as they say, "out of town." The song might have remained at the bottom of the Gershwins' vaunted "trunk," had it not been rescued by an unlikely savior—Lady Edwina Mountbatten. She had heard George perform the song at a New York party and asked him for a copy of the sheet music. When she returned to London, she had the Berkeley Square Orchestra play it in their concerts, where it was picked up by other London bands and then, across the Channel, by black jazz bands in Paris. Its popularity abroad induced the publisher, Max Dreyfus, to try to plug "The Man I Love" directly through Tin Pan Alley channels, rather than work it into another musical. First, however, he insisted the Gershwins take a cut in the sheet-music royalties; instead of receiving the usual three cents each, they agreed to take two cents apiece.

One problem with marketing "The Man I Love" as a straight pop song was that Ira had neglected one of the finer, but important, points of his new trade: in order for a song to get the maximum exposure through recordings, live and radio performance, its lyric needed to be androgynous—a genderless "me" cooing to an equally unisex "you"—so that it could be sung as easily by a male as by a female vocalist. The problem with "The Man I Love" was not so much the title, which easily became "The Girl I Love," but, as Ira himself admitted, with such obdurate lines as "and she'll be big and strong—the girl I love." Once Helen Morgan and other torch singers of the 1920s recorded it, "The Man I Love" quickly sold 100,000 copies of sheet music. Thus the song that evinced Ira's full mastery of the mosaic craft of fitting witty, singable, and memorable words to musical notes also demonstrated to him that the success of his work would depend not only on its artistry but upon the whims of producers, publishers, and public taste.

3

That Certain Feeling
1924–1927

Knowing him [Ira] personally so well, I have often wondered
how his leisurely temperament ever managed to keep pace
with George's supersonic velocity. As a mutual friend once
remarked, "Ira's a hard man to get out of an easy chair." The
answer is that there was a chemistry between the two that
touched off sparks, flames, explosions. Together they created
musical history.

— Arthur Schwartz

IF the Jazz Age, as F. Scott Fitzgerald claimed, was
born with the May Day riots of 1918, the era came
to full-blown adolescence at 3 P.M. on February 12,
1924, at New York's Aeolian Hall. Until the wail of Ross Gorman's
clarinet glissando opened the premiere performance of *Rhapsody in
Blue*, the afternoon's program had been a stuffy sequence of "jazzed"
classics and "concertized jazz," put together by Paul Whiteman, the
self-anointed "King of Jazz." Once George Gershwin strode to the piano
to perform his *Rhapsody*, however, the program turned electric. Originally entitled *American Rhapsody* (until Ira Gershwin suggested a
change after gazing at Whistler's brooding blue "nocturnes" and "sym-
phonies" at the Metropolitan Museum), *Rhapsody in Blue* captured the
rhythmic vitality of New York at the height of the Roaring Twenties.
By the end of that year George and Ira Gershwin had infused the same
Jazz-Age spirit into musical comedy when *Lady, Be Good!*, their first
successful musical, opened at the Liberty Theatre on December 1.
    Before *Lady, Be Good!*, the fortieth musical produced in 1924,
Broadway productions had run the gamut from sonorous operettas,

such as *The Student Prince* and *Rose-Marie*, to flippantly satirical revues like the *Greenwich Village Follies* and the *Grand Street Follies*. When the Gershwins teamed up to write songs for *Lady, Be Good!*, the American musical theater finally found its native idiom. George's score revealed his assimilation of blues and jazz, and Ira's lyrics registered his equally hard-won skill at setting such music to the American vernacular. The Jazz Age was, above all, an era intoxicated with its own language—*The American Language*, as H. L. Mencken had pugnaciously dubbed it with his volume of 1919. By 1927 it was clear to another linguistic innovator, Walter Winchell, coiner of "pfft" and "whoopee," that the "slang capital of the world" was the area around Broadway and Forty-second Street. There the worlds of music and theater, newspapers and magazines, sport and gambling, collided. Figures such as Ring Lardner and Damon Runyon, Ben Hecht and Charles MacArthur, Dorothy Parker and Robert Benchley, mingled at the Algonquin Round Table, Jack Dempsey's Cafe, and Lindy's. Out of that Babel emerged a "talk of the town" that Jack Conway of *Variety* acclaimed as the "national slanguage": terms like "ballyhoo," "click," "hit," "fan," "flop," "baloney," "turkey," "cinch," "hooch," "phoney," "racket," and "squawk," as well as such phrases as "Sultan of Swat," "Yes, We Have No Bananas," and Tex Guinan's greeting to the "big butter-and-egg men" who frequented her "speakeasies": "Hello, Suckers!" In 1937, after having edited several editions of *The American Language*, H. L. Mencken looked back upon Broadway in the 1920s and proclaimed: "It is from this quarter that most American slang comes."[1]

In *Lady, Be Good!*, and a string of Jazz-Age musicals that followed in its wake, Ira Gershwin set that language—its terms like "crush" and "mush," phrases such as "It's all bananas," and even "'s wonderful" way of clipping syllables from words—to his brother's music. The shows that provided the Gershwin brothers the opportunity to work their alchemy were produced by Alex Aarons and Vinton Freedley, two men who set out to resuscitate the Princess Theatre tradition—but jazzed up for the new decade with larger-scale productions and greater emphasis on dancing. Originally, however, Aarons and Freedley planned to have P. G. Wodehouse supply the lyrics for their shows. In turning from Jerome Kern to George Gershwin, the producers felt they had given the Princess tradition enough of a Jazz-Age face-lift and could retain Guy Bolton to write the book and Wodehouse the lyrics.

George, however, envisioned something beyond a resuscitation of the Princess Shows. As he described it to his father one night, his ambition was to "write an absolutely new type of musical show, with

modernistic words as well as modernistic tunes." "But where," he wondered aloud, "can I find a librettist? The well-known guys want the show
written their way." "Try Ira," was Morris Gershwin's reply.[2] Whether it
stemmed from fraternal (and paternal) loyalty, George's decision was
a fortuitous one, for the songs the Gershwins wrote for *Lady, Be Good!*
and the other Aarons and Freedley musicals that followed during the
decade had a rhythmic "thrust" that was their hallmark. That over-all
pace was quickened with energetic dance numbers, blackouts, and
"crossovers" (brief musical scenes played in front of the curtain while
scenery was changed, keeping the "action in a state of nearly perpetual
motion").[3] Even the scenery, designed along sleek and gleaming Art
Deco contours by Norman Bel Geddes, was as streamlined as the Gershwins' songs and reflected the world of the "smart set"—luxury hotels,
country clubs, and playboy mansions.

To achieve that all-important thrust a show had to be extensively
doctored throughout rehearsals—and sometimes even after opening
night. Songs had to be rewritten, shunted from scene to scene, thrown
out or tossed in, all in the interests of that magical rhythm. Since the
book was constantly undergoing revision, a lyricist was well advised
not to integrate his song too closely into a dramatic situation or tie it
to a particular character whose role might be cut after the next rehearsal. It was rhythmic pace, rather than integration between songs
and story, that melded these shows into organic wholes. Not only did
the book not matter, the fact of its not mattering—its open display of
its own frivolousness—highlighted the energetic fusion of the other
elements of the show—the dances, the sets, and, above all, the songs.

When the stars of *Lady, Be Good!*, the brother-and-sister dance
team of Fred and Adele Astaire, first read the script, they thought it
was "pretty stupid." Although it met their demand that they no longer
be cast as lovers but as brother and sister, Adele worried about the
"tacky book" and "weak plot" right up to the out-of-town opening in
Philadelphia. Fred, however, reassured her:

> I told her that I thought this was one instance where it might not matter
> because the whole thing had a new look to it, a flow, and also a new
> sound . . . This was no hackneyed ordinary musical comedy. It was slick
> and tongue-in-cheek, a definite departure in concept and design.[4]

Fred Astaire's concerns about the book had been allayed from the
moment he first heard the song "Oh, Lady Be Good," which indicated
to him how genuinely new—"smart" and slickly paced—this musical
was to be. "Oh, Lady Be Good" so epitomized the spirit of this musical

that once Guy Bolton and Fred Thompson heard it they changed the title of the show from *Black-Eyed Susan* to *Lady, Be Good!* Years later, the sculptor Isamu Noguchi, who created a streamlined, modernist bust of George Gershwin, marveled at the song's ability to transfix the "timely, yet timeless image of an era"[5]—the heady, glistening aura of the Jazz Age. The title itself was a 1920s slang plea for sexual favors, which, Ira found, could serve as a ready-made fit for George's plaintive blue-note melody. The whole lyric is confected of tongue-in-cheek catch-phrases, from "I tell you I am so awf'ly misunderstood" to "I'm going to end it all." Together they form a seamless fabric, woven through with perfectly "singable" long vowels and even some clever light-verse rhymes:

> I must *win some*
> *winsome miss;*
> can't go on like *this.*

While it gave the show its title, "Oh, Lady Be Good" was not at all integral to the book. Sung not by a lover pleading for romance but by a lawyer beseeching the aid of the heroine in his latest scheme, even lines such as "please have some pity—I'm all alone in this big city" are completely unrelated to the setting—a country estate in Rhode Island.

Equally imbued with the energetic pace of *Lady, Be Good!* (and equally irrelevant to the book) was "Fascinating Rhythm," the biggest hit to emerge from the show. As a recent discovery has revealed,[6] George had previously written a composition called "Syncopated City" (another reflection of his fascination with the rhythm of New York in the Jazz Age). When he played it for the producers, Alex Aarons asked him to save it for a future musical. As the brothers Gershwin set to work on *Lady, Be Good!*, George played "Syncopated City" and suggested he and Ira adapt it into a song for the show. Frances Gershwin, their sister, recalled Ira's reaction to the music: "George, what kind of a lyric can I write for that?" Then, after a pause, he mused, "Still . . . it is a fascinating rhythm." While that bemused phrase, as Ira himself said, was not "*the* brilliant title" it "*did* sing smoothly."[7]

Not only was the title-phrase singable, it fit the asymmetrical pattern of George's melody. Another composer would have handled the rhythm much more conventionally, giving his lyricist a simple sequence of parallel four-bar phrases, such as:

> Fas-ci-na-ting rhy-thm! (*rest*)
> You've got me on the go! (*rest*)

> Fas-ci-na-ting rhy-thm! (*rest*)
> I'm all a-qui-ver! (*rest*).

George Gershwin repeats his melodic fragment, but each time on a different beat and at a different point in each bar:

> Fas-ci-nat-ing rhy-thm! (*rest*) You've
> got me on the go! (*rest*) Fas-ci-
> na-ting rhy-thm! (*rest*) I'm all a-
> qui-ver (*rest*) (*rest*).

It's the "fascinating" that begins on the downbeat in measure two that catches the singer and listener by surprise, then by stretching that second "fascinating" across "the boundary between measures two and three," the "downbeat falls in the third measure without any new word to announce it—a downbeat both felt and missed."[8] The surprises are compounded, when, almost magically, words and rhythm come out right by the end of the fourth measure.

Not surprisingly, Ira said that "Fascinating Rhythm" was "the hardest song I ever had to fit words to."[9] Once he had come up with a title that fit George's unusual music, Ira went back to a song he had written in 1923, "Little Rhythm, Go 'Way," and reworked some of its phrases. In the earlier song he had set a much more conventional melody by William Daly and Joseph Meyer with such simple words as

> It's so persistent
> the day isn't distant, I know,
> when I'll go mad.

Inspired by George's intricate rhythm, Ira now recast those lines into the more vernacular—and percussively alliterative—

> so darn persistent
> the day isn't distant
> when it'll drive me insane!

Ira found that contractions keep a lyric colloquial, providing a verbal equivalent for George's frequent syncopations. In the most common of American catch-phrases Ira discovered verbal shards that perfectly fit the rhythms of George's musical phrases: "take a day off," "run along," and "make it snappy."

"It was a tricky rhythm for those days," Ira said, "and it took me several days to decide on the rhyme scheme."[10] When he showed his rhymes to his brother, however, George did not approve. "There was many a hot argument between us," George recalled, "over where the accent should fall."[11] Ira thought the last two notes of each phrase were accented equally and thus called for strong masculine rhymes (a rhyme on a single, accented syllable, such as *wake, quake,* a-*shake*). George maintained that since his downbeat fell on the next to the last note of the bar, the verbal accent should fall there as well and wanted Ira to provide feminine rhymes (two-syllable rhymes, with the second syllable unaccented, such as *hop*ping, *stop*ping). "The ear just didn't get it," Ira admitted, until George "had to explain it to me" by conducting it; once he saw his brother's hands describe that "funny beat—*Tah-tee-ta-ta-tah-ta*—" Ira realized the need for feminine rhymes:

> What a mess you're *ma*king!
> The neighbors want to know
> why I'm always *sha*king
> just like a *fliv*ver.

In "*fliv*ver" he found not only a match for the tremulously romantic "a-*quiv*er" that dangled at the end of his opening phrase but a nickname for the automobiles that set the new pace of American life in the 1920s. "When one considers," observed composer Arthur Schwartz, that Ira "was required to be brilliant within the most confining rhythms and accents," "Fascinating Rhythm" is "a truly phenomenal feat."[12]

Where "Oh, Lady Be Good" is a sly and slangy Jazz-Age proposition, "Fascinating Rhythm" captures the plight of a doped-out addict of the nervous energy of the era. In a recording made by the Astaires and George Gershwin during the London run of *Lady, Be Good!*, it is clearly Fred who has seized that new rhythm. While Adele sings the tricky chorus in a traditionally strict tempo, Fred experimented with a "rubato approach" that indicated he was "beginning to explore a new genre."[13] As he would prove again and again in musicals and films, Fred Astaire was the singer who best captured the intricate musical and verbal interplay of a Gershwin song.

Lady, Be Good! fulfilled a dream George Gershwin had had years earlier when he was a plugger on Tin Pan Alley and Fred Astaire a young hoofer in vaudeville: "Wouldn't it be great," George had said back then, "if I could write a musical show and you could be in it?"[14] Fittingly, *Lady, Be Good!* also gave Fred Astaire a number in which he could step out on his own. Ever since he was four years old, when his mother packed him and Adele on a train and left Omaha for New York and vaudeville, Fred had always danced with his sister. Now that he and Adele were playing siblings rather than lovers, Fred got to do a solo.

The dance evolved one day during rehearsals, when he embellished one of George's melodies with an impromptu tap routine. The melodic line echoed the clarinet glissando that opens *Rhapsody in Blue*, and Ira found a ready-made fit for it in another of the era's catch-phrases, "The Half of It, Dearie, Blues." According to Astaire, the title-phrase originated with a female impersonator in vaudeville, then quickly became part of the period's argot. F. Scott Fitzgerald had used it in "May Day," a short story about the birth of the Jazz Age, where the heroine muses about an upcoming dance:

> . . . she would talk the language she had talked for many years—her line—made up of the current expressions, bits of journalese, and college slang strung together in an intrinsic whole, careless, faintly provocative, delicately sentimental. She smiled faintly as she heard a girl sitting on the stairs near her say, "You don't know the half of it, dearie!"[15]

Taking that catch-phrase, Ira shrewdly couched it within the "I've got the . . . blues" formula to create a perfect "line" for George's melody, a line that keeps the syntax driving forward, piling up its sinuous modifier until it reaches "blues":

> I've got the—
> you don't know
> the half of it,
> dearie—
> blues.

On the recording of *Lady, Be Good!* Astaire sings the long-limbed line in an extended rhythmic curve as effortless as one of his dance moves, then throws in other slang terms, such as "bunk" and "duffer," with the steely precision of his taps. What Astaire said of George Gershwin also went for Ira: "He wrote for feet."[16]

Such vernacular songs set the rhythmic pace of *Lady, Be Good!* right from the opening number. When the curtain rose, Fred and Adele, just evicted from their apartment, are pluckily setting-up housekeeping on the street. As Adele searches for an outlet to plug in a lamp, a rain shower begins, and Fred nonchalantly launches into "Hang On to Me," a syncopated and colloquial reworking of the formulaic pollyanna weather song. As one critic noted, *Lady, Be Good!* "started at such a lively and melodious gait that it did not seem possible that it could last for any great time"; nevertheless as song flowed into song, "speed and hilarity and the lilting music were continuous."[17] Another singled out Ira for his contribution to that over-all pace: "There is a decidedly humorous poesy to Ira Gershwin's lyrics which stamp them as the most distinctive words to music we have listened to in the longest time."[18]

Lady, Be Good! inaugurated a series of streamlined musicals that ran through the rest of the decade. All had the same basic components—which usually came in twos: the two producers, Alex Aarons and Vinton Freedley; a book, by two writers; an orchestra that featured the twin pianos of Phil Ohman and Victor Arden, and, of course, songs by the two Gershwins. After *Lady, Be Good!* and *Tell Me More* (1925), George thought it brought good luck if a show's title was kept to two words: *Tip-Toes* (1925), *Oh, Kay!* (1926), *Funny Face* (1927), *Treasure Girl* (1928), and *Girl Crazy* (1930). All of these shows placed a premium on songs of romantic euphoria and other upbeat sentiments that were the perfect basis for Ira Gershwin's linguistic playfulness. What was taboo in these shows, however, were songs of romantic heartache or loss. Even when a ballad with just a touch of wistfulness, such as "The Man I Love," threatened to slow the frenetic energy of the production, it was cut.

While Ira expressed no regrets that such a "simple" lyric was dropped from *Lady, Be Good!*, he had some other qualms about his score:

> I had adequately fitted some sparkling tunes, and several singable love songs and rhythm numbers had resulted. Yet I was a bit bothered by there being no lyric I considered comic.[19]

By "comic," as opposed to "simple," Ira meant lyrics that not only fit singable words to music but infused a song with the light-verse wit of Gilbert and Wodehouse. To achieve such a fusion, Ira Gershwin knew his lyrics would have to be more integrated into the dramatic context of the show and more closely tied to particular characters.

Tip-Toes, in 1925, provided just such an opportunity for, as Ira put it, "some development in craftsmanship":

> *Tip-Toes* contained longer openings, many of the songs had crisp lines and the first-act finale carried plot action for four or five minutes. Also I liked the trio, "These Charming People," which seemed to amuse the audience. Up to then I'd often wondered if I could do a comedy trio like the ones P. G. Wodehouse came up with.[20]

The trio clearly was a lyrical lodgment that emerged from a specific occasion in the script—the heroine, a saucy flapper, and her villainous uncles scheme to "comport themselves" like "society folks" in order to swindle a millionaire. The lyric would have to be so integral to its dramatic context that it would advance the plot and gain particularity from its close association with the characters. While such witty patter songs were common in Gilbert and Sullivan, Ira would have to craft a "comic" trio, as P. G. Wodehouse had done, by following the un-Gilbert-like practice of fitting together words and musical notes.

Taking his inspiration from the dramatic context, Ira had the three culprits reveal their naiveté even as they lay plans to impersonate sophisticates. Thus one uncle boasts:

> When those million-dollar blokes pass,
> I will never make a faux pas.

The second uncle then condescends:

> Merely social climbing varmints;
> *ours* was made in undergarments,
> so you see before you one who's B.V.D.

Then Tip-Toes tops them with her own smattering of ignorance, when the acronym she flaunts (literally, "free on board") also reveals her as "fresh off the boat":

> If that's pedigree, enjoy it;
> my old man comes from Detroit,
> so I'll have you know that I am F.O.B.

Any concerns Ira had about his ability to follow Wodehouse's lead in fusing light verse and song must have been assuaged by the reviewer who wrote that "'These Charming People' has the best lines of any patter song since P. G. Wodehouse stopped turning out lyrics for Jerome Kern's tunes."[21]

Although "These Charming People" gave Ira a chance to write a comic lyric, in the other songs for *Tip-Toes* he had to continue to ply his verbal playfulness within the confines of George Gershwin's intricate music. "That Certain Feeling," one of George's trickiest melodies, takes a simple five-note phrase, such as an Alley tunesmith might compose, but laces it with surprising syncopations. Those subtle departures from the formulas of Tin Pan Alley, according to Alec Wilder, make "That Certain Feeling" "mint Gershwin," a quintessentially "native" song, marked by the qualities of "boldness," "wit," and "unexpectedness" that demonstrate Gershwin's "flair for the idiom" of American music.[22]

Such musical innovation, obviously, demanded the same kind of skill from the lyricist, and the blend of words and music in "That

Certain Feeling" is a perfect illustration of how Ira achieved his comic effects. What he did in this case was to match the musical syncopation with the way Americans fuse syllables. So intricate was the interplay between words, notes, and rests that Ira had to spell out the way a singer had to collapse two syllables into one:

> That cer-tain feel-ing
> (BEAT) *Thefirst* time I met you!
> I hit the ceil-ing!
> (BEAT) *Icould* not for-get you!

What he found, however, and would find time and again, was that many singers failed to catch the close matches (and even cleverer mismatches) between his words and his brother's music. In "That Certain Feeling," Ira complained, most singers missed "the rhythmic point" by "giving equal value to the first three notes and words,"[23] straightening them out by singing,

> No use concealing
> I've got what they call love

instead of

> No use concealing
> *I'vegot* what they call love.

Ira's lyrical syncopation wittily refreshes the formula of romantic euphoria with a verbal imbalance that registers the giddiness of "love-at-first-sight" (which gets a further jolt by an expression, "I hit the ceiling," usually used to register outrage).

Tip-Toes opened in December of 1925 at the Liberty Theatre, where *Lady, Be Good!* had closed after a strong run of 330 performances, and garnered reviews that, for the first time, took significant notice of Ira's contribution. While George received his usual lion's share of the credit in the *New York Herald Tribune*, the critic also singled out "the other Gershwin, Ira," for his "engaging lyrics."[24] The *New York Evening Post* gave him yet more ink:

> The lyrics for these creations are by the elder Gershwin, Ira, and combine sufficient freshness of rhyme and simplicity of appeal to make them popularly ideal. Occasionally an excursion into the playful mood would bring such rhyming as "enjoy it" and "Detroit" or "folks pass" and "faux pas."[25]

It was the dean of all newspaper critics, Alexander Woollcott, however, who made the most of Ira. Noting that "all the good tunes ever trolled will not make a musical comedy," Woollcott cautioned:

> care must even be taken to see that all the wreaths addressed to Gershwin do not go to the composer, for it is his elder brother, Ira Gershwin, who writes the lyrics which helped George Gershwin's tunes in their journey across the land. He has worked cleverly and engagingly this time. The result is good.[26]

As pleased as Ira must have been to receive critical recognition for himself—and for the importance of lyrics in musical comedy—he must have been even more elated by a letter from his brilliant contemporary Lorenz Hart. Hart wrote that the lyrics in *Tip-Toes* "gave me as much pleasure as George Gershwin's music," then took "the liberty of saying that your rhymes show a healthy improvement over those of *Lady, Be Good!*" In addition to the wit of "These Charming People" and "That Certain Feeling," Hart's fancy would have been tickled by "When Do We Dance?," an obligatory dance number, which Ira enlivened with better than obligatory rhymes, such as "I'm fed up with discussions about the music of Russians" and "Conversation so highbrow is much too heavy for my brow." Similarly, in "Sweet and Low-Down" (where he updated the traditional lullaby "Sweet and Low" with 1920s "lowdown"), he rhymed "th*is city*" and "electr*icity*," "nation" and "syncopation," and "crisis" with "my advice is." Even in some of his simplest lyrics, such as the winsome "Looking For a Boy," he tossed off another of his "apocopated rhymes"—"where one word rhymes with only part of another":

> I'll be blue until he comes my w*ay*;
> hope he takes the cue when I am s*aying*—.

Little wonder that Lorenz Hart, who had long railed against Tin Pan Alley's ignorance of the intricacies of masculine, feminine, near, eye, slant, assonantal, and other kinds of rhyme, took special delight in Ira's achievement in *Tip-Toes*. Hart concluded by saying, "It is a great pleasure to live at a time when light amusement in this country is at last losing its brutally cretin aspect" and praising Ira's "delicacies" as evidence that at last "songs can be both popular and intelligent."[27]

What Hart glimpsed in 1925 was the dawning of a lyrical renaissance. Before then, he and Richard Rodgers had seen their witty songs summarily dismissed by producers as "too collegiate," and Rodgers was on the verge of giving up songwriting for the children's underwear business. Then in 1925 the pair was invited to supply songs for a satirical revue, the *Garrick Gaieties*. Designed by young actors to raise funds for the Theatre Guild, the *Garrick Gaieties* was originally planned for a two-night stand, but Hart's lyrics, bristling with pyrotechnic rhymes and literate allusions to Strindberg and Ibsen, kept it running for more than a year. Some of Hart's wittiest lyrics, such as the patter song "Manhattan" and the trenchantly unsentimental "Sentimental Me," went on to become independently popular on Tin Pan Alley and were reprinted in newspapers across the country. Such success surprised even the lyricist, who, in an interview,[28] confessed his amazement that a lyric with "very intricate and elaborate rhymes" should be "the hit of the show," which "is usually a very simple one with monosyllabic words." Rodgers and Hart's success challenged another assumption—that "the cleverest lyricists"—and here Hart cited P. G. Wodehouse—"are seldom big-hit writers." Hart's success, along with that of Ira Gershwin, Howard Dietz, and other young lyricists who brought light-verse techniques to bear on songwriting, was clearly proving that it was no longer just "banal lyrics" that garnered "royalty statements from the music publishers" of Tin Pan Alley.[29]

By the end of 1925 *Variety* gave its official seal of approval to this lyrical renaissance:

> It hasn't been so long ago when a maudlin group of words strung to a tune constituted a "heart song." An inane collection of funny sayings run off to simple music was a "patter" song. Whenever it came time in our musical pieces for the hero or heroine to sing, the action of the play simply stopped until they were finished. Nothing was advanced in the lyrics; they were repetitious. Throughout every few bars came the words "I love you" and usually a sad sweet finale set to the words "and love like ours will never die."

While noting some exceptions, such as Wodehouse's lyrics for the Princess Shows, *Variety* went on to lament that the "general run of musical comedies were stupidly worded." But, it trumpeted, "in the last two or three seasons, things have taken a change." As evidence, *Variety* quoted numerous lyrics by Lorenz Hart, openly comparing him to Gilbert, but also praised Ira Gershwin's "great lyrics . . . great principally because they fitted the music precisely."[30]

Such praise must have doubled Ira's determination to write more "comic" lyrics, but the next Aarons and Freedley show provided him with even less integration and particularity to inspire a light-verse curve to his lyrics. During the summer of 1926 he and George wrote songs in New York while Guy Bolton and P. G. Wodehouse worked on the book in England—a transatlantic division of labor that made integration between lyrics and story even more difficult. Originally called *Mayfair*, the title of the show was first changed to the even more Anglophile *Cheerio*, then finally became *Oh, Kay!* Whether "okay" originated in Choctaw phrase "Okeh" ("It is correct") or as an abbreviation for Martin Van Buren's nickname ("Old Kinderhook"—after his New York hometown), it elicited H. L. Mencken's praise as "without question the most successful of all Americanisms."[31] As such, it was the perfect title for the most spirited musical of the Jazz Age.

In September, "doctoring" began in earnest on *Oh, Kay!*, with director, composer, writers, choreographers, and lyricist alternately tugging the show together—and apart. As with *Lady, Be Good!* the rhythmic pace was set by songs, dances, and snappy one-liners ("Is my face dirty or is it my imagination?" "Your face is clean, but I don't know about your imagination"). The book was a lightweight spoof of Prohibition: an English Duke, reduced by British taxation policies to using his yacht for rum-running off Long Island, stores his bootleg wares in the basement of an American millionaire's mansion. The Duke's sister, Lady Kay, falls in love with the playboy millionaire through the usual gamut of mistaken identities and disguises. After considerable revision, the book was streamlined to a main plot, rescuing the playboy from his marital commitments and engaging him to Kay, and a subplot, keeping the Duke and his bumbling accomplices out of the clutches of the revenue officer, in order to highlight songs and dances.

The show that emerged from such doctoring, as Guy Bolton himself observed, captured the rhythm of the era:

> It was the "Hooch Age," and the spirit that made bathtub gin (the human spirit, not the stuff you bought at the druggist's with a doctor's prescription) was the same devil-may-care quality that accounted for flagpole sitters, marathon dancers and the bull market.[32]

Throughout rehearsals the songs were reworked to maintain the heady pace of the show. Of the nineteen songs the brothers wrote, only eleven were used, the others discarded to make way for plot revisions, dance numbers, or cast changes. Most that remained were free-standing rhythmic songs like "Fidgety Feet" and "Heaven on Earth," which, as Edward Jablonski notes, have nothing to do with the story and "would serve in any scene," but were nevertheless "carefully plotted and paced to keep the show moving."[33]

While none of the songs are closely integrated into a particular dramatic scene, Ira did manage to achieve a more general level of integration between songs and story by weaving through his lyrics the thematic motif of time so central to the book and to the whole conception of an Aarons and Freedley musical. Thus a romantic duet, "Maybe," plays with the catch-phrase "soon or late," while the spiritual, "Clap Yo' Hands," has a warning at once terpsichorean and philosophical: "Don't you lose time! Don't you lose time!"

The motif of seizing time recurs in "Do, Do, Do," as the archly elegant catch-phrase title is followed by the skewed grammar of "what you done, done, done before." In this lyric Ira did manage to take somewhat more specific inspiration from the script. In a scene where Lady Kay and her playboy impersonate honeymooners to keep out of the clutches of the revenue officer, the dialogue is drenched in baby talk. Taking the standard Tin Pan Alley term of endearment, "baby," Ira wrote a plea that oozed the same gooey babble:

> Baby, see
> it's A B C—
> I love you and you love me . . .
> So don't, don't, don't
> say it won't, won't, won't
> come true, baby!

The word "do" itself was a staple double entendre of 1920s lyrics, from Buddy DeSylva's "Do It Again" (1922) through Cole Porter's "Let's Do It" (1928), but Ira adamantly insisted that his "do" was purely about kissing and did not smack of "musical comedy 'smart smut.'" It had "face not body value."[34]

The lyric's plea for seizing the moment may reflect not only the fast-paced rhythm of *Oh, Kay!* in general but the flurry of the song's composition. While his lyrics usually took days of labor, Ira completed "Do, Do, Do" in a remarkably short time. He had suggested to George that a song could be built around the current catch-phrase, and just as they sat down at the piano, Ira's fiancée, Leonore Strunsky, called to say she was coming over by taxi. By the time she arrived, the brothers had finished the chorus.

Somehow in the midst of rehearsals and doctoring, Ira and Leonore managed to seize some time to get married. Ira, characteristically, had let Leonore take the lead, from courtship to the altar. They had met at one of the many soirées George, occasionally with Ira in tow, attended in Greenwich Village. There, while George held forth at the piano, usually flanked by starlets, Ira would withdraw to a corner. It was Leonore, the attractive "dynamo" of the literate and artistic Strunsky family, who sought him out and, by her own admission, fell in love "before he did" and even "proposed marriage."[35]

Ira's courtship, as well as his work on *Oh, Kay!*, were suddenly interrupted by an emergency appendectomy. Confined to his hospital bed for six weeks, he finally persuaded the doctors to release him with his own plea to seize the time—"They're waiting for me to finish the lyrics."[36] Even then he could work only sporadically, so another young lyricist, Howard Dietz, was brought in to help. Dietz had also started as a light-verse poet, a self-styled "literary aficionado" who, along with F.P.A. and Dorothy Parker, "lived by a code of scansion."[37] When he turned to lyric-writing, he, too, had to learn the simple crafts of singability and memorability that distinguish song lyrics from poetry.

Those newly mastered skills prompted Dietz's greatest contribution to *Oh, Kay!*—a suggestion for the title of one of the show's ballads, "Someone To Watch Over Me." Originally, Ira recalled, the melody for "Someone To Watch Over Me" had begun as a "fast and jazzy" dance number:

> Early in 1926 George wrote a rather exciting tune which he played at a brisk tempo. Obviously it was destined to be a stage dance-and-ensemble number—one that features rhythm, delights the dance director, receives applause in the theater, but makes little or no progress outside. The book for the new show wasn't ready, so there was little use thinking up a lyric notion until we knew the exact spot where it would fit and what dancer or dance team would do it. Then one day, for no particular reason and hardly aware of what he was at, George played the dance tune in a comparatively slow tempo. The melody hadn't reached the halfway mark when both of us had the same reaction: this was no . . . rhythm tune but rather a wistful and warm one—to be held out until the proper stage occasion arose for it.[38]

It was at this point that the fresh ear of Howard Dietz came in; after throwing out several seven-syllable suggestions for the main phrase, Dietz hit upon the rich vowels and soft consonants of "Someone To Watch Over Me." Ira, who always complained that coming up with a title was the lyricist's most difficult task, snatched the phrase and retreated to work out the rest of the lyric on his own.

At first he could take inspiration from where his lyrical lodgment would fit into the book. In the original script, Bolton and Wodehouse had inserted a parenthetical request for a "lady-in-waiting" song early in Act I and even suggested using "'The Man I Love' (or an equivalent)." Their only stipulation to the Gershwins was that the song allow a

change of scenery: "NUMBER MUST BE LONG ENOUGH TO COVER CHANGE."
The character of Lady Kay also helped Ira create a lyric with more
particularity; the female leads of *Lady, Be Good!* and *Tip-Toes* were
generic flappers, but Lady Kay is at once sophisticated and innocent,
hard-boiled and tender, urbanely flippant yet romantically vulnerable.
The comparatively rich role went to the English stage sensation Gertrude Lawrence, whose voice and dramatic ability far exceeded that of
any actress the Gershwins had yet written for. When Guy Bolton and
P. G. Wodehouse first saw Gertrude Lawrence in an English revue,
their reaction, as they put it, was much like that of Keats to Chap-
man's *Homer*.

> She had everything. She could play sophisticated comedy, low comedy,
> sing every possible type of song, and she looked enchanting.[39]

Although she had never done musical comedy, when Gertrude Lawrence learned that George Gershwin would compose the songs, she
promptly signed on. The lyrics Ira wrote for Gertrude Lawrence in
Oh, Kay! were merely an overture to what he would provide for her,
fifteen years later, when she starred in *Lady in the Dark*. In both musicals, however, Ira would also find that the star could be imperious,
changing his most carefully crafted lyrics to suit *her* sense of the "proper
stage occasion."

With character and situation in mind, Ira lodged his lyric near the
end of the first scene, where Gertrude Lawrence makes her initial
appearance, braving revenue officers to search for a man she has rescued in her launch. Since she never learned his name (he turns out,
of course, to be the playboy millionaire), she vows, "I'm sure I'll meet
him again *someday!*" (a clear echo of "The Man I Love"). Integrating
his lyric into this dramatic context, Ira gave a world-weary twist to the
standard "lady-in-waiting" formula. That transformation is established
in the verse, which opens with a biblical allusion that foreshadows the
closing plea of "where is the shepherd for this lost lamb":

> There's a saying old
> says that love is blind;
> still, we're often told
> "Seek and ye shall find."

He also uses the dramatic situation to give this innocent singer an
imaginary "big affair" and even a torch to carry:

> Looking ev'rywhere,
> haven't found him yet;
> he's the big affair

> I cannot forget—
> only man I ever think of with regret.

While such jaded lines made perfectly good sense in the first scene, they were pointless when the song was moved to the middle of Act II—to ensure that it did not impede the all-important pace of the show. There, coming long after Kay has met, kissed, and cavorted with her beloved millionaire, the witty twist made little sense—the "penalty," as Wayne Shirley points out, "for writing lyrics too closely connected with the plot of a show."[40]

Yet if the lyric made little integral sense in its new position, it was now sandwiched in between two rhythmic dance numbers and stood out as the major ballad in the score. It also retained its particularity from a character who was a combination of hard experience and innocent yearning. In the hands of Gertrude Lawrence, "Someone To Watch Over Me" received a rendition that, as one reviewer put it, "wrung the withers of even the most hard-hearted"[41] and provided the audience "with an experience they would remember and relate for years."[42] Instead of singing the song in traditional fashion—from center stage and directly to the audience—she made it much more introspective by standing off to one side and singing to a rag doll she held in her arms (a doll George Gershwin had noticed in a Philadelphia toy store and bought for her to use in the number). Even the costuming added to the emotional effect, for at this point in the story Lawrence was in disguise as the maid (giving her an opportunity to show off a Cockney accent). Up until then, she had been tough-talking, rum-running, sophisticated Lady Kay, who initially confronted the man of her dreams with a pistol in her hand. With "Someone To Watch Over Me," however, she became the "dear little girl," yearning for protection.

To heighten the poignancy, Gertrude Lawrence even went so far as to alter Ira's lyric, dropping the vernacular and comic touches he used to keep it from lapsing into sentimentality. In the initial A-section Ira had used a colloquial contraction—"someone who'll watch over me"—but Lawrence reverted to the formality of Dietz's title-phrase: "someone *to* watch over me." Similarly she dropped the 1920s catch-phrases Ira so carefully wedded to the show's over-all themes of time's passage and the need to seize the moment:

> Won't you tell him, please,
> to put on some speed,
> follow my lead?
> Oh, how I need
> someone to watch over me.

Instead, Gertrude Lawrence sang the more elevated and sentimentally strained,

> Won't you tell him
> all my love I will save,
> I'll be his slave,
> Oh, how I crave
> someone to watch over me.

If Lawrence's revisions turned "Someone To Watch Over Me" even further away from the kind of "comic" lyric Ira wanted to write, it showed how powerfully a song could be showcased when performer, staging, and dramatic moment coalesced.

Even as *Oh, Kay!* marked the acme of Aarons and Freedley musicals of the 1920s, changes were under way that would eventually spell the demise of such frothy shows. On the one hand, those changes in musical theater would give Ira his long-sought opportunity to write comic lyrics that were thoroughly integrated into the book of a musical. At the same time, however, change would come gradually enough to allow him to continue to write some of his greatest simple lyrics, using the confines of his brother's music to refresh the tiredest romantic formulas with his playful handling of the American language.

4

'S Wonderful
1927–1930

Now, in song lyric writing, sound is one of the most important things, and I don't think anybody surpasses my brother, Ira, when it comes to inventing song titles. He fancies abbreviation. For example, "Sunny Disposish" and "'S Wonderful." And don't ever let Ira hear you say, "It's Wonderful." Just "'S wonderful, 'S marvelous."

—George Gershwin

ONE indication of the changes that would transform Broadway came in 1927 when Oscar Hammerstein and Jerome Kern approached Edna Ferber about turning her novel *Show Boat* into a musical. Ferber was understandably puzzled, for the nature of the American musical in the 1920s, epitomized by the shows of Aarons and Freedley, seemed an odd vehicle for her book's tragic themes of racism and miscegenation. When Hammerstein and Kern played "Ol' Man River" for her, however, Ferber realized that something genuinely new had emerged—an American musical drama, in which songs could be integrally related to a serious plot and fully developed characters. While its roots were in traditional European operetta, the story, characters, and setting of *Show Boat* were indigenously American. *Show Boat* was an enormous success, running for 527 performances, but the change it heralded would not be evident for a number of years. Although Hammerstein pleaded with Kern to collaborate on similar musical dramas, the composer insisted they return to lighter fare, such as *Sweet Adeline* and *Roberta*. Not until 1943, when Hammerstein teamed with

Richard Rodgers on *Oklahoma!*, did musical drama fully establish itself on Broadway.

Another indication that the American musical was moving toward integration of songs and story came with the Gershwins' 1927 production. *Strike Up the Band* integrated songs into the story and even used them to advance the plot in lengthy stretches of lyrical pastiche, where soloist and chorus sing rhymed dialogue. For George, *Strike Up the Band* represented the chance to compose music that resonated with its dramatic context; for Ira, it was a unique opportunity to write lyrics that were intimately related to particular scenes and characters. If *Show Boat* was an American adaptation of traditional European operetta, *Strike Up the Band* was a native version of the comic operettas of Gilbert and Sullivan. *Show Boat* was a success, whereas, *Strike Up the Band* closed, out of town, in Philadelphia. The Gershwins would successfully revive *Strike Up the Band* in 1930 and then go on to write other satirical operettas, but for the remainder of the 1920s they were confined to formulaic musicals cast in the mold of *Lady, Be Good!*

That formula, moreover, was beginning to show signs of strain. The next production that rolled off the Aarons and Freedley assembly line at first seemed to have all the lineaments of another success: Fred and Adele Astaire, fresh from completing the successful London run of *Lady, Be Good!*, were slated to star; Guy Bolton and Fred Thompson would write the book; and the Gershwins, of course, would supply the songs. The source of the problems, as usual, was the book. Originally entitled *Smarty*, the show's genesis, as Fred Astaire recalled it,reveals how far such musical comedies were from dramatic substance, let alone integration of songs and story:

> We had discussed it with Alex and Vint [Alex Aarons and Vinton Freedley] and finally came round to having an idea written up whereby I would be the legal guardian of three girls, one, of course, being Adele. Her romance would concern another fellow. This seemed to be a good idea, but we had no thought about what would happen from there on.[1]

Problems began when Guy Bolton, committed to too many different projects, had to back out. As his replacement he recommended Robert Benchley, a brilliant humorist but hardly the skilled playwright needed to set the streamlined pace such musicals required. "The script was a problem," Astaire recalled, "one of those things that wouldn't work—even in rehearsals." Dress rehearsal for the Philadelphia opening was so bad that the producer asked the cast to run through the entire show again—at 1:30 in the morning. Afterwards, an exhausted Fred Astaire still felt that "opening anywhere with that mess was not pleasant."[2]

The Philadelphia reviewers pounced on the lengthy and ragged production, and Alex Aarons calmly informed the dejected cast that he was holding the show on the road for a few extra weeks while the script was completely rewritten. Robert Benchley was in no mood for such extensive doctoring. Noted for his skewering of other people's plays—most pitilessly of *Abie's Irish Rose*—Benchley's experience in mounting a musical left him chastened. "Gosh," he admitted, "how can I criticize other people's shows from now on?"[3] Pleading other commitments, he backed out of the show and gave up all royalties, though it embarrassed him that some of the sheet-music for songs from *Smarty* had already been printed and carried his name.

In Benchley's place, Paul Gerard Smith was brought in for what amounted to major surgery. The cast carried the patient from Philadelphia to Washington to Wilmington, rehearsing the revised version during the day while performing the moribund turkey at night. As Ira recalled, "Everyone concerned with the show worked day and night, recasting, rewriting, rehearsing, recriminating—of rejoicing, there was none."[4] In all, he and George wrote twenty-four songs for the production, eleven of which had to be cut to accommodate changes in the script. Cast changes only added to their woes. The replacement of Stanley Ridges by Alex Kearns (in the lead role of an aviator—a staple of many shows that year, designed to cash in on the Lindbergh ballyhoo) meant cutting "How Long Has This Been Going On?," one of George's most sensuously beautiful melodies. Ira's title, a catch-phrase associated with finding one's mate in the arms of another, is transformed into the exclamation of lovers experiencing their first truly passionate kiss. In the verse, one of his very best, Ira gave a curve to the formula of love-at-first-kiss with clever, light-verse rhymes:

> As a tot,
> when I trot-
> ted in little velvet panties,
> I was kissed
> by my sist-
> ers, my cousins, and my aunties.
> Sad to tell,
> it was hell,
> an inferno worse than Dante's!

As good as the song was, "How Long Has This Been Going On?" had to be replaced with "He Loves and She Loves," a melody more in Kearns's vocal range and a simpler lyric that, as Ira put it, "managed to get over" to the out-of-town audiences.[5]

While most of the changes were in the direction of greater simplicity, one bit of doctoring provided Ira with the opportunity to write a "comic" lyric. In a scene added to "punch up" the script, two characters get drunk on bootleg punch and exchange a series of platitudes:

> Where you from?
> Omaha.
> Omaha? You don't tell me—
> Yes, sir—Omaha.
> Well well well—it's a small world, isn't it?
> Yes, sir—You from Omaha?
> No-no—just the same—it's a small world.[6]

Reminded of Sinclair Lewis's satire on the jargon of the 1920s, Ira wrote "The Babbitt and the Bromide," a lyric about two "sub-stan-ti-al" and "solid citizens" who meet on the avenue and strike up a conversation that consists of nothing but inanities:

> "Hello!"   "How are you?"
> "How-za folks?"   "What's new?"
> "I'm great!"   "That's good!"
> "Ha-ha!"   "Knock wood."
> "Well, well!"   "What say!"
> "How-ya been?"   "Nice day."

When they encounter one another again after ten years, they only repeat the same litany of clichés, then, after they die and meet again in heaven they run through the same catch-phrases "as they were strumming on the strings." The song was set up by Adele's satiric observation that "Everybody is cuckoo these days. The dumber you talk, the more intelligent everyone thinks you are." She and Fred then launched into their classic "runaround" routine, peddling around the stage with deadpan faces, utterly oblivious to one another as they sang the clichés. So adroitly had Ira joined light verse and song that Louis Kronenberger included "The Babbitt and the Bromide" in his 1934 *Anthology of Light Verse*—the first time a song lyric was so honored.

The book for *Smarty* poked fun at another of the era's linguistic foibles—the "flapperese" that F. Scott Fitzgerald described as a "mental pablum" voiced by the uncorseted, bobbed, and berouged "new" women of the 1920s. One of the characters speaks in this idiom continually:

It's so incredibly—whatever the word is—I mean after all I have done for him when I *actually* stepped in and saved him from—well, I mean, you can't blame a girl—or can you . . . it's so *excruciating*, in a way, here am I—or rather you can't blame me for feeling a little miffed. In fact I'm simply *seething* with *spleen*—I mean I am *honestly* all of a bib-and-tucker at this point because, after all—.

Her befuddled auditors ask, "Do you speak any other language than English?" and, when another addle-brained lovely launches into the same babble, they wonder: "My God! Do they all talk that way?"

One feature of such flapperese was the clipping of syllables from words, as in "Don't be ridic'" and "Positively sil'." Light-verse writers had parodied that linguistic penchant, and Ira Gershwin now used it to render the clichés of romantic euphoria:

> Don't mind telling you
> in my humble fash',
> that you thrill me through
> with a tender pash'.

Such snippings undercut the sentimental hyperboles and refreshed the tritest of rhymes:

> When you said you care,
> 'magine my emosh';
> I swore, then and there,
> permanent devosh'.

All of this linguistic byplay and foreplay took place in the verse; when Ira turned to the chorus, he clipped and fused his syllables to register the giddiness of romantic union:

> 'S wonderful! 'S marvelous!
> You should care for me!
> 'S awful nice! 'S paradise!
> 'S what I love to see!

Little wonder that Ira was miffed by singers who blithely restored his lyric's truncated terms to "It's wonderful, it's marvelous . . ."

His other lyrics for the show also bristle with catch-phrases of the era: "The World Is Mine" calls for "making hay," "Let's Kiss and Make Up" assures "everything is jake," and "My One and Only" confesses "my cards are on the table" then matches George's percussive twelve-note outburst with "what am I gonna do if you turn me down?" Ira turned one catch-phrase, "High hat!," into a formula for romantic success:

> High hat!
> You've got to treat them high hat!
> Don't let them know that you care;
> but act like a Frigidaire.

To stage the number, the director decked out Fred Astaire and the male chorus in what would soon become Fred's trademark garb—top hat and tails.

Changes in *Smarty* continued right up to the New York opening. Even with all the doctoring, Fred Astaire still feared that after five years of playing in nothing but successes he and Adele were in for trouble. In an uncharacteristic blow-up in the dressing room he shouted, "I hate flops—and this is one. We might as well face it, this damn turkey hasn't got a prayer." But, with one final bit of doctoring, a change of title to *Funny Face* (the song "Funny Face" had been added in Atlantic City), the show opened to rave reviews and ran for 244 performances, just a dozen short of *Oh, Kay!*'s run. Astaire was pleasantly amazed:

> The over-all something was there. What a pleasant surprise! Having gone through such a series of mishaps and revisions on the road, we simply didn't know what we had.[7]

Astaire's realization was echoed by the critics, who lambasted the book as "perishable" but exulted in the songs, the dances, and the brisk pace of the production. One reviewer, Robert Benchley, ruefully recalled his lack of faith in the "doctoring" that created such musicals:

> Every once in a while we drop in at *Funny Face* to count the house and figure out how much money we lost (it is well up in the four figures already) and we are putting it with the money we didn't bet on Tunney and are planning to buy a town car with it.[8]

Funny Face was the first production at Alex Aarons and Vinton Freedley's new Alvin Theatre (named, 1920s style, by clipping and fusing a syllable from each man's first name). Given the extraordinary resuscitation of what had seemed a dead show, one would think that the Alvin could count on full houses for an endless series of fast-paced musicals in the formula set by *Lady, Be Good!* For the Gershwins, however, that formula had nearly exhausted itself, and, despite the failure of *Strike Up the Band*, the brothers still longed to work on a show where songs and story could be fully integrated.

Their next assignment, unfortunately, offered even less opportunity for such integration than an Aarons and Freedley musical. Florenz Ziegfeld, holding the brothers to a commitment they had made earlier to do a show for him, summoned them aboard his new musical, *Rosalie*—despite the fact that Sigmund Romberg and P. G. Wodehouse had already written a score for the show. The great impresario was determined that his star Marilyn Miller would sing "The Man I Love" (though it again was cut before the show opened), and he summarily instructed the Gershwins to supply some additional numbers from their "trunk" of songs.

George and Ira dutifully recycled "How Long Has This Been Going On?" from *Funny Face*, "Show Me the Town," a reject from *Oh, Kay!*, and "Yankee Doodle Rhythm" from the failed *Strike Up the Band*. None of these, of course, bore any relation to the story of *Rosalie*, which shrewdly cashed in on the ballyhoo over the Queen of Roumania's visit to America in 1926. "Rosalie" is a princess from operetta-land, "Romanza," who, naturally, falls in love with a commoner—a West Point cadet who, like Lindbergh, flies solo across the Atlantic to join her. Not only were the Gershwin trunk songs out of step with the story, they clashed with Wodehouse and Romberg's rousing operetta numbers such as "The Hussars March" and "The West Point Song." Ira and Wodehouse collaborated with George Gershwin on a few new songs for *Rosalie*, but the slangy exuberance of "Oh, Gee!—Oh Joy!" and "Say So!," replete with such terms as "gotcha" and "sappy," seemed out of place amid the swashbuckling score. Amazingly, however, the mélange held together, helped by Joseph Urban's spectacular set and costume design. At one point, an enraptured reviewer gasped, "fifty beautiful girls in simple peasant costumes of satin and chiffon" rush on stage from one side while "fifty hussars in a fatigue uniform of ivory white and tomato bisque" march on from the other.[9] And so they rushed and so they marched, from its opening night on January 10 of 1928, on and on, for 335 performances of *Rosalie*.

For the Gershwins, however, *Rosalie* meant merely marking time in their progress toward writing songs for an integrated musical, but their next project did little to realize that goal. Another Aarons and Freedley venture, *Treasure Girl*, starred Gertrude Lawrence, but neither her considerable talents nor those of the Gershwins could redeem the book, a tedious and convoluted tale of a treasure hunt. Fred Thompson and Vincent Lawrence tried to fashion a more complex character for Gertrude Lawrence. Building on her role in *Oh, Kay!*, they made her more worldly and cynical and her leading man equally so, but to the point of being sadistic. While audiences and critics found the play an "evil thing,"[10] however, Ira was inspired by such characters to write love songs with greater particularity.

Given characters who feel "love is a wash-out," he ventured into the anti-romantic sentiments that were the staple of Lorenz Hart and Cole Porter lyrics. In one duet, Ira has the lovers consider the prospect of marriage—only to reject it after questioning one another about mundane practicalities. "Do you sleep with window shut?" she inquires; when he answers in the affirmative, she snaps, "Charming, *but*—I don't think I'll fall in love today." He, in turn, hearing her speculate about opening cans and laying out "kippers," asks,

> "Don't you know how to cook?"

to which she replies,

> "I could look—in a book."

But then she gives the matter a bit more thought and concludes:

> Imagine signing up for life,
> then finding peas roll off his knife.

Finally the two agree that, given their "incompatibility" (a seven-syllable word which Ira wittily rhymed with "A B C") they should not be like "the other sheep" who fall in love only to end up in "marriage—maybe divorce."

Ira admitted that for "I Don't Think I'll Fall in Love Today" he took inspiration from G. K. Chesterton's "A Ballade of Suicide," with its refrain of "I think I will not hang myself today." The inspiration carried over to an even darker duet, "What Causes That?," which begins with the man's harsh accusation,

> You're so full of trickery;
> life is bitter as chicory,

then his resolve,

> I go contemplating suicide
> You're much too much for me!

The rest of the lyric catalogues his plans for self-destruction:

> If I should climb the Brooklyn Bridge and jump off—
> Oh, I suppose you'd ask, "What causes that?"
> If I should get a gun and bump this chump off—
> Oh, I suppose you'd ask, "What causes that?"

To all of this the woman nonchalantly responds with some helpful suggestions:

> Really, you don't have to mope around
> and burn up as you do;
> There's a cannon and a rope around—
> There's lots of poison too.

He then gives her a backhanded compliment: "You're not so dumb that you don't know the answer: loving you is what causes that!"

While such acerbic sentiments exercised Ira's wit in new directions, they did not please audiences. The only song from *Treasure Girl* to become popular, "I've Got a Crush on You," confines its mordant curve to the verse, where an egoistic oaf, reversing gender roles, congratulates his lover on *her* catch of *him*:

> How glad the many millions
> of Annabelles and Lillians
> would be
> to capture me,
> but you had such persistence
> you wore down my resistance.

After she agrees, tongue-in-cheek, "How I won you I shall never, never know," he blithely adds insult to injury:

> It's not that you're attractive—
> but oh, my heart grew active
> when you
> came into view.

In the chorus, the sentiment is more straightforward, though Ira subtly portrays this narcissist as less infatuated with his beloved than with his own newly discovered emotional depths:

> I never had the least notion
> that I could fall with so much emotion.

Significantly, "I've Got a Crush on You" did not become popular as a result of its presence in *Treasure Girl*, where it was performed as a fast-paced dance number, but several years later, when torch singer Lee Wiley recorded it, to Ira Gershwin's surprise, at a much slower tempo. Backed by a tremulous accompaniment, Wiley overrode all of the Gershwins' efforts to keep the song comically unsentimental. Usually, he explained, he restricted himself to only the most common terms of endearment—"baby," "dear," "honey"—militantly avoiding the like of "sweetheart." In "I've Got a Crush on You," he was sure that, in this case "sweetie pie" "wasn't too diabetic." The way Wiley coos those words must have given Ira second thoughts, however, and her throaty delivery of "The world will pardon my mush" melts all the irony out of the slangy boast. Still, "after the third playing," he admitted, "I liked the new interpretation."[11]

The failure of *Treasure Girl* only strengthened Ira's conviction that individual songs "alone do not make a show"[12] and fueled the brothers' desire to write a truly integrated score. With that goal in mind they accepted Ziegfeld's invitation to write the songs for a musical adaptation of *East Is West*, a successful play about Americans in China. On the one hand, the Gershwins knew that Ziegfeld, ever since he launched his annual *Follies* in 1907, was synonymous with the loose-knit formula of Broadway musical "revues." It was Ziegfeld, however, who had also produced *Show Boat*. With the impresario's assurance that there would be equally close integration of songs and story in *East Is West*, the Gershwins studied the play for places where character and story could blossom into song. For one such moment they wrote "In the Mandarin's Orchid Garden," about a Chinese girl who feels like a common "buttercup" who "did not grace the loveliness of such a place." Their other songs—"Sing Song Girl," "Under the Cinnamon Tree," "We Are Visitors Here," and "Lady of the Moon"—were all closely tied to particular characters and integral to the dramatic context of *East Is West*.

Their hopes for a fully integrated musical were dashed, however, when the whimsical Ziegfeld, upon reading a novel about a young actress who longs to become a Ziegfeld girl, decided it could be transformed into a musical that would celebrate his own *Follies*. Summoning the Gershwins into his office, he told them to shelve *East Is West* and get to work on his new brain child—*Show Girl*—which would go into rehearsal in two weeks. To a flabbergasted George Gershwin, Ziegfeld imperiously explained that all he had to do was "dig down in the trunk and pull out a couple of hits."[13] To Ira, Ziegfeld was more magnanimous; he would have the help of a collaborator on the lyrical rush job—none other than the great Gus Kahn, whose string of hits spanned the Roaring '20s, from "Ain't We Got Fun" (1921) to "Makin' Whoopee" (1928). (Ziegfeld didn't mention that he owed Kahn an assignment and this would fulfill his obligation.)

From the prospect of writing songs for an integrated musical, the Gershwins had now fallen back into the formula of the fast-paced frothy musical of the 1920s. In Ziegfeld's hands, moreover, that formula received one of its worst incarnations. Whereas Aarons and Freedley were skilled at the doctoring process that gave such shows their streamlined pace, Ziegfeld's imagination worked by grandiose accretions. From the start he decided that *Show Girl* would feature the comedy trio of Clayton, Jackson, and Durante, dancer Eddie Foy, Jr., Duke Ellington's orchestra, and, for good measure, an entire ballet company to perform George Gershwin's *An American in Paris*. Where Aarons and Freedley centered their shows on one or two versatile stars, such as Gertrude Lawrence or the Astaires, Ziegfeld clustered his galaxy of big names around nineteen-year-old Ruby Keeler, even though her major accomplishment until then had been to marry Al Jolson.

To compound the problems, Ziegfeld hired the desultory William McGuire to do the script—a difficult task since the novel that had inspired the show was epistolary, relating its story through telegrams, letters, and greeting cards. "Genial Bill McGuire," as Ira dubbed him, had only the first scene ready when rehearsals began and seemed content to wait for the songs to inspire him with ideas for scenes and dialogue. "You never can tell," he would say as he listened to anything they played for him. "Maybe I'll get a good idea for a scene from one of the songs."[14] McGuire's procedure was the exact opposite of what the Gershwins were seeking—the chance to work from a strong script and choose appropriate places for songs, letting characters and situations in the story inspire a lyric.

All these liabilities, compounded by the production's feverish timetable (*Show Girl* went into rehearsal with only a third of the book completed), took their toll on the lyrics Ira and Gus Kahn wrote. In all, they had to set words to twenty-seven songs, nearly a dozen of which were cut from the show. Some of George's most beautiful melodies, such as "Feeling Sentimental," were hastily conjoined with cliché-ridden imagery—"When the sun goes down and the stars come out and the moonbeams kiss the blue"—and well-worn platitudes—"every day had the gladness of spring." Only one song from the show, "Liza," has endured, and its initial success can be attributed primarily to Ziegfeld's showmanship. The producer had secretly arranged for Al Jolson to leap up from the audience, just as Ruby Keeler (backed by one hundred chorus girls in minstrel garb) was about to sing "Liza," and serenade his new bride by singing the number himself. The gimmick overcame the weakness of the lyric, which clearly bears the marks of rushed composition. The abrupt opening phrases of the chorus had

Ira and Gus Kahn reaching for the most hackneyed pollyanna weather imagery, first with a wrenching internal rhyme,

> Li*za*, Li*za*,
> sk*ies* a-
> re gray

then with an awkward string of twelve syllables that struggle to follow George's sinuous melodic turns with liquid consonants:

> but if you smile
> on me all
> the clouds'll
> roll away.

Although Jolson contributed his "impromptu" rendition to several performances, "Liza" could not keep *Show Girl* rolling, and when Keeler abruptly quit the show, it closed. Blaming the Gershwins for the failure, Ziegfeld refused to pay them; by the time the brothers sued, the stock market crash had wiped out Ziegfeld's fortune.

The grim end of *Show Girl* is an apt symbol for the demise of a musical—and a decade—long on rhythm, pace, and "numbers." A formula that was born with *Lady, Be Good!*, peaked with *Oh, Kay!* and *Funny Face*, then slumped with *Treasure Girl*, now had collapsed with *Show Girl*. In 1930, before they went on to a very different kind of musical, the Gershwins gave that frothy formula one glorious finale with *Girl Crazy*. Aarons and Freedley cast this new musical in the same mold as all their other shows—the requisite two-word title, the twin pianos of Ohman and Arden, and a jazz orchestra that, on opening night at the Alvin Theatre, included Benny Goodman, Glenn Miller, Jimmy Dorsey, Jack Teagarden, and Gene Krupa. *Girl Crazy* not only had the over-all rhythmic energy of Aarons and Freedley musicals at their best, it produced the greatest array of hits of any Gershwin musical: "I Got Rhythm," "Embraceable You," "But Not for Me," "Bidin' My Time," "Could You Use Me?," "Sam and Delilah," and "Boy! What Love Has Done to Me." These songs reveal Ira's complete mastery at balancing simple and comic lyrics, infusing popular-song formulas with light-verse flourishes, making his wit perfectly singable, and avoiding both flippancy and sentimentality as he registered genuine feeling.

Ira was helped by a book that, while hardly a dramatic masterpiece, was considerably stronger than the typical script of an Aarons and Freedley show. In Guy Bolton and Jack MacGowan's tale of New York

playboy Danny Churchill, banished to Arizona by his father to cure
his "girl-craziness," there was enough of East-versus-West conflict and
gender role reversals to spark Ira's lyrics. Instead of opening with the
usual bevy of chorus girls, for example, the rising curtain belied the
show's title by revealing a quartet of cowboys, standing behind a sign
proclaiming that in the town of Custerville there were NO WOMEN.
When they break out their ukuleles to croon "Bidin' My Time," they
reveal themselves to be incarnations of that Hollywood monstrosity
the singing cowboy. In another departure from formula, Ira suggested
that George eliminate the second eight-bar A-section of the chorus;
with an ABA structure, he thought, it would sound more "folksy"[15] than
it did with the slick, urban AABA pattern of Tin Pan Alley.

That opposition of musical formulas may have inspired Ira's verse,
where the cowboys lampoon a succession of Tin Pan's Alley's most
hackneyed lyrical clichés:

> Some fellers love to Tip-toe Through the Tulips;
> some fellers go on Singin' in the Rain;
> some fellers keep on Paintin' Skies with Sunshine;
> some fellers must go Swingin' Down the Lane.

After these cloying sentiments, the cowboys proclaim their impervi-
ousness to love: "while other folks grow dizzy I keep busy—bidin' my
time." Invoking the example of the henpecked Rip Van Winkle, who
wisely "bided his time," these unromantic mavericks brag, "like that
Winkle guy I'm."

Danny, however, transforms their sleepy male retreat into a boisterous dude ranch, replete with casinos and imported chorus girls. The
clash between East and West, as well as between male and female
stereotypes, provided Ira considerable elbow room for reversing the
standard romantic formulas. Here in the West the women are strong
while the Eastern men are effete—a contrast made even stronger by
the casting. "Molly," the gun-toting hard-riding postmistress who lives
outside of town, was played by Ginger Rogers, who had recently made
a sensation in the movies as a tough-talking dame (her line, "Cigarette
me, Big Boy!" had quickly become a national catch-phrase).

When Danny first encounters Molly, it is the usual love-at-first-
sight on his part, but he pleads with the unusually business-like catch-
phrase, "Could You Use Me?":

> Have some pity on an Easterner;
> show a little sympathy.

> No one possibly could *be* sterner
> than you have been with me.

Molly, however, rejects him with a brusque recipe for the kind of man she really wants:

> There's a chap I know in Mexico
> Who's as strong as he can be
> Eating nails and drinking Texaco—
> He is the type for me.

Once again, Ira's wit flourished within the tight confines of George's music as he set the abrupt, turnaround phrases with a lyric that gives Danny's pleas a whining, sing-song quality:

> I'd shake the mat out
> and put the cat out
> I'd clean the garret
> and feed the parrot.

Taking those same terse musical phrases, however, Ira provided Molly with a slangy curtness:

> For you're no cowboy;
> You're soft—and how!—boy!
> I feel no muscle
> That's fit for tussle . . .
> Your ties are freakish
> Your knees look weakish;
> go back to flappers
> and high-ball lappers.

The pugnacious character of Molly also enabled Ira to refresh the formula of romantic heartache—which he playfully dubbed "Ladies in Lament." Throughout Act One, Molly shuns Danny's overtures and, when he tries to play the role of the Western he-man she longs for, she pulls out her pistols and fires at his feet to make him "dance." Only after he storms off in humiliation—another role reversal—does her remorse set in. The script called for a plaintive "Someone To Watch Over Me" number, but for Ginger Rogers, Ira concocted a tough-nosed and literate torch song. The verse for "But Not for Me," another of the Gershwins' gems, opens with Molly's angry attack on all the clichés of theatrical romance:

> Old Man Sunshine—listen you!
> Never tell me Dreams Come True!

> Just try it—
> and I'll start a riot!

After a litany that includes "Final Curtain," "He Will Care," and "Fate Supplies a Mate," she brassily dismisses the whole shebang with a Winchellesque "It's all bananas!"

In the chorus, however, those clichés again insinuate themselves into her reverie, though she puts them in quotes to keep them at arm's length:

> With "Love To Lead the Way,"
> I found more "Clouds of Gray"
> than any Russian play
> could guarantee.

Such artful bracketing also enables Ira to weave in some subtle rhymes:

> I was a "Fool to F*all*"
> And "Get That Way."
> "Heigh-ho!" "A*las*!" and *al*-
> so, "Lackaday!"

At the conclusion Ira caps his catalogue with a pun that transforms his own title-phrase into yet another theatrical cliché:

> The climax of a plot
> should be the marriage knot
> but there's no knot for me.

As bittersweetly comic as some of Lorenz Hart's romantic laments, "But Not for Me" showed that Ira could handle even the torch song formula without forsaking his linguistic playfulness.

In another duet for Danny and Molly, Ira takes the formula he dubbed "The Importunate Male" and injects it with the sensuous urgency of Cole Porter. "Embraceable You" goes Gilbert's patented three-syllable rhyme one better by wedding four-syllables to a rhythmic pattern of notes and rests that kick George's music along:

> Embrace me, my sweet em*brace*- (rest) (rest) *a-ble you*
> Embrace me, you irre*place*- (rest) (rest) *a-ble you* . . .
> my heart grew *tip*- (rest) (rest) *sy in me*
> you and you alone bring out the *gyp*- (rest) (rest) *sy in me*.

These gently erotic urgings are sung by Danny; Molly's more robust and insistent response claims the bragging rights normally reserved for men:

> But hang it,
> come on, let's *glor-i-fy love*
> Ding dang it!
> You'll shout *"En-core"* if I love.

Molly's energy, in turn, elicits more genteel, East Coast sensuousness from Danny as he envisions her as "Dear lady" and "My silk-and-*lace-a-ble you.*"

If Ginger Rogers inspired Ira to write spunky lyrics, it was Ethel Merman, *Girl Crazy*'s other new star, who demanded even more explosive words. In the original script, the part of Frisco Kate, a rough-and-tumble "floozy" from San Francisco's Barbary Coast, was listed as played by a mysterious "Miss Barry," but whoever Miss Barry was she gave way to a young unknown, Ethel Zimmerman. After Vinton Freedley heard her project lyrics to the back rows of the cavernous Brooklyn Paramount, the producer whisked the soon-to-be-renamed Merman over to the Gershwins' apartment complex on Riverside Drive. There, despite her awe at the Art Deco luxury, she auditioned for George Gershwin. When George, taken with her voice, offered to change anything in the songs she did not like, the stunned novice responded with a remark as brassily streamlined as the decor—"No, Mr. Gershwin, they'll do very nicely."[16]

Merman stole the show because, more than any other performer, she was the living embodiment of its rhythmic energy. As script doctoring went on during rehearsals, Merman got more and more sarcastic lines (as her mother gleefully told neighbors after she saw the show, "Ethel can TALK too!").[17] What gave her role even more punch was that her first song did not come until well into the first act. Until that point, the audience assumed Ethel Merman was purely an actress, not one of the singing members of the cast. For the surprised audience to learn that Ethel Merman could sing was a kick in itself. Hearing her belt out "Sam and Delilah," the show's first full-scale rhythmic number, bowled them over.

The song was designed for Kate to illustrate her former career as a Barbary Coast chanteuse, and Ira gave Merman a lyric laced with slang to recount the tale of Delilah, "a floozy" who "never gave a damn" until the day she "fell for a swell buckaroo whose name was Sam." In typical Frankie-and-Johnnie fashion, their affair ends tragically, and Ira detailed the gruesome end with plenty of guttural consonants:

> Delilah, she got jealous
> and she tracked him

> and hacked him
> and dug for Sam a grave.

The name Delilah gave him the chance to rhyme playfully—in the warning "run cowboy, run a mile-a" as well as in verifying the fact that Delilah was hanged for her crime: "the records are on file-ah." For other rhymes, however, he had to scramble to keep up with George's raucous, bump-and-grind melody. Pronunciation "and exigency," he explained, enabled him to rhyme "passion" with "cash in" and "distressin'" with "lesson," but only Merman's incredible skill let him get by with placing the clipped consonants of "hooch" and "kootch" on long, full notes:

> These words should be uttered quickly so that the listener hears them as monosyllables; not duo, as "hoo-ch" and "koo-tch." I got away with it, thanks to Merman's ability to sustain any note any human or humane length of time. Few singers could give you *koo* for seven beats (it runs into the next bar, like intermission people) and come through with a terrifically convincing *tch* at the end.[18]

Writing for such a voice enabled him to take new liberties with the rules for singability, confident that every syllable of his lyric would be heard in the last row of the balcony.

For all her brass, Kate is hopelessly in love with a gambler named Slick, who, in another role reversal, is utterly inept with cards. Kate's romantic addiction inspired Ira to write the kind of torch song called a "Mon Homme" lyric—"Boy! What Love Has Done to Me!":

> I fetch his slippers,
> fill up the pipe he smokes.
> I cook the kippers,
> Laugh at his oldest jokes.
> Yet here I anchor—
> I might have had a banker!
> Boy! What love has done to me.

The lost banker (like her other complaint, "and here's the joker—I might have had a broker") would have evoked an ironic laugh in the wake of the stock-market crash and bank holidays.

Her litany is laced with the wry imagery and wrenched rhymes of light verse:

> His brains are minus—
> never a thought in sight—
> and yet his highness

> lectures me day and night.
> Oh where was *my* sense
> to sign that wedding license.

Even as she acknowledges his faults, Kate, true to the "Mon Homme" formula, admits her helpless enthrallment:

> Where will I wind up?
> I don't know where I'm at.
> I make my mind up
> I ought to leave him flat.
> But I have grown so
> I love the dirty so'n'so!
> Boy! What love has done to me.

The number that gave the Gershwins the most difficulty in *Girl Crazy* was the apparently artless "I Got Rhythm." Originally, the melody had been a slow ballad for *East Is West*; when George quickened the tempo, Ira was frustrated to find that he could not devise the proper words to allow the song, as he put it, to "throw its weight around." Almost as abrupt a melody as "Fascinating Rhythm," the A-sections consist of three brief, parallel, four-note phrases, each beginning on an upbeat after a rest, followed by a long phrase that begins, surprisingly, on a downbeat. After struggling with the unusual melodic pattern for three weeks, Ira realized that the problem lay with rhyme. When he used rhymes, they reduced the song to a "jingly Mother goose quality,"[19] as he could see in his dummy lyric:

> *(rest)* Roly-poly,
> *(rest)* eating solely
> *(rest)* ravioli—
> Better watch your diet or bust!

He therefore abandoned rhyme altogether and let parallel verbal phrases outline the rhythmic bursts:

> I got rhythm
> I got music
> I got my man
> who could ask for anything more?

Along with dropping rhyme, Ira eschewed long, singable vowels. What gives the song its kick are the consonants—the guttural and dental of "got" and the alliteration of "rhythm," "music," and "my man." He also made the crisp opening phrase the title of the song (and always railed against singers who tried to "correct" his grammar by singing "I've got rhythm"). "I Got Rhythm" thus triumphed over the more logical choice of a title—"who could ask for anything more," a phrase, repeated four times in the lyric, which is far richer in singable vowels and "memorable" rhymes (*for* and *more*). Clearly, Ira was artfully violating the very principles of simple lyrics he had mastered only a few years earlier.

The percussive consonants, the grammatical nose-thumbing, the rhymeless rhythmic punch all were tailor-made for Ethel Merman at the finale of Act I. In utter contrast to the laconic "Bidin' My Time" that opened the show, "I Got Rhythm" was the apt description not only of *Girl Crazy* itself but the whole string of Aarons and Freedley musicals inaugurated by *Lady, Be Good!* With Merman's extended barbaric yawp held for a breathtaking eight bars, "I Got Rhythm" was a dynamic exclamation point to an era and the Gershwin songs that registered the musical and verbal rhythms of the Jazz Age. In recognition of the perfect coalescence they had achieved, George gave his brother an opening-night gift—a silver cigarette lighter engraved with the inscription, "To Ira, the Words, from George, the Music." While they could justifiably bask in their long line of successful shows since *Lady, Be Good!*, in their next ventures in the American musical theater, the Gershwins would indeed be asking for something more.

5

SWEEPING THE COUNTRY
1930–1933

Lyric writing, like tea tasting and hitting the chimes for half-hour station announcements, has become a profession. A precarious profession, no doubt—one that the east side marriage broker has as yet put no valuation on, one that is looked down on as a racket in some literary fields, but one which nevertheless requires a certain dexterity with words and a feeling for music on the one hand, and, on the other, the infinite patience of the gemsetter, compatibility with the composer and an understanding of the various personalities in a cast.

—Ira Gershwin

DURING the Philadelphia tryout of *Strike Up the Band*, Ira Gershwin, lyricist, and George S. Kaufman, playwright, were standing outside the Shubert Theatre before a Saturday night performance. As the pitifully small audience filed in, two bearded, stout, and formally dressed men stepped up to the box office. Kaufman wondered aloud who they could be. "Oh, that's Gilbert and Sullivan," Ira said, "coming to fix the show." "Why don't you put such funny lines in your lyrics?" Kaufman retorted. Neither book nor lyrics could save *Strike Up the Band*, which never made it out of Philadelphia, closing "out of town" in 1927. From the debacle, Kaufman managed to fashion one of his classic one-liners: "Satire is what closes on Saturday night."

Ira's joke was equally apt, since Edgar Selwyn, the producer of *Strike Up the Band*, had explicitly set out to "Americanize" Gilbert and Sullivan. In contrast to the rhythm-driven musicals of Aarons and

Freedley, *Strike Up the Band* was a full-fledged operetta, right down to the orchestra pit, where saxophones were excluded in favor of French horns, violas replaced guitars, and, instead of the trademark twin pianos of Aarons and Freedley shows, there was only the solitary harp of classic operetta. If such an elegant ensemble challenged George Gershwin's musical skills, *Strike Up the Band* gave Ira Gershwin the demanding task he had long hoped for—writing lyrics that were thoroughly integrated into the book of a musical. Instead of songs that "stopped" the dramatic action to say "I love you" in thirty-two bars, he could at last write comic lyrics that "carried" plot, as characters sang dialogue in long stretches of recitative or, as he termed it, "lyrical pastiche." Those lyrics, moreover, had to underscore the satirical themes of the book, rubbing light-verse salt into the wounds inflicted by Kaufman's exposé of war and profiteering.

In uniting the brothers Gershwin with "The Gloomy Dean of American Comedy," Selwyn boasted he had put together "the ultimate collaboration of the generation."[1] Also known as "The Great Collaborator," George S. Kaufman had risen, via light-verse contributions to F.P.A.'s "Conning Tower" and luncheon barbs around the Algonquin Round Table, to eminence through his work with such other writers as Marc Connelly, on *Beggar on Horseback*, and Edna Ferber, on *The Royal Family*. From the team of Kaufman and the Gershwins, Selwyn promised the press, with typically 1920s ballyhoo, would come an "entirely new genre" in American musical theater.[2]

While *Strike Up the Band* was indeed innovative in many ways, in one important respect it followed the standard practice of musicals of its time by dividing the tasks of writing the book and the lyrics. It therefore differed from Gilbert and Sullivan operettas, for which Gilbert always wrote both book and lyrics and thus could tailor a dramatic context to highlight his songs. Lyricists such as Ira Gershwin and Lorenz Hart, who longed to integrate their songs fully into the book, always had to take their lyrical cues from the playwright, who naturally thought in terms of plot and dialogue rather than moments when speech could flower into song. The major exception to this division of labor was Oscar Hammerstein, who, in *Show Boat*, adapted Edna Ferber's novel into his own libretto, where he could weave songs into the flow of action and dialogue. By 1943, when Hammerstein adapted *Green Grow the Lilacs* into *Oklahoma!*, the practice became standard, and the typical Broadway marquee carried the credit "Book and Lyrics by . . . ." From then on lyricists such as Hammerstein, Frank Loesser, and Alan Jay Lerner transformed literary works as diverse as James

Michener's *Tales of the South Pacific*, Damon Runyon's *Guys and Dolls*, and George Bernard Shaw's *Pygmalion* into libretti bursting with song. While Ira Gershwin lived and worked during that great era of the "integrated" musical, he never once wrote or adapted his own book, always remaining a lyricist, one who worked with a composer's music as well as with a playwright's dialogue as he crafted his witty—and singable—syllables.

Working with George S. Kaufman could be especially trying for a lyricist. While he had written books for musicals, the playwright was notorious for hating to have his dialogue interrupted by songs. When he and Irving Berlin collaborated in 1925 on *The Cocoanuts*, the Marx Brothers revue, playwright and songwriter treated each other with "flinty discourtesy."[3] Whenever a song was about to be sung, Kaufman left the theater, coming back only when dialogue resumed, at which point Berlin would walk out. For love songs—and love itself—Kaufman had the greatest disdain. When Berlin played "Always" for his collaborator, a song the composer so treasured that he gave it to his bride as a wedding present, Kaufman listened, then acidly suggested Berlin change the opening line to "I'll be loving you—Thursday."

While such cynicism was perfect for literary satire, it did not suit musical comedy, where, as Gilbert and Sullivan had shown, you must love what you satirize. In *Iolanthe*, for example, Gilbert poked fun at the House of Lords, a hopelessly outmoded institution, that he, like most Britons, nonetheless cherished. Only because of his affection for the House of Lords could Gilbert expose its laziness, foibles, and egregious privileges. In *Strike Up the Band*, by contrast, Kaufman satirized a subject he despised. It is frequently said that *Strike Up the Band* failed because its vitriolic portrait of war profiteering was too shocking for audiences of the time. One wonders, however, how audiences in 1927 could have been so politically naive as to be offended by the story of Horace Fletcher, a cheese factory magnate, who finances a war against Switzerland to maintain America's 50 percent tariff on imported cheese. As John Mueller has observed, the "glib anti-capitalist premise" that "wars are brought about by the nefarious machinations of profit-seeking businessmen" enjoyed such favor in the late 1920s that Kaufman was "basically preaching to the choir."[4]

Although Kaufman by his own admission gave the Gershwins a "lousy" book, Ira was delighted to have the opportunity to write lyrics that would be totally integrated into the story. He was especially proud of the "finaletto" of Act I, where his lyrics carry plot for a full fifteen minutes. In that stretch of recitative, Fletcher is confronted by the pacifist hero, Jim Townsend, who discloses that Fletcher's cheese is secretly made from Grade B milk. Such a dramatic turn inspired Ira to write a solo for Jim, in which he first trots out his agricultural credentials:

> Folks, I was born
> down on a farm—
> There 'midst the corn,
> far from all harm—
> I learned about cows and their ilk,
> so, my friends, I know milk!

In typical Gilbert and Sullivan fashion, the chorus echoes his silliness with operatic bombast:

> He knows milk!

Jim then reveals that "Fletcher's cheese is made of milk—grade B" and, when the shocked chorus asks,

> Not A?

Jim resoundingly answers:

> No—B!

When Fletcher and his cohorts shoot back in righteous indignation with the businessman's clichéd pledge,

> We always use the best ingredients!

Jim rebuts them with a triple rhyme worthy of Gilbert:

> You're using Grade B for expedience!

The chorus recounts its charges and counter-charges, then adds an even more thumping rhyme of its own:

> He says they do not use the best ingredients,
> but that they're using Grade B for expedience;
> and Fletcher told us when he beg*an it, he*
> was only making cheese to help hum*anity*!

Ira could justly take pride in such recitative, but in other stretches his inspiration sagged under the cumbersome plot his lyrics had to carry.

In Act II, for example, America wins the war with Switzerland when the American general decoys the Swiss army with a yodel, luring them into a trap where his soldiers surround them. Since all of the action takes place off stage, the general and his troops must explain all of this in song:

> There we were way up in an Alp
> (Up in an Alp, up in an Alp)
> out to get the enemy scalp-
> (Get the enemy scalp!)
> I told my men to hide—
> (We scattered far and wide—).

After this uninspired lyrical stretch, the music mercifully stops, and song gives way to chanted dialogue as the general narrates the rest of the convoluted events.

If the burden of a silly plot could drag down Ira's lyrics, those lyrics, in turn, could take with them some of George Gershwin's finest music. A plaintive blues fragment that George had kept in one of his musical notebooks—his "tunebooks," as he called them—was wasted when it was used in sung dialogue between Jim Townsend and Fletcher's daughter (who has, naturally, fallen in love with her father's enemy). When Jim accuses her father of chicanery, she bursts out with:

> Jim, how could you do such a thing?
> Oh Jim, unworthy of you, such a thing!

Caught between the demands of Kaufman's script and his brother's tricky melody, Ira had to rely upon inverted word order—his lyrical Achilles heel—weighing down one of George's most sinuously haunting melodies.

At other points in *Strike Up the Band*, however, George's music could assert itself over both Kaufman's book and Ira's lyrics. Kaufman not only turned his satiric guns on war but on its accompanying hoopla of flag-waving and parades. Kaufman was probably the one man who did not love a parade, but his satire backfired when George wrote a march so infectious that it undercut its anti-patriotic reason for being. Normally, George's musical ideas came quickly, and he was sometimes vexed at Ira, "The Jeweller"'s, protracted "polishing." In this case, however, their roles were reversed. After days of work, George had written no fewer than four different melodies, and Ira was pressing his brother to finish so he could "write it up." Still, George kept putting him off by saying, "Not bad, but not yet." Finally, one night George came to Ira's room in pajamas and awakened his brother with the news that he had finally completed the march. When George played it on the piano, Ira listened and asked if this were truly the final version. When assured it was, Ira snapped, "That's good. Don't forget it," meaning he not only wanted George to remember the melody but his promise that this, indeed, was the final version.[5]

With his ear to the satirical script, Ira crafted a lyric for the verse that mocked jingoism:

> We're in a bigger, better war
> for your patriotic pastime.
> We don't know what we're fighting for—
> but we didn't know the last time!

When he got to George's stirring chorus, however, Ira's words got caught up in the very martial fever "Strike Up the Band" was supposed to mock:

> Let the drums roll out,
> let the trumpet call,
> while the people shout,
> strike up the band!

George had managed to cram a Sousa-like march into the confines of Tin Pan Alley's thirty-two-bar AABA structure, and Ira gave in completely to the music's spirit, creating an inspiring, yet thoroughly vernacular, call to arms:

> There is work to be done, to be done!
> There's a war to be won, to be won!
> Come, you son of a son of a gun!
> Take your stand!

The rousing power of "Strike Up the Band" was demonstrated time and again. Louis B. Mayer, shrewdest of the Hollywood moguls, made a movie out of *Strike Up the Band* solely because he found the title song "so patriotic." The song was the only link to the original stage production; Mayer threw out Kaufman's script to film a musical about Judy Garland, Mickey Rooney, and the neighborhood kids—what else?—putting on a show.

In 1936, Ira turned the supposedly satirical march into a football fight song, "Strike Up the Band for U.C.L.A.":

> We're Sons and Daughters of the Bear,
> we're the California Bruins.
> We fight the foe and do and dare
> and the foe is left in ruins.

He was rewarded for his efforts with two lifetime tickets to UCLA home football games.

With World War II on the horizon, Ira again gave the music its patriotic due:

> We hope there'll be no other war,
> but if we are forced into one—
> the flag that we'll be fighting for
> is the red and white and blue one!

Then in 1942, when the war looked darkest, he retooled the lyric yet again:

> Again the Hun is at the gate
> for his customary pastime;
> again he sings his Hymn of Hate—
> but we'll make this time the last time!

One can sympathize with the confusion of Philadelphia audiences at the original run of *Strike Up the Band*, torn, as they must have been, between such stirring strains and their satiric context.

Despite failure in 1927, Edgar Selwyn clung to his dream of Americanizing Gilbert and Sullivan and mounted a revised version of *Strike Up the Band* in 1930. With the onset of the Depression, he reasoned, audiences might be more receptive to political satire, and he called upon Morrie Ryskind to revise Kaufman's original script. Ryskind had also begun as a light-verse contributor to F.P.A.'s "Conning Tower," making a successful transition to the theater by writing satirical sketches for Rodgers and Hart's *Garrick Gaieties* in 1925. When Ryskind sat down with Kaufman's script, he compared the task to rewriting "*War and Peace* for the Three Stooges."[6] Thinking in those terms, he was able to move the libretto more fully into the absurdly theatrical orbit of Gilbert and Sullivan. Ryskind also toned down some of the satiric barbs and sweetened the story with plot revisions, one of which—having Fletcher's factory produce chocolate, rather than cheese—was suggested by his chocolate-loving lyricist.

Sweeter still was the addition of more love songs. Taking the beautiful melodic snatch that in the 1927 production had been saddled with "Jim, how could you do such a thing?," George and Ira fashioned it into a standard thirty-two-bar ballad. With the burden of plot-carrying lifted, Ira could set the opening long note, not to "Jim," but to the more singable "Soon," following it with more long vowels and liquid and nasal consonants: "our lonely nights will be ended." Yet even in this

simple lyric he slipped in some triple rhymes that keep sentimentality
at bay:

> When I'm with you who cares what time it is
> or what the place or what the climate is?

With the addition of "Soon" and "I've Got a Crush on You" (interpolated
from the failed 1928 production of *Treasure Girl*), the new *Strike Up
the Band* played in New York for nearly 200 performances—a strong
run on a Depression-dimmed Broadway. Reviewers took more notice
of Ira's lyrics than they ever had: in the *Post*, John Mason Brown
observed that "Ira Gershwin's lyrics, especially in the chorus numbers
are ingenious in their rhymes, witty in their writing, and possessed of
an uncommon felicity"[7]; *World* reviewer Robert Littel pointed out that
"George Gershwin has a brother, Ira, whose contribution to last night's
party was . . . the extraordinarily gay, neat words and endlessly re-
sourceful rhymes of his lyrics."[8]

Another important factor in the success of the revival was its gently
satiric swipe at the American presidency. The 1927 production of *Strike
Up the Band* had poked fun at "Silent Cal" Coolidge. Though the President was never portrayed on stage, his "Unofficial Spokesman," Colonel
Holmes, extolled the virtues of taciturnity:

> Like a Massachusetts resident
> who once became a President
> I never, never, never say a word!

The chorus echoed that wisdom but with an ironic twist:

> He never said a thing that was absurd,
> because, you see, he never said a word.

For this patter song, Ira's words, for once, took precedence over
George's music. As usual, however, there was give-and-take between
the brothers. Sensing that the metrics were too regular, "*too* Gilbert
and Sullivan," George suggested Ira have the chorus interject several
four-syllable words and phrases, such as "unofficial," "interview me,"
and "tell 'em nothing," "creating a stammering effect that transformed
the song from English to American."[9]

By 1930, with the Depression deepening despite Herbert Hoover's
assurance that "Prosperity is just around the corner," the presidency
seemed even riper for satire. The revised production of *Strike Up the
Band* was therefore augmented with another song, "If I Became the
President," in which Colonel Holmes voices his own presidential ambi-

tions and woos a wealthy widow with the prospect of her becoming
First Lady:

> We could receive ambassadors,
> The kind the upper class adores,

The regular iambic meter suggests that, once again, Ira's words pre-
ceded George's music, as do the fractured light-verse triple
rhymes—"tell of it"/"vel-a-vit," "Executive"/"de-tec-a-tive," "politish-i-
on"/"Prohibish-i-on." At one point Holmes's longings lead him all the
way to the standard presidential preoccupation with his "place" in
history:

> I'd never go so far afield
> as Tyler, Polk, or Gar-a-field.

With such jibes, *Strike Up the Band* made fun of the presidency "in a
way it had never been lampooned before."[10]

The success of *Strike Up the Band* launched the Gershwins, along
with both Kaufman and Ryskind, on an even more significant political
operetta, *Of Thee I Sing*. As Ira recalled,

> Kaufman was sick when he saw the 1930 revised version of *Strike Up
> the Band* doctored for public taste. He said then and there that he wanted
> to write one show that would make no concessions to anyone. This is it.
> He hasn't been hampered at all.[11]

While Kaufman wasn't hampered, his naturally acerbic wit had found
a much more appropriate satiric object than war. What he and Ryskind
discovered was that the popularly elected office of the President, and
even more that of the Vice-President, was precisely the kind of quirky
yet beloved American institution that could be satirized in the same
way Gilbert had skewered the House of Lords. Their script surveyed
all the theatrical hoopla surrounding the presidency, from political
conventions to election campaigns, and the Gershwins matched it with
a perfectly integrated score. From the moment the curtain opens on a
chorus of marchers carrying banners that tout such slogans as "WIN-
TERGREEN FOR PRESIDENT—HE KEPT US OUT OF JAIL" while
singing, "He's the man the people choose—loves the Irish and the Jews,"
song and story are completely wed.

That wedding became firmer still when Kaufman and Ryskind
linked politics with love. The first scene takes place in a hotel room,
where assorted party hacks express post-convention relief that they

"put the ticket over," a ticket headed by John P. Wintergreen, nominated primarily because his name sounds presidential, and Vice-President Alexander Throttlebottom, whose name, picked out of a hat, nobody can remember. Still, they are concerned about the coming election; the people "seem to be getting wise to us," one laments, and another concurs, "we should have never sold Rhode Island." Inspired by the hotel maid's remark that, next to money, she values love, they devise a campaign based on romance: Wintergreen will court the winner of an Atlantic City beauty contest, wooing her in every state along the campaign trail, proposing on election day, and marrying her at his inauguration.

In a detailed, fourteen-page scenario Kaufman and Ryskind sent to the Gershwins in Hollywood, they outlined this plot and noted: "They will need a song, of course—a love song that will sweep the country." Taking his cue from that political cliché, Ira penned "Love Is Sweeping the Country," in which he pulled triple rhymes out of vernacular contractions—"passion'll soon be national"—and gave the most hackneyed metaphors new, literal life—"waves are hugging the shore." In keeping with the operetta character of the show, Ira suggested they add a "patter" section to "Love Is Sweeping the Country" to differentiate it from the standard AABA pattern of Tin Pan Alley songs. He went into the Gershwin trunk for a patter song they had written for *East Is West*, where he had "slanged up" a quartet for Chinese Mandarins who look over a "bevy of Sing-Song Girls":

> I come here to seek
> a high-tone baby, *Class* A—
> beautiful and chic
> and up-to-date, not *pass-é*.[12]

Ira then reset that music to express the amorous politics of "Love Is Sweeping the Country":

> Spring is in the air—
> each mortal loves his neighbor.
> Who's that loving pair?
> That's Capital and Labor.

The coalescence of love and politics enabled Ira to focus on his favorite motif of language, demonstrating that the slogans of a political campaign were akin to the romantic clichés of Tin Pan Alley. For a title song, he simply tacked the Alley's favorite apostrophe—"baby"—to the patriotic convolution "of thee I sing," to produce a hybrid catch-phrase that shocked even the cynical Kaufman. Instead of offending audiences, the affectionate satire of "Of Thee I Sing, Baby" showed that the clichés of politics and love were interchangeable. Unfortunately, the original lyric he sketched for a verse did not make it into the show:

> From the rock-bound coast of Maine
> to California's climate,
> there is something I'd explain,
> but it's awf'ly hard to rhyme it.
> (He feels the need of poesy,
> needs it badly so as 'e
> can explain to one and all
> what holds him in thrall).

"Love Is Sweeping the Country" and "Of Thee I Sing, Baby" were written in the Gershwins' usual manner—music taking the lead. The rest of the score for *Of Thee I Sing* was done Gilbert-and-Sullivan fashion, with Ira's words calling George's tune. As a result, Ira boasted to an interviewer, he could avoid the Tin Pan Alley format of saying "I love you" in thirty-two bars:

> We—George and I—have done something I think is new and something I think is good. In the show there are no verse-and-chorus songs. There is a sort of recitative running along and lots of finales and finalettos. It has meant easier work for both of us, It is hard to sit down and stretch out some single song for thirty-two measures. That is what you do with the usual song. In this show you develop ideas, condensing pages of possible dialogue into a few lines of song. And George found it easier to write these measures, too, though he works much the same at anything he attempts.[13]

One can detect a note Ira would sound increasingly in years to come—a weariness of writing romantic ballads.

One ballad Kaufman and Ryskind's script called for, however, must have delighted Ira, for it was as openly theatrical and contrived as anything in Gilbert and Sullivan. Wintergreen falls in love with Mary Turner, secretary for the beauty contest, after he samples one of her corn muffins; when she boasts, "I'm the only person who can bake them without corn" (a gag that got a laugh from a Depression-era audience used to making do), he is so smitten he proposes marriage on the spot. In doing so, however, he must break his campaign promise to marry the winner of the beauty contest—Diana Devereaux, "the most beautiful blossom in all the Southland."

In their scenario Kaufman and Ryskind stipulated that "all of this" would have to be recounted "in music and lyric," and Ira came up with a most unusual love song for Wintergreen to explain his change of heart to the contest judges and the press:

> Some girls can bake a pie
> made up of prunes and quinces;
> some make an oyster fry—
> others are good at blintzes.
> Some lovely girls have done
> wonders with turkey stuffin's,
> but I have found the one
> who can really make corn muffins.

For a lyricist tired of romantic ballads, such an absurdly culinary passion inspired a delicious addition to the formula of love-at-first-sight.

Although the Gershwins usually followed playwrights' suggestions for the placement of songs, Ira sometimes found his own lodgments in their scenario. The French Ambassador takes umbrage at Wintergreen's refusal to marry Diana Devereaux, because, as the scenario explains, "she had a French father, so the French government is up in arms about the slight that has been inflicted on her." It was Ira, however, who struck upon a way "to musicalize a French father for her":

> Should he be a baker in Lyons, or prefect of police in Dijon, or what? More and more I kept thinking that his political or economic or social importance had to be important, else why France's fuss? Not wishing to use the names of any contemporary personages, I went historical. And, illegitimacy being not too socially disadvantageous among many broad-minded Europeans, I scribbled this possible genealogy for her on the margin of page 11: "She was an illegitimate daughter of an ill. nephew of Louie-Philippe (or Napoleon)."[14]

That scrawl then blossomed into a patter song for the pompous French Ambassador that is worthy of Gilbert:

> I've been looking up her family tree
> and I have found a most important pedigree:
> she's the illegitimate daughter of an illegitimate son
> of an illegitimate nephew of Napoleon.

In contrast to the Ambassador's convolutions, the chorus demands, in vernacular directness, that Wintergreen marry Diana or face impeachment:

> you so-and-so
> we didn't know
> she had a tie-up
> so very high up!

The Ambassador is accompanied by the French Honor Guard, for whom Ira provided some bilingual lyrical nonsense to unused music from *Girl Crazy* that George had saved in his tunebooks:

> *Garçon, s'il vous plaît,*
> *Encore, Chevrolet coupé,*
> *Papah, pooh, pooh, pooh!*
> *À vous toot dir vay à vous?*
> *Garçon qu'est-ce que c'est?*
> *Tra la, Maurice Chevalier?*
> *J'adore crêpes-Suzette*
> *Et aussi Lafayette!*

All of this the Frenchmen translate roughly as "we're fifty million and we can't be wrong."

Just as Ira's integrated lyrics could advance the plot, the script could enhance the show's one free-standing romantic ballad. Taking a bit of American slang—"Who cares?"—Ira constructed a Depression-era pledge of love in the face of global and financial catastrophe that balances flippant wit with passionate devotion:

> Who cares—if the sky
> cares to fall in the sea?
> who cares what banks fail in Yonkers—
> long as you've got a kiss that conquers?

In Act I, as Ira noted, "Who Cares?" is sung "brightly"—"even glibly"— as Wintergreen and Mary Turner fend off reporters inquiring about his jilting of Diana Devereaux. Later, in Act II, however, it is reprised during the impeachment hearings. When Wintergreen refuses to accede to the Senate's demand that he divorce Mary, the "lights dimmed down, the music slowed up, and the tongue-in-cheek refrain was now sung with such sincerity that this moment became a quite sentimental, even a touching one."[15] For all of his growing antipathy to romantic ballads, Ira had written one of his best and saw "Who Cares?" movingly show-cased by its dramatic context.

While Kaufman and Ryskind's script could inspire and enhance Ira's lyrics, it could also constrain his imagination as much as the most rigid of romantic formulas. By far the most difficult stretch of plot-carrying lyrics he had to write was for the original ending of *Of Thee I Sing*. As the United States draws to the brink of war with France over Wintergreen's refusal to marry Diana Devereaux, the Senate tries the impeached Wintergreen. Mary saves the day, however, when she announces she is pregnant, prompting the Senate to find Wintergreen innocent (on the grounds that there is no precedent for removing an expectant father from office). The original script then resolved the conflict with France by having Mary give birth to twins. Since France had struggled with a low birth rate after World War I, Wintergreen gives one of the newborns to France; the Ambassador is appeased, and war is averted. That Kaufman and Ryskind could imagine that this ending, as they noted in the script, "makes everyone happy" indicates that they knew even less about parenthood than they did about love.

Ira, however, dutifully carried all of this in wittily comic lyrics that run for some twenty pages of typescript—only to see all of his work thrown out when, in the course of script doctoring, it occurred to someone that no parents, not even politicians, blithely give away a baby just because they have two. Ira's lyrics, however, almost manage to make such baby-bartering funny, as Wintergreen greets the news that Mary's given birth to twins with unfatherly irascibility:

> Ye gods, but there's a crew of them!
> First one—and now there's two of them!

He then turns to the French Ambassador and proposes the solution Kaufman and Ryskind thought would make for a universally "happy ending":

> Squalling infants are a bother—
> you'll admit that that is true.
> Though I yearn to be a father,
> it's to one and not to two . . .
> so I ask consideration
> for a father and a mother;
> take one for your population
> and let us retain the other.

The French Ambassador gleefully accepts:

> By these friendly arbitrations,
> mortal combat's been averted;
> we resume all our relations
> and nobody will get hurted.

Then Ira's lyrics wrap up the final loose end of the playwrights' original plot as the scorned Diana Devereaux appears, forgives Wintergreen, and announces that she will no longer press her marital suit because she has married the Ambassador himself:

> There he stands, the bold and daring!
> I the May and he December.
> That's the man whose name I'm bearing,
> but a name I can't remember.

In the revised ending the plot conflicts are resolved much more comically by employing the Vice-President. From the opening scene, the bumbling Alexander Throttlebottom, played by Victor Moore, had stolen the satiric show as he kept trying to find out what the Vice-President is supposed to do. In the new ending, the Vice-President is officially called upon to fulfill a duty that the President cannot—marrying Diana. By that marriage Throttlebottom heroically saves the day, the baby—and probably *Of Thee I Sing*.

Of Thee I Sing was an enormous success with critics and public alike. Comparisons with Gilbert and Sullivan were rife, so much so that George told an interviewer:

> if people knew more than they do they would not always be using that famous team as a handle, but would go back to the source from which they eventually got their inspiration. That source, he says, is Mozart's "Don Giovanni." "As much Gilbert and Sullivan as 'Pinafore'," he says.[16]

With such heady talk, it is not surprising that *Of Thee I Sing* won the Pulitzer Prize—the first musical ever to do so—then was the first musical whose book and lyrics were published. Ira's only regret was that the Pulitzer committee, reasoning that George's music was ineligible for a "literary" award, awarded the prize only to Kaufman, Ryskind, and him.

With their success at its height, the Gershwins were sought out by Alex Aarons and Vinton Freedley. The producers of the slick-paced shows of the 1920s had been hit hard by the market crash and were trying to get back on their feet—and on the bandwagon of satirical musicals—by mounting a musical spoof of Freudian psychiatry. From the very beginning, Ira "disliked enormously the central notion of the project—duo-personality or schizophrenia or whatever the protagonist's aberration was supposed to be."[17] A few years later, in the hands of playwright Moss Hart, the theme of mental illness would give Ira his most inspiring dramatic vehicle in *Lady in the Dark*, but *Pardon My English* only gave him "a headache from start to finish." Against their better judgment, the Gershwins relented under pressure from Aarons, who insisted that he was strapped by several recent flops and had only obtained financial backing on his assurance that he could "deliver" the Gershwins. "No Gershwins, no show," was his plea, "and he would be finished on Broadway."[18]

When the Gershwins saw the book, their doubts were confirmed. The original script, by Herbert Fields and Morrie Ryskind, had already undergone major surgery by several "play-doctors" and now limped along on a few tiresome jokes about psychiatry, things Germanic, and, of course, sex. With his recent success at writing integrated lyrics, Ira deftly managed to weave all three subjects into a single song, "Freud and Jung and Adler," a stretch of Marx Brothers patter for six Viennese psychiatrists:

> We're ein, zwei, drei, fuhr, funf, *sechs*—
> *Sechs* psychoanalysts analyzing sex . . .
> When we make our diagnosis,
> with results it always checks:
> if you want to know *vos los is*,
> then our answer is, it's sex!

This song was cut during tryouts and, along with most of the rest of the score from *Pardon My English*, was effectively "lost" after the show's failure. When the score, along with scores from many other musicals of the 1920s and '30s, was discovered in a New Jersey warehouse in the 1980s, newspapers hailed the recovery and reprinted some of the "lost" lyrics. Actually, Ira had retained his copies of all the songs for *Pardon My English*, but he felt staunchly, as George had, that "if a show flopped, it was best to forget its songs."[19]

Not all that was lost glittered, however. Amid the jettisoned was the title song, a last-minute addition which Ira Gershwin described as "the worst lyric I ever wrote." When he learned that the discovery of the treasure trove of lost scores in the New Jersey warehouse included material from *Pardon My English*, his wry response was, "I hope you didn't find the lyric to the title song." As it turned out, Ira had secreted a copy in his own files. "Much as he disliked it," observes Robert Kimball, "he had not thrown it away."[20] While it merits Ira's low opinion, "Pardon My English" does illustrate, in an unsuccessful way, the tension between Tin Pan Alley clichés and the vernacular inventiveness with which he normally could subvert them:

> You have got that certain something
> makes me sing of you till it hurts—

> you'll pardon my English
> but you're the nerts!

Of the twenty-four songs the Gershwin brothers wrote for *Pardon My English*, only three managed to attain something of a life of their own—"The Lorelei," "My Cousin in Milwaukee," and "Isn't It a Pity?" Each of these had an integral relation to the book but could also stand as an independent number. In "The Lorelei" the mythic Rhine monster diagnoses her "yen for all the sailors" in clinical fashion, calmly balancing sadistic against nyphomaniac tendencies:

> I'm treacherous—*ja, ja*!
> Oh, I just can't hold myself in check!
> I'm lecherous—*ja, ja*!
> I want to bite my initials on a sailor's neck!

Where the Lorelei lures sailors to their death with her seductive song, her American counterpart, "My Cousin in Milwaukee," is an American blues singer with a "voice so squawky"; nonetheless, like the Lorelei, "how she gets the men!"

> Her singing isn't operatic,
> it's got a lot of static,
> but makes your heart get acrobatic.

One of the Gershwins' best romantic ballads, "Isn't It a Pity?" survived *Pardon My English*. Ira's catch-phrase title, with its short vowels and internal rhyme (*it*/*pity*), was a ready-made fit for George's delicate six-note melodic phrase. Even such a purely singable and memorable lyric was integrated into the satiric context of the show: when the hero, suffering from amnesia, muses on all that might have been had he met the heroine earlier, his romantic euphoria lapses into Germanic gloom:

> What joys untasted! You, reading Heine—
> I, somewhere in China.

She concurs, recounting her own bouts with pessimistic *Angst*:

> My nights were dour—
> spent with Schopenhauer.

Such comic and simple lyrics could not redeem the book for *Pardon My English*. Foreseeing the imminent disaster, the star, Jack Buchanan bought his way out of the show, and was replaced by an actor whose specialty, a Greek accent, complemented the German accent of the lead comic and the heroine's "polyglot of Polish, German, and near-Hungarian."[21] After opening on Broadway in January of 1933 the aptly dubbed *Pardon My English* was silenced after a run of only forty-six performances.

Such a dismal failure made the Gershwins receptive to a proposal from Kaufman and Ryskind that the foursome reunite on a sequel to *Of Thee I Sing*. Ignoring Broadway folk wisdom—which counsels "never do a sequel"—they conceived *Let 'Em Eat Cake*, which would trace Wintergreen's campaign for re-election. The political scene of 1933, however, did not lend itself to the kind of gentle satire that made for successful musical comedy; FDR had taken hold of a shaken economy and an equally shaken population, while, in Europe, Fascism gripped Germany and Italy. Kaufman and Ryskind reflected those tense times in their script, as Wintergreen, having been thrown out, and succeeded in office by President Tweedledee, leads an army of "blueshirts" in a revolution that establishes an American dictatorship. "If *Strike Up the Band* was a satire on War," Ira mused, "and *Of Thee I Sing* one on Politics, *Let 'Em Eat Cake* was a satire on Practically Everything."[22] Such unalleviated satire was hardly the stuff of musical comedy, however, and *Let 'Em Eat Cake* closed after only ninety performances.

Once again, the division of labor between book and lyrics was the source of most of the show's problems. The first outline the playwrights sent the Gershwins reveals that, from the outset, Kaufman and Ryskind had little sense of where songs might be placed. Their typescript is peppered with hesitant parentheses asking if "(MUSIC?)" could be inserted and such uncertain musings as "Perhaps this decision, worked up to a climax, could be followed by a concerted NUMBER for all of them, perhaps not. Would a duet be any good?" One can sympathize with Ira's difficulties in taking inspiration from such tentative suggestions as "Perhaps a number for Cleo and the girls. More likely not." What, moreover, was a lyricist to do when told, "Supreme Court were to have been shot, but they ran out of ammunition," then asked, "What chance for musical stuff here?"

If Kaufman and Ryskind were tentative, however, the Gershwins were not. Although they did not renew their experiment of writing words before music, the brothers did try another "unconventional approach."

> Working from the libretto, the Gershwins blocked out the musical se-
> quences to blend into the plot; there are few conventional songs, all are
> subordinate to the structure and movement of story. Nor was it a case

of music first, lyrics later. George worked from his brother's conception
of what at any point in the musical, the mood, the focus, should be.
Music and lyrics grew out of this.[23]

George immediately seized upon the musical principle of counterpoint.
As he explained to an interviewer: "I've written most of the music for
this show contrapuntally, because it's that very insistence on sharpness
of form that gives my music the acid touch."[24] Following that lead,
George went on, his brother wove counterpoint into "the words of the
lyrics" to make them integral "to the satire of the piece." The contrapuntal note, musically and lyrically, is sounded at the very beginning of
the show as competing campaign parades, brandishing banners and
chanting slogans, clash in raucous dissonance. The Wintergreenites,
as they did at the beginning of *Of Thee I Sing*, boom,

> He's the man the people choose,
> loves the Irish and the Jews,

but now they are countered by the opposition's shrill screams:

> Tweedledee, Tweedledee!!
> He's O.K.

Ira had originally planned to add more lyrics for the Tweedledee marchers, such as:

> He's the man the country needs
> loves the Pollacks and the Swedes . . .
> Ev'ry candidate he tops,
> Loves the Hunkeys and the Wops.

He had even sketched out some mud-slinging:

> He's the man for you and me
> Wintergreen's an S.O.B.

In deciding to use only the two competing monotonous chants, Ira
reduced political sloganeering to its lowest common denominator.

After that contrapuntal opening number, however, no music is
heard for an entire scene—a gloomy election night at the White House
that lacks the witty dialogue of *Of Thee I Sing*. Contrapuntal music
returns powerfully in the next scene, however, as Wintergreen, booted
out of office, opens up a shabby storefront factory on Union Square.
Although the script provided no suggestions for musical numbers,
the brothers took inspiration from the setting, America's version of
London's Hyde Park Corner. Recasting the opening clash of cam-

paign parades, they transposed it into a struggle between competing radical groups, who wave banners that sport such slogans as "Peace on Earth—Kill the Capitalists." While their slogans are fiery, however, the radicals sing a sweet paean to world brotherhood:

> Our hearts are in communion
> when we gather down on Union
>   Square, heigh ho. . .
> We may not fill our stomics,
> but we're full of economics
> down on Union Square!

This blissful radical hymn, in turn, is interrupted by a new burst of soapbox demagoguery from an ominously fascistic character named Krueger. In clear echoes of Hitler and Mussolini, he opens his speech with a seemingly reasonable call for strong action:

> Conditions as they are
> cannot go very far;
> the world must move
> and we are here to move it.

As Krueger outlines his "plan" for the "Brotherhood of Man," however, his rhetoric turns into a mad catalogue of hateful "patter" that has none of the affectionate satire that mitigated *Of Thee I Sing*:

> Down with one and one make two,
> Down with ev'rything in view!
> Down with all majorities;
> likewise all minorities!
> Down with you and you and you!

Even when the radicals endorse his speech, Krueger rejects their support:

> Somehow I abominate
> anything you nominate.
> That's the torch we're going to get the flame from!
> If you don't like it,
> why don't you go back where you came from?

As George's march tempo builds to a frenzied goose step, Ira's catalogue becomes a collage of nihilistic images:

> Let's tear down the house of Morgan . . .
> Let's burn up the Roxy organ . .
> Down with music by Stravinsky!

snapped at the cynical playwright, "Don't knock love, Kaufman—without it, we'd be out of business!" The only love song in the show was "Mine," and it proved to be the one enduring success. Kaufman and Ryskind's outline called for a "number which can stand by itself in the same way" that "Who Cares?" did in *Of Thee I Sing*. The Gershwins again came up with an independent song but one that was still integral to the show—and the score's stress on counterpoint. "Mine," like Irving Berlin's "Play a Simple Melody," was based on two melodies played against one another. Ira found that coming up with a "simple" lyric for George's first melody proved even more difficult than usual:

> With only fifty-four notes to this stately refrain, and with a one-syllable title, "Mine," fitted in four times, the lyricist couldn't exactly be brilliant in setting the remaining fifty syllables.[26]

Faced with such a spare melodic sequence, Ira resorted to utter simplicity, down to what he termed an "obvious" rhyme:

> Mine—more than divine—
> to know that love like yours is mine.

What turned this simple song "comic," however, was the counterpoint lyric. As the lovers softly intone the first melody, the chorus undercuts their sentimentality:

> It does a person good to see
> such happy domesticity;
> the way they're making love you'd swear
> they're not a married pair.

Here, too, Ira could indulge his characteristic pronoun play:

> He says, no matter what occurs,
> whatever *he* may have is *hers*;
> the point that *she* is making is—
> whatever *she* may have is *his*.

Even such a contrapuntal love song could not alleviate the bitterness of *Let 'Em Eat Cake*, whose book, as Brooks Atkinson tersely noted, proved that Kaufman and Ryskind's "hatreds have triumphed over their sense of humor."[27] As with the original *Strike Up the Band*, unmitigated satire had proven inimical to song, and a musical that was to have built upon the achievement of *Of Thee I Sing* only ended the Gershwins' venture into satirical operetta.

Kaufman, characteristically, salvaged a one-liner, describing the failure of *Let 'Em Eat Cake* as a "*succès d'estime,*" which he translated as "a success that ran out of steam." For Ira, however, the failure represented unalleviated disappointment. Having tasted the pleasures of writing completely integrated and particular lyrics, he was not eager to return to the simple fare of standard romantic ballads. Even in 1969, as he prepared his and George's manuscripts from *Let 'Em Eat Cake* for the Gershwin Archive at the Library of Congress, he surveyed all of the wonderful words and music that had gone down with the show and wrote on the cover sheet, "All I can say 36 years later is 'Alas.'"

6

NECESSARily So
1933–1935

The brothers Gershwin, after their extraordinary fashion, would get at the piano, pound, wrangle, swear, burst into weird snatches of song and eventually emerge with polished lyrics.

—DuBose Heyward

IN 1925, during one of his frequent insomniac nights, George Gershwin picked up DuBose Heyward's best-selling novel *Porgy*, hoping it would help him fall asleep. Instead, he was inspired by the possibilities for operatic passion and violence in the tale of the crippled Porgy, who challenges Crown for the love of Bess. His ambition to compose an opera was already evident in 1922, when he persuaded George White to include a one-act opera, *Blue Monday*, in that year's annual *Scandals*. Buddy DeSylva, George's primary lyricist at the time, had concocted a Harlem version of Frankie and Johnnie in a libretto so bombastic it guaranteed the failure of the piece. When White insisted, over George Gershwin's objections, that white actors perform the opera in blackface, *Blue Monday*, turned into a travesty that was dropped after opening night.

George's determination persisted, however, and soon he was thinking in larger terms—an opera set in the "melting pot" of New York that could draw on "many kinds of music, black and white, Eastern and Western" and "catch the rhythms of these interfusing peoples, to show them clashing and blending." For a librettist, he longed for "a philosopher, a poet, and a man who understands America," a writer such as Carl Van Vechten, the white impresario of the Harlem Renaissance.[1] Never, it seems, did George think of his brother in that role, presumably because for opera he needed someone who was not only a lyricist but a dramatist as well. While the book and lyrics of a musical comedy could be divided, the continuous singing of opera, alternating only between recitative and aria, required a seamless libretto.

Thus when he struck upon *Porgy*, George Gershwin seemed to have found in DuBose Heyward, a white poet from South Carolina, a collaborator who could write such a libretto. When George proposed an opera, Heyward was enthusiastic, but at that point he and his wife Dorothy were adapting *Porgy* into a play, which eventually had a successful run in 1927. Plans for an operatic version were postponed, and, with the onset of the Depression, the extensive financial backing required for an opera, particularly an opera with the black cast George Gershwin insisted upon, was difficult to find. At one point Heyward was so desperate for money that he considered a proposal by Jerome Kern and Oscar Hammerstein to make *Porgy* into a musical. While he envisioned a success to equal *Show Boat*, Heyward was leery of their suggestion that Al Jolson could play Porgy—in blackface!

In 1933, however, the Theater Guild stepped in and offered its support, and George Gershwin, after the back-to-back failures of *Pardon My English* and *Let 'Em Eat Cake*, was eager to strike out in a completely new direction. Travelling to Charleston to begin collaboration with Heyward, George insisted from the outset that all the dialogue be set to music, as recitative, despite Heyward's belief that much of it should simply be spoken. Heyward deferred to his composer, particularly when he saw how George Gershwin resonated to the music of the local Gullah blacks. On a trip to the islands off the coast of South Carolina, Heyward marvelled at the way George joined in their "shouting"—rhythm chants "beaten out by feet and hands to the spirituals." "I think," Heyward observed, "that he is probably the only white man in America who could have done it."[2]

After that first collaborative session, however, Heyward and Gershwin found it increasingly difficult to get together. It was the Depression, and Heyward was too financially strapped to make extended trips to New York; besides, he found his "creative ability practically paralyzed in a new environment." Even George Gershwin felt the effects of the Depression; finding "royalties from shows and sheet music were down," he agreed to do a weekly series of radio programs, "Music By Gershwin," where he showcased his own songs as well as the work of other songwriters.[3] Although some friends accused him of selling out and made jokes about the program's sponsor, Feen-A-Mint laxative gum, and George's constant complaints about his "composer's stomach," the radio show helped support him for the nearly two years it took to complete the score of *Porgy and Bess*. While it helped him financially, however, the radio commitment prevented George from travelling to South Carolina for the extended periods he and Heyward needed to integrate words and music.

Collaboration by correspondence clearly did not work. George, for example, would write to Heyward:

> I would like to write the song that opens the 2nd Act, sung by Jake with fish nets, but I don't know the rhythm you had in mind especially for the answers of the chorus, so I would appreciate it if you would put dots and dashes over the lyric and send it to me.[4]

As primitive a device as dots and dashes were, they were more promising than Heyward's attempts to suggest rhythm via the mail:

> I have done my best to convey my own rather vague idea for the rhythm on the enclosed copy of Jake's song. If you will imagine yourself at an oar and write the music to conform to that rhythm that will give you a better idea than anything I can write.[5]

After a few such exchanges, the collaborators found a better way to solve their long-distance problem. "The solution came quite naturally when we associated Ira Gershwin with us," Heyward recalled. "Presently we evolved a system which, between my visits North or George's dash to Charleston, I could set scenes and lyrics. Then the brothers Gershwin, after their extraordinary fashion, would get at the piano, pound, wrangle, swear, burst into weird snatches of song and eventually emerge with polished lyrics."[6]

While Ira may initially have been drawn into the orbit of *Porgy and Bess* as a convenience, his role as the mediator between Heyward's words and George Gershwin's music quickly became vital to the opera's success. "DuBose was a poet," Ira explained, "which I am not."[7] With songs such as "Summertime," Heyward wrote the words first, then, "he would turn in his poetry and George would set it to music."

> With me it worked the other way. I cannot read music. I must hear a tune before I can write lyrics. My job was to sit and listen to music that George created and then set words to it.

Ira marvelled at his brother's ability to work from Heyward's confected folk poetry:

> All his fine and poetic lyrics were set to music by George with scarcely a syllable being changed—an aspect of this composer's versatility not generally recognized. These many years . . . and I can still shake my head

in wonder at the reservoir of musical inventiveness, resourcefulness, and craftsmanship George could dip into. And no fraternal entrancement, my wonderment. He takes two simple quatrains of DuBose's, studies the lines, and in a little while a lullaby called "Summertime" emerges—delicate and wistful, yet destined to be sung over and over again. Out of the libretto's dialogue he takes Bess's straight, unrhymed speech, which starts: "What you want wid' Bess? She's gettin' old now," and it becomes a rhythmic aria; then he superimposes Crown's lines, "What I wants wid other woman? I gots a woman," and now is heard at once a moving and exultant duet. . . . all I'm trying to say is that George could be as original and distinctive when musicalizing words (as in the above examples, plus "A Woman Is a Sometime Thing," "The Buzzard Song," and others) as when composing music which later would require words . . . Regardless of which procedure was used, the resultant compositions sang so naturally that I doubt if any listener, lacking the mentions in this note, could tell which came first—the words or the music.[8]

As usual, however, when Ira talked about George, he told only half the story.

The number of songs for which George set Heyward's poetry to music constitute fewer than a third of the opera. Even those required minor, but crucial, revisions to make them singable. According to Dorothy Heyward, Ira "polished many of Heyward's lyrics,"[9] and when Heyward's biographer pressed Ira on the point, Ira responded with characteristic modesty:

In all honesty I don't recall having had much to do with polishing any of DuBose's lyrics. True, if a scene was too long or a substitute line was required here and there in the text, I was always available and if DuBose wasn't around I would help my brother cut, edit, or change.[10]

It is difficult to ascertain how extensive Ira's polishing actually was, but if the revisions for "Summertime" are representative, his contribution was minor but crucial. In their play, the Heywards had used some lines from an old spiritual, "All My Trials":

Hush, lil' baby, don' you cry
Fadder an' mudder born to die.

For the lyric of "Summertime" Heyward reworked these lines into:

Yo' Daddy's rich, chile, an yo' ma's good-lookin',
So hush, little baby, don' yo' cry.

George, presumably with Ira's help, then altered the first line ever so slightly to conform to the contour of his melody and to eliminate the back-to-back *ch* sounds, giving the singer more long vowels to "lean on":

> Oh—your Daddy's rich and your Ma is good-lookin
> So hush, little baby, don't yo' cry.

For most of the songs in *Porgy and Bess*, Ira had a fuller—and sometimes exclusive—hand. In DuBose Heyward, Ira met someone every bit as self-effacing as he, and it is thus difficult to ascertain the exact extent of each man's contribution to the score. Notes among Ira Gershwin's papers indicate that he was the sole or primary lyricist for "There's a Boat Dat's Leavin' Soon for New York," "A Red-headed Woman," "I Can't Sit Down," "I Ain't Got No Shame," and "It Ain't Necessarily So."[11] Even with these, however, Ira maintained "I'm pretty sure I was indebted, theme-wise, to a word or phrase borrowed from the text."[12] His notes also indicate that he and Heyward collaborated on the lyrics for "I Got Plenty O' Nuthin'," "I Loves You, Porgy," and "Oh, Bess, Oh Where's My Bess" (though Ira's name alone is listed on the sheet music for this last song). Ira also insisted that Heyward share copyright credit for "Bess, You Is My Woman Now," for while he and George had written the song on their own, Ira maintained he "took the title from one of the lines in the text and probably used three or four lines from the libretto in the body of the song."[13]

In their collaborations, it was apparent to Ira that Heyward, fine poet that he was, simply was not skilled in the lyricist's craft of writing singable and memorable words:

> This is no reflection on DuBose's ability. It takes years and years of experience to know that such a note cannot take such a syllable, that many a poetic line can be unsingable, that many an ordinary line fitted into the proper musical phrase can sound like a million.[14]

On one occasion, when the three men were able to get together, Heyward actually tried his hand at the mosaic art of the lyricist. George Gershwin suggested that "Porgy might sing something lighter and gayer than the melodies and recitatives he had been given in Act I." When he improvised a song at the piano, Ira had a rare response:

> A title popped into my mind. (This was one out of only three or four times in my career that a possible title hit me on first hearing a tune. Usually I sweat for days.) "I got plenty o' nuthin" I said tentatively. And a moment later the obvious balance line, "An nuthin's plenty for me." Both George and DuBose seemed delighted with it.

When Ira promised, with his Van Winkle mask in place, to "work on it later," DuBose Heyward responded with a request:

> Ira, would you mind if I tried my hand at it? So far everything I've done has been set by George and I've never written words to music. If it's all right with you I'd love to take the tune along with me to Charleston.[15]

With the help of Dorothy Heyward, a dummy lyric was devised for DuBose to work with in Carolina, with lines such as "I got a horse and a shoe," that helped him remember the rhythmic contours of the music. Two weeks later Heyward sent the Gershwins a strong lyric, but, while it fitted the melody's notes, its vowels and consonants were not sufficiently "singable":

> Some folks make plenty o' money
> laborin' all o' de time,
> sweatin' in de sun all day for a dolluh,
> or diggin' for a dime.

While Heyward's effort struck Ira as having many "usable lines," others "looked good on paper but were awkward when sung, so on this song I did have to do a bit of 'polishing.'" Ira's polishing, as he modestly termed it, laced the lyric with a simple—but singable and memorable—pattern of alternating long *a* and *e* vowels:

> D*e* folks wid plent*y* o' plent*y*
> got to pr*ay* all d*e* d*ay*;
> s*ee*ms wid plent*y* you sure got to worr*y*
> how to k*ee*p d*e* Debble aw*ay*,
> a-w*ay*.

For all of its operatic character, the parallel structure of the lyric to "I Got Plenty O' Nuthin'" is similar to that of "I Got Rhythm," and even a line such as "I got my gal, got my song, got Hebben de whole day long," is reminiscent of "I got starlight, I got sweet dreams, I got my man." Perhaps sensing such an intersection between Heyward's poetic and his own lyrical art, Ira said, "All in all, I'd consider this a 50-50 collaborative effort."[16]

For some of the opera's greatest songs, however, Ira was the sole lyricist—in particular, for Sportin' Life's numbers. In both the novel and the play, Sportin' Life remained a relatively minor and one-dimensional figure. As Ira's role in the collaboration increased, however, so did the character of Sportin' Life, whose presence grew at once more comical and ominous—a discordant urban intrusion into the pastoral setting of the opera. "Ira's gift for the more sophisticated lyric," Heyward realized, "was exactly suited to the task of writing the songs for Sportin' Life."[17] The song that most defines Sportin' Life's big-city condescension toward his country cousins is one he leeringly delivers to the churchfolk at a community picnic. While the title for "I Got Plenty O' Nuthin'" came to Ira immediately, the melody for this number had him completely stumped. For days, he had been using the title phrase merely as a dummy lyric, until George finally suggested he try making the dummy title the real one. Pleased at the suggestion, Ira was thankful that the eight-syllable phrase, which could have been "An order of bacon and eggs," "Tomorrow's the Fourth of July," or "Don't ever sell Telephone short," was, instead, "It Ain't Necessarily So."[18] An equally pleasing discovery was that it had the metrical pattern of a limerick, and Ira sensed that the irreverent poetic form was perfect for Sportin' Life to make a mockery of biblical fundamentalism:

> Methus'lah lived nine hundred years,
> Methus'lah lived nine hundred years,
> but who calls dat livin'
> when no gal'l give in
> to no man what's nine hundred years.

Cast in the sophisticated form of a catalogue song, "It Ain't Necessarily So" goes on to list other biblical tales, such as the story of Moses in the bulrushes, only to debunk them with an equally naughty wink: "Ole Pharaoh's daughter she fished him—she says—from dat stream." As with successful catalogue songs in 1930s musicals, the lyricist had to supply extra lyrics in the likely event the audience's applause demanded more items. Sportin' Life had this "Encore Limerick" in reserve:

> 'Way back in five thousand B.C.
> Ole Adam and Eve had to flee,
> Sure, dey did dat deed in
> De Garden of Eden—
> But why chasterize you an' me?

Ira also gave the character of the Harlem dope peddler a verbal playfulness not present in either the original novel or play:

> De t'ings dat yo' li'ble
> to read in de Bible—
> it ain't necessarily so . . .
> oh, I takes dat gospel—
> whenever it's pos'ple. . . .

Ira wanted to share the copyright for "It Ain't Necessarily So," but Heyward demurred, saying, "You're very sweet, Ira, but no one will ever believe I had anything to do with that song."[19]

Sportin' Life's other great song, "There's a Boat Dat's Leavin' Soon for New York," grew out of a simple line of dialogue in Heyward's script: "Listen, there's a boat leaving soon for New York, an' I'm goin'." When George first read it, he instinctively jotted "song" in the margin, but it fell to Ira to craft a lyric that revealed another, more sinister dimension to Sportin' Life. Whereas Crown seduces Bess with his overwhelming sexual force, Sportin' Life plies her with "happy dust"—cocaine—and clearly foresees a profitable future for himself as her pimp. Ira's deft use of contractions captures the sleazy charm of Sportin' Life:

> I'll buy you de swellest mansion
> up on upper Fi'th Avenue
> an' through Harlem we'll go struttin'
> we'll go a-struttin'
> an' dere'll be nuttin'
> too good for you.

While the Fifth Avenue domicile Sportin' Life promises Bess would make a Harlem resident scoff, the allure of New York to rural blacks was, Sportin' Life knows, as seductive as the "happy dust" he gives her.

Ira used "There's a Boat Dat's Leavin' Soon for New York" to defend himself and Heyward from charges that they had written lyrics in a dialect that demeaned blacks:

> Spelling "there" as such in one spot and as "dere" in another wasn't an oversight. It didn't matter too much if dialect was exact or not, considering the stylized and characteristic music. All that was required was a suggestion of regional flavor; and if the artist preferred—for personal literacy or racial righteousness—to enunciate any words formally rather than colloquially, that was all right.[20]

The criticism of dialect was only one of many made—and still made—against *Porgy and Bess* on racial grounds. While admitting that the music was "grand," Duke Ellington said that "the times are here to debunk Gershwin's lampblack Negroisms,"[21] and Hall Johnson, a distinguished black musician, attacked such songs as "It Ain't Necessarily So" as "a pathetic Gilbert and Sullivan vainly trying to go slumming in a very smudgy coat of burnt-cork."[22] While the racial criticisms of *Porgy and Bess* on musical and dramatic grounds have faded over the years as the work has assumed its place in the canon of American opera, the use of dialect in the lyrics has remained a continuing problem.

That it should be is ironic, for Ira Gershwin and DuBose Heyward came as close as any lyricists, white or black, to using that dialect as a medium of dignified and passionate expression. To understand the extraordinary nature of that achievement requires some understanding of how black dialect had been used in songs for the American musical theater for nearly a century before *Porgy and Bess*. It has long been debated whether such a dialect was totally confected by white minstrels in blackface or whether, as one such minstrel, Dan Christy, claimed, it was based upon the actual speech of black workers. William Mahar has recently tried to resolve the debate by arguing that it is a "literary dialect, compiled, created, and presented by blackface actors who borrowed some of their material from black culture." While "that dialect may seem absurd to modern readers," Mahar insists, "it is in fact based upon such phonetic and orthographic features of the 'Black English Vernacular' as the regular substitution of /d/ for /th/, /b/ for /v/, and the deletion of final consonants, such as /g/ (courtin'), /d/ (an'), and /t/ (a' home)."[23] Such substitutions can go even deeper, down into the syntactic and morphological principles of grammar that govern such elemental rules as subject-and-verb agreement. From the dialect's origins in nineteenth-century minstrel shows, however, lyricists were content to use merely its superficial phonetic and orthographic features to create an idiom for comic racial caricature in what were then called "coon songs." By the turn of the century, this dialect was so entrenched in American musical theater that even black songwriters employed it. In 1898, Will Marion Cook, a classically trained composer, asked the poet Paul Dunbar to write lyrics for the first major black musical, *Clorindy,* or *The Origin of the Cake Walk*. Dunbar had long been writing comic poetry in that dialect and unblinkingly adapted it for his lyrics:

> Blame de lan', let the white folks rule it
> I'se a lookin' fu a pullet,
> Who dat say chicken in dis crowd?

Another black songwriting team, Bob Cole and the brothers John Rosamond Johnson and James Weldon Johnson, tried, in such songs as "Under the Bamboo Tree," to elevate and refine the dialect. On the one hand, they felt that black performers ought to express romantic passion in an idiom that differed from that used by white performers; still, they had to obey the theatrical taboo of their day against portraying romantic love between blacks in anything but comic terms. To balance these demands, Cole and the Johnsons sometimes portrayed lovers not as American blacks but as African royalty, though why two royal "Zulus from Matabooloo" would woo in such dialect terms as

> If you lak-a me and I lak-a you
> and we lak-a both the same,
> I lak-a say, this very day,
> I lak-a change your name,

seems never to have been questioned. What is significant about "Under the Bamboo Tree" is that it anticipates the structural use of dialect features. Not content simply to substitute "dis" for "this," Cole makes the "lak-a" construction an integral match for the musical syncopation of eighth- and sixteenth-notes. As a result, the lyric cannot be transformed into standard English; a singer can turn "dis" into "this" but substituting "like" for "lak-a" would upset the relation of words to music.

Any advances Cole and the Johnsons might have made in the use of this dialect on Broadway ended with Cole's death in 1911. The same year saw the death of George Walker, who, with Bert Williams, had formed the only other major black songwriting team on Broadway. For a decade there were no black musicals on Broadway, and the use of dialect was left almost exclusively to white songwriters, who employed it in endless "mammy" songs. Not until *Shuffle Along* (1921) would black songwriters again achieve success on Broadway. In that musical, which, more than any other event, launched the Harlem Renaissance, Eubie Blake and Noble Sissle finally broke the taboo against black performers singing passionate love songs, but in those songs they avoided any trace of dialect. Sissle recalled his fears on opening night that the audience would pelt the performers with rotten eggs. Instead, it gave songs such as "Love Will Find a Way" several encores:

> Love will find a way,
> though skies now are gray.
> Love like ours can never be ruled,
> Cupid's not schooled
> that way.
> Dry each tear-dimmed eye,
> clouds will soon roll by,
> though fate may lead us astray.

While such lyrics are free of dialect, there is nothing at all about them to suggest the lovers are black. Indeed, they are indistinguishable from the standard pollyanna weather songs of the day—"Till the Clouds Roll By," "Look For the Silver Lining," and Ira's own "Waiting For the Sun To Come Out."

Just as black songwriters abandoned the dialect, so did black poets of the Harlem Renaissance, such as Claude MacKay and Countee Cullen, who were embarrassed by the dialect poetry of Paul Laurence Dunbar. By 1927, James Weldon Johnson, who had put songwriting behind him to become one of the major literary voices of the movement, could proclaim, that "practically no poetry is being written in dialect by the colored poets of today":

> The passing of dialect as a medium for Negro poetry will be an actual loss, for in it many beautiful things can be done and done best; however, in my opinion, *traditional* Negro dialect as a form for Aframerican poets is absolutely dead.[24]

Later he speculated that had black poets "been the first to use and develop the dialect as a written form . . . to work it in its virgin state, they would, without doubt, have created a medium of great flexibility and range, a medium comparable to what Burns made of the Scottish dialect."[25]

Black dialect, black poets felt, was too weighted down by the "coon song" tradition to ever be used for serious poetic expression. Thus, when a poet such as Langston Hughes wanted to express the themes of suffering and endurance in "The Negro Speaks of Rivers," he rigorously avoided any trace of dialect:

> I've known rivers:
> Ancient, dusky rivers.
> My soul has grown deep like the rivers.

Ironically, just as black poets were abandoning the dialect, white lyricists were employing it as a medium for more dignified expression. In the very year that James Weldon Johnson proclaimed the death of black dialect, Oscar Hammerstein, in *Show Boat*, attempted to forge that dialect into an instrument of powerful expressiveness, most notably in "Ol' Man River." For all of its poetic imagery, however, "Ol' Man River" relies upon those same superficial dialect features—phonetic and orthographic substitutions—that had been the mark of "coon" songs. One can thus easily substitute "tote that barge" for "tote dat barge" without any loss of lyrical power. Indeed, singers, both black and white, from Joe Williams to Frank Sinatra, have long performed the song by making such standard substitutions. Even when Hammerstein delves deeper into the structural features of the dialect, with "Tired of livin' but feared of dyin'," the line can easily be sung as "tired of living but scared of dying."

DuBose Heyward and Ira Gershwin, by contrast, drew upon structural features of black dialect to construct love songs whose lyrical power is lost if the dialect is altered. In the novel *Porgy*, Heyward had used little dialect, recounting much of the action in the elevated language of a third-person narrator. When he and Dorothy Heyward adapted the novel into a play, dialogue became much more central, and Heyward, who knew the dialect firsthand from working with blacks in Charleston, helped his wife by suggesting such structural substitutions as "Lord, I be tired tonight" for "I sure am tired tonight." When DuBose Heyward collaborated with George and Ira Gershwin, the recitatives and arias offered an even greater opportunity to experiment with that dialect in poetic ways. Heyward's knowledge, matched with Ira's remarkable sensitivity to vernacular patterns, produced a lyrical idiom that grows out of the most fundamental syntactic and morphological features of black dialect. Heyward's libretto vibrates with such a line as "what I likes less than I does you"; and in "My Man's Gone Now" he has Serena mourn her slain husband in powerful terms:

> I'm ole now,
> since I lose my man.

Then the chorus echoes her lament:

> since she lose her man.

The poignancy of the cry would clearly be "lost" if the verb tenses were brought into accord with standard English.

Such a loss would be even greater in Porgy's aria, "Bess, You Is My Woman Now," where Ira Gershwin wove structural features of the dialect into one of his greatest songs of romantic euphoria, setting the syntactic clash of

> You is!
> You is!

to George's exultant octave leaps. The singular verb "is" creates an off-rhyme with "Bess" that reflects the passionate mismatch of the world-weary Bess with the crippled Porgy. To gauge the crucial importance of the dialect, one need only imagine what would be lost if the lyric were changed to standard English:

> Bess, you are my woman now!
> You are! You are!

The power of the dialect is further heightened when Bess responds,

> Porgy, I's yo' woman now!
> I is!
> I is!

At the climax of the song Ira weaves pronouns and verbs together to reflect their romantic union:

> we is one now.

These deep features of the dialect run throughout the libretto, from Crown's threatening

> What I wants wid other woman,
> I gots a woman

to Bess's fragile plea to Porgy,

> If you kin keep me,
> I wants to stay here

to Porgy's exultant cry:

> What the hell!
> I is glad
> I's alive!

The poetic expressiveness of the dialect culminates in Ira's lyric for "Oh, Where's My Bess," when the simplest terms carry an extraordinary poignancy:

> Where Bess gone?
> . . . I ain' care what she say,
> I ain' care what she done.

Here the delicately ungrammatical off-rhyme, *gone/done*, subtly underscores the separation of the mismatched lovers. Ira Gershwin and DuBose Heyward's handling of structural features goes far beyond the superficial phonetic and orthographic substitutions that mark earlier dialect lyrics, making *Porgy and Bess* the greatest fulfillment of James

Weldon Johnson's hope that a dialect so long used for racial caricature might become a medium for the full range of poetic expression.

Despite the achievement of Ira Gershwin and DuBose Heyward, despite George Gershwin's magnificent score and the over-all quality of the production, *Porgy and Bess* initially failed to win over critics or the public. Both were confused by what one reviewer called its "hybrid" character.[26] Audiences used to musicals were baffled by the sung dialogue, and critics regarded the presence of "song hits," particularly "such sure-fire rubbish as 'I Loves You, Porgy'" as a "blemish upon its musical integrity."[27] *Porgy and Bess*, it seemed to critical consensus, was little more than "an aggrandized musical show."[28] A few critics, however, recognized *Porgy and Bess* for the great work it is, and one, Pitts Sanborn, specifically attributed an important measure of that success to Ira Gershwin. Praising George Gershwin for being "more fortunate than most of our native opera writers have been in his choice of text," Sanborn found *Porgy* a "play that lends itself readily to operatic treatment."

> Mr. Heyward and Ira Gershwin have been unusually adroit in adapting its language to the needs of music . . . Owing partly to Mr. Gershwin's valuable Broadway experience and partly to the superior singableness of the text, there is in *Porgy and Bess* little of that fatal discrepancy between word and note that has been the bane of American opera.[29]

It seems fitting that Ira Gershwin's skill in setting "singable" words to music should be the catalyst that fused the poetry of DuBose Heyward with the music of George Gershwin into what is rightly called "the first authentic American opera."[30]

7

Fun To Be Fooled
1934–1936

Our tribe of songsmiths always wrote for our peers. We were very much ashamed of ourselves if we wrote anything clichéd, if we took an idea from another person. By "our tribe" I'm talking about Cole Porter, Ira Gershwin, Hart, Dietz, all those people who got together every week, usually at George Gershwin's house . . . something like Fleet Street in Samuel Johnson's time—an artistic community where people took fire from one another.

—E. Y. "Yip" Harburg

WHEN George Gershwin plunged into the composition of *Porgy and Bess* in 1934, Ira Gershwin also struck out in a new artistic direction. The twin failures of *Pardon My English* and *Let 'Em Eat Cake* had been as hard on him as they had been on his brother and induced him to explore other forms of musical theater as well. Even though he was drawn into the orbit of *Porgy and Bess*, he found his contribution "required nowhere near the time George needed, and I was able to work on two other properties during the twenty months."[1] The shows Ira termed "properties," *Life Begins at 8:40* and *The Ziegfeld Follies of 1936*, were both "smart" 1930s revues. Traditional revues, such as Earl Carroll's *Vanities*, George White's *Scandals*, and Ziegfeld's early *Follies*, were lavish but loose productions that featured an array of songs, comic sketches, and titillating dances. After the stock-market crash, however, Broadway revues were scaled down. Beginning with *The Little Show* of 1929, songs and sketches took a wittier turn, held together by an over-all, usually satirical, theme.

Ira's invitation to try his hand at such "smart" and "little" revues came from his old high-school friend, Yip Harburg. After graduating from the City College of New York (CCNY), Harburg had shelved his dreams of becoming a light-verse newspaper poet to go into business. During the 1920s he developed a successful electrical appliance store, but the crash ruined him, so, as he whimsically put it, having "had my fill of this dreamy abstract thing called business, I decided to face reality by writing lyrics."[2] With Ira's help, Harburg teamed up with several different composers and had his first hit song in the 1932 revue *Americana*—"Brother, Can You Spare a Dime?" The song's remarkable sense of character and dramatic situation—it portrays a veteran bitterly questioning why he must stand in a bread line—quickly made it an anthem of the Depression. Although Harburg always remained a social radical, he could also write straightforward romantic songs such as "April in Paris" (1932) and "It's Only a Paper Moon" (1933).

It was in the newer smart revues that Harburg established himself as a lyricist. The self-contained satirical sketch, he found, could inspire the witty curve he, like Ira, always sought in his lyrics, while a clever lyric could, in turn, provide an idea for a sketch. Early in 1934 Harburg was approached by the Shuberts for a much more ambitious revue, one "that mixed the wit and critical spirit of the smaller revues with the budget and spectacle of the larger ones."[3] The Shuberts offered him the opportunity to write for such comic stars as Bert Lahr and Ray Bolger and to collaborate on a score with Harold Arlen. Arlen had also started out in revues, primarily staged at the Cotton Club, where his jazz and blues style produced rhythmic hits such as "I've Got the World on a String" and torch songs like "Stormy Weather." When George Gershwin heard Arlen's songs, he took the young composer under his wing as a kindred spirit who could bend the standard formulas of Tin Pan Alley into distinctively individual songs. In agreeing to work on the Shubert revue, Arlen was trying to move beyond the Cotton Club's "familiar world of ballads, production numbers, and torch and rhythm songs to the newer terrain of comic parody numbers, patter songs, mock marches, and extended send-ups of opera."[4]

When Harburg and Arlen found Ira Gershwin with free time on his hands, they urged him to join them in their new venture. Arlen later confessed to some trepidation at the prospect of working with two lyricists bent on literate satire. He knew that Ira was being hailed as "the American Gilbert" and that "Yipper" was "a Gilbert and Sullivan lover." Understandably, the composer was concerned that his music, like Sullivan's, would have to take a back seat to a "torrent of lyrics."

He was relieved, however, that he "didn't have to set lyrics—we really collaborated." Still, he said of his two witty collaborators, "Man, they sure gave me an interesting time."[5]

As envisioned by Harburg, the revue would be completely different from any musical Ira Gershwin had worked on before:

> Lacking a story line, the Broadway revue was at least latently anti-illusionary: it was a comic's medium, allowing for acknowledgment of and interplay with the audience, for running commentary in comedy and song on the show itself. *8:40* was particularly insistent upon its proclamation of artifice and illusion.[6]

Ira quickly grasped the self-reflexive satire of the genre and, at an early production meeting, suggested *Life Begins at 8:40* as a title—a doubly allusive wink, at a current best-seller, *Life Begins at 40*, as well as at the standard curtain time of a Broadway show. Instead of integrating his songs into the plot and characters of a script, in the revue Ira had the opportunity to create a special dramatic context around each song, and he is credited with writing not only lyrics but some of the satirical skits as well.

The sketches and songs parodied the clichés of Broadway, Hollywood, and Tin Pan Alley, as well as the New York political scene and its two theatrical mayors, Jimmy Walker and Fiorello LaGuardia. One day Bert Lahr, who was synonymous with slapstick humor, suggested Ira and Harburg jettison that comic persona and write a song for him as a *bon vivant*, replete with an Inverness cape. "Yip" and "Gersh" came up with "C'est la Vie," then wrote a skit around the song that had Lahr and Bolger playing rejected lovers, both poised to jump from a bridge over the Seine. Before they leap, they strike up a conversation:

> BOLGER: Monsieur, you too?
> LAHR: I'm afraid that—yes.
> BOLGER: Ah, monsieur, la depression?
> LAHR: Non, monsieur, la dame. And you, monsieur?
> BOLGER: La same.
> BOTH: Cherchez la femme.

When each displays a photo of his beloved, they realize they have been rejected by the same woman—Luella Gear—who then enters and explains her Gallic hard-heartedness thus:

> But you do not understand. I tell you I do not love you because I love you each so much and if I tell one, I hurt the other.

To solve her dilemma she suggests a *ménage à trois*, and they launch into a merry waltz:

> C'est la vie,
> sans souci,
> in a cute little love nest for three,
> breakfast will be set
> tête à tête à tête . . .
> Three hearts beating as one!
> C'est Paree!
> C'est la vie!

The French phrases took Ira and Yip back to their light-verse roots, as did their swipe at Joyce Kilmer, whose solemn sentiments were the antithesis of their own "smart" urbanity:

> Duets are made by the bourgeoisie-o,
> but only God can make a trio!

They aimed another blow at Kilmer—and gave Lahr another parodic role as a pompous concert-hall tenor presenting a program of art songs. In formal regalia, Lahr stepped on stage to introduce "the first number of my second group," which "was written while I was lying in a little garret on the left bank." After alerting his audience to its "polychromatic undulations, its rhythmic reverberations, and its purely American chichi based on legendary folklore," he launched into "Things":

> Things that ease the rocky way,
> things that look at God all day,
> things, sweet misery of things!

Warring with his accompanist, the orchestra, and his own loose toupee, Lahr fought his way through a welter of poetic clichés from "When the frost is on the punkin" to "the clouds in the West are sunken."

Another parody, "My Paramount-Publix-Roxy Rose," made fun of the standard revue number that featured chorus girls dressed as flowers, with Luella Gear recounting her roles "on the world's biggest stages":

> A poppy for Loew's, a pansy for Pantages,
> Oh, I've been a tulip for Shubert . . .
> a daisy for Fanchon and Marco,
> a cactus for Balaban Katz.
> Yes, I was an orchid for Carroll,
> asleep in a garden of rocks,

and awoke as poison ivy
for Paramount, Publix, and Fox.

In "Quartet Erotica," Rabelais, De Maupassant, Boccaccio, and Balzac
lament the recent advances in literary smut:

> We thought that our erotica
> was very, very hotica . . .
> the dirt we used to dish up,
> sad to say,
> wouldn't shock a bishop
> of today;
> a volume like *Ulysses*
> makes us look like four big sissies.

With such literary lyricizing, Yip and Ira delighted in "experimenting
with words" and "using the language, twisting it, bending it."[7]

Their most skillful parodies were of Tin Pan Alley romantic formulas, formulas each had had to refresh, time and again, with light-verse
curves; now they revelled in the opportunity to take each of those
constricting formulas and wring its romantic neck. In the category of
"let's get away from it all" travel itinerary songs, "Let's Take a Walk
Around the Block" has two poor lovers working in a travel agency
dream of faraway—but hardly romantic—places:

> In winter, at Christmas,
> we'll visit the Isthmus
> to see how they lock up a lock;
> and then in Caracas,
> on a jackass . . .
> we'll take a ride around the block.

In the torch-song category, Luella Gear, poised for suicide, laments,
"I Couldn't Hold My Man," but blames Madison Avenue:

> I'm through with yeast by Fleischmann,
> I'm through with Kellogg's Bran.
> I fell for Listerine and Zulac—
> but I couldn't hold my man!

Yip and Ira's ultimate parody, "What Can You Say in a Love Song (That
Hasn't Been Said Before?)," posed the problem each had faced with every
romantic ballad they wrote. They solved it with inspired idiocy:

> Mn, mn, mn, surrender,
> Mn, mn, mn, so tender,
> Mn, mn, mn, forevermore . . .

> Mn, mn, mn, so sweetly,
> Mn, mn, mn, completely,
> Mn, mn, mn, *je vous adore*—
> What can you say in a love song
> that hasn't been said before?

Thus Gershwin and Harburg playfully bit the hand that fed them, all the time knowing that while such songs worked wonderfully in the satirical revue, they could not possibly transcend the show to become independently popular.

Two songs from *Life Begins at 8:40* did, however, manage to balance satire with sentiment. In "You're a Builder-Upper" the two lyricists spoofed romantic paeans by playing with suffixes as if they were still in high school English class:

> You're a builder-upper,
> a breaker-downer,
> a holder-outer,
> and I'm a giver-iner,
> sad but true
> I love it, I do,
> being broken by a builder-upper like you!

Still, the satiric point does not overwhelm the sentiment, and "You're a Builder-Upper" achieved independent popularity, though most singers omitted the "tag" ending where Yip and Gersh went over the top with "taker-inner," "chaser-outer," "goer-wither," "pusher-frommer," "clinger-toer," "shaker-offer," "smiler-atter," and "squeezer-outer like you."

The most wittily poignant song in the show, "Fun To Be Fooled," unites cynical sophistication with genuine heartache. The singer knows the clichés of love are all a sham, yet still takes masochistic pleasure in falling for them:

> Fun to be fooled, fun to pretend,
> fun to believe love is unend-
> ing.

The dangling "ing" belies the very unendingness it affirms, and the word "fun" comes off as bitterly as "nice" does in the next section:

> Nice—when you tell
> all that you feel.
> Nice—to be told
> this is the real thing.

In the release, the well-worn clichés of romance hold the singer help-lessly in thrall even as she recognizes their duplicity:

> It's that "old devil moon"
> "having its fling" once more,
> selling me "spring once more,"
> I'm afraid "love is king" once more.

Thus romantic sentiments "do double duty as agents of entrap-ment and illusion" and the "sale is transacted" even though "the sales pitch is made plainly visible."[8] Despite its iron-clad irony, "Fun To Be Fooled" became an independent hit when Lee Wiley recorded it. As she had with "I've Got a Crush on You," Wiley took away the lyric's tongue-in-cheek and breathed new life into those sentimental "once more"s.

Writing lyrics with Ira Gershwin, Harburg found, was "like doing a crossword puzzle—one making up one line one day, the other making up the next line the next day." While they worked on *Life Begins at 8:40*, George was busy writing *Porgy and Bess*:

> He had a penthouse across the street on 72nd Street. Ira lived on the north side of the street and George lived on the south. We would get together at George's place [and he would play] what he was doing on *Porgy and Bess* and we would play him what we were doing on *Life Begins at 8:40*. They were glorious days.[9]

No two musical productions could have been more different. That Ira was able to make key contributions to both at the same time is eloquent testimony to his collaborative skills.

Although *Life Begins at 8:40* is barely remembered today and *Porgy and Bess* is in the standard operatic repertoire, their positions were reversed in their own time. The revue had a very successful run, but *Porgy and Bess* was coolly received both by critics and the public. Running for little more than a hundred performances, it fell far short of George's enormous hopes for the "folk opera" he had labored on so long and with such energy. For the first time in his life, he admitted to creative exhaustion and took a rare vacation; telling himself that an exotic locale might inspire him to a new concert work, he sailed for Mexico in the fall of 1935. Ira, once again adrift, accepted an invitation to write songs for a revival of *Ziegfeld's Follies*. Florenz Ziegfeld had died, deeply in debt, in 1932, and his widow, Billie Burke, had to resort to collaborating with the rival Shubert Brothers to produce *The Ziegfeld Follies of 1936*. They assembled an enormous array of talent—Fanny

Brice, Eve Arden, Bob Hope, Judy Canova, the Nicholas Brothers—even Josephine Baker in a ballet choreographed by George Balanchine.

Yet Burke and the Shuberts were shrewd enough to realize that audiences now demanded more than a lavish string of "acts" and "numbers." The emphasis in the 1936 edition of Ziegfeld's *Follies* was as much on satire as pulchritude, and sketches were built around songs in the style of the little smart revues. The producer paired Ira with the sophisticated Russian composer Vladimir Dukelsky (who earlier, at George Gershwin's suggestion, had changed his name to Vernon Duke). Steeped in "all of that Noel Coward/Diaghilev/Paris/Russia background,"[10] Duke had composed the sensuous melody of "April in Paris" (1932) and had both words and music of the equally brooding "Autumn in New York" (1935).

While Ira had a different group of comic performers to write for, the basic premise of the revue was the same as that of *Life Begins at 8:40*—parodies of theatrical clichés. Yet that very similarity seems to have struck a discomfiting note with him, for he found himself repeating the same satirical strategies. In *Life Begins at 8:40*, for example, he had written, "Shoein' the Mare," a send-up of new "dance-craze" numbers, and now for the *Follies* he wrote another:

> First you take a step,
> and then you take another,
> and then you take another,
> and then you take,
> and then you take,
> and then you,
> and then you,
> and then you,
> and that's "The Gazooka."

Cranking out parodic numbers for revues, it seems, had begun to produce something of the same "and then you take another" feel for him.

Still, Ira could take inspiration from the comic talent in the show, particularly Fanny Brice, whom he admired as "one of the most versatile and accomplished personalities in our musical theater":

> In the skits she played Baby Snooks; then a tough Tenth-Avenue girl; then the most elegant English drawing-room matron in "Fawncy, Fawncy"; then a Bronx housewife who has misplaced her winning Sweepstakes ticket; then a starlet in a satire on Hollywood musicals—all exquisitely and incomparably executed.[11]

Given that versatility, Ira could write lyrics for her that parodied virtually any kind of song. "Please Send My Daddy Back to Mother" was a throwback to the "sob ballads" of the 1890s, with Fanny playing a little girl beseeching her father's mistress to "send my daddy back home," only to conclude with a very un-1890ish sentiment:

> Oh, my mother she really is worried,
> for it seems, if you must know the truth,
> that it happened she first met my daddy
> in a joint just like this in Duluth.

In "Modernistic Moe," a satire on Martha Graham's modern dance movement, Brice played a former stripper:

> I used to work in a nightclub
> for sixty bucks a week.
> To please the chumps
> I did the bumps
> and turned the other cheek.

After meeting "Modernistic Moe," however, she is transformed into an "expressionistic dancer" in an avant-garde theater, interpreting "the rhythm of the masses":

> Staccato and dynamic—
> The Movement That Revolts—
> A future panoramic
> of nuts and screws and bolts.
> The Movement of the Masses
> on the economic scene—
> Every Movement has a Meaning,
> but what the hell does it mean?

But "the masses," she discovers, "won't even come on passes."

The best song Ira provided for Fanny Brice was "He Hasn't a Thing Except Me," which she delivered, in the classic pose of a torch singer, under a lamp-post. A parody of the "Mon Homme" songs popularized by such singers as Helen Morgan, the lyric is a list of complaints a helpless woman can add up against the louse who holds her in thrall:

> I give you His Highness,
> a pain worse than sinus . . .
> His talk isn't flow'ry,
> it's straight from the Bow'ry . . .
> The one thing he's mastered

> is just getting plastered . . .
> Of money he's got less
> than someone who's potless.

At one juncture Brice would suddenly stop singing and launch into a diatribe against the absurdity of such "Mon Homme" lyrics:

> You know, I've been singing about this bum for twenty-five years. Sometimes he's called "Oh My Gawd, I Love Him So!" Or "He's Just My Bill." Or "You Made Me What I Am Today." Once he was even called "The Curse of an Aching Heart." But he's always the same low-life, always doing me dirt, and I just keep on loving him just the same. Can you imagine if I really ever *met* a guy like that what I would do to him?[12]

A rap from the conductor's baton would then shock Fanny back into character, and she would continue her litany of laments until she exited—escorted by the lamp-post.

"He Hasn't a Thing Except Me" was one of many parodic "catalogue" songs in the show. While such lyrical lists went back to Gilbert and Sullivan patter songs, they were enjoying a new rage in the wake of Cole Porter's 1934 hit, "You're the Top." Porter was the master of such witty catalogues, but other lyricists of the day wove lists of clever allusions, each new item "topping" another, in a seemingly endless display of imaginative fecundity. Ira skewered this formula in such numbers as "The Economic Situation," where Eve Arden and the chorus girls complain that men nowadays talk only about politics—not love—and that in the most arcane terms:

> Discussing Germanism,
> and Economic Determinism
> and H. G. Wells' latest Utopia,
> and Mr. Borah on Ethiopia,
> and Morgenthau on the Surtax,
> and Jaeckel on the Fur Tax.

Another parodic catalogue lyric, "Does a Duck Love Water?," leaps from item to item, none of which bears any relation to any other—"Does the land of Dante love Chianti" is followed by "Are the Chinese fond of rice?" "Do Postmen love to ring twice?" and "Do New Deal officials love initials?" precedes "Do the Minsky Mammas love to shed pajamas?" The frankly scattergun character of the references turns the genre on its head by threatening to go on forever, as the singers indicate when they boast "we've got lots more . . . we've a thousand pages." Where

Ira Gershwin, George Gershwin, Arthur Gershwin, and Rose
Lagowitz (cousin), Coney Island, N. Y., 1912. *The Gershwin Trusts.*

Ira Gershwin and E. Y. "Yip" Harburg, Finley Club Picture, Townsend Harris Hall, circa 1914. Ira Gershwin sits at the far left of the middle row, and "Yip" Harburg stands behind him, hands on Ira's shoulders. *The Gershwin Trusts.*

Vincent Youmans and Ira Gershwin in Larchmont, N. Y., 1921. *The Gershwin Trusts.*

Fred and Adele Astaire in *Lady, Be Good!*, 1924. *The New York Public Library.*

Gertrude Lawrence performing "Someone to Watch Over Me" in
Oh, Kay!, 1927. *The New York Public Library.*

George Gershwin and Ira Gershwin on the terrace of their twin penthouses at 33 Riverside Drive, New York City, 1929. *The Gershwin Trusts.*

Ethel Merman and Chorus in *Girl Crazy*, 1930. *The New York Public Library.*

Scene from *Of Thee I Sing*, 1931. *Museum of the City of New York.*

Scene from *Let 'Em Eat Cake*, 1933. *The New York Public Library.*

DuBose Heyward and Ira Gershwin working on *Porgy and Bess,* 1935.
Museum of the City of New York.

Act I, Scene I from the original production of *Porgy and Bess,* 1935.
The Gershwin Trusts.

Right top: Ginger Rogers and Fred Astaire performing "Let's Call the Whole
Thing Off" from *Shall We Dance,* 1936. *Museum of Modern Art, courtesy Turner
Entertainment and Mrs. Fred Astaire.*

Right bottom: Bob Hope and Fanny Brice in the *Ziegfeld Follies of 1936. The
New York Public Library.*

Harold Arlen and Ira Gershwin on the tennis court of the Gershwin home at 1019 North Roxbury Drive, Beverly Hills, Calif., 1936. *The Gershwin Trusts.*

Ira and George Gershwin, Spring 1937, also at 1019 Roxbury Drive, Beverly Hills. *The Gershwin Trusts.*

Vernon Duke and Ira Gershwin, circa 1940. *The New York Public Library.*

Kurt Weill and Ira Gershwin, circa 1940. *The Gershwin Trusts, courtesy the Weill-Lenya Trust.*

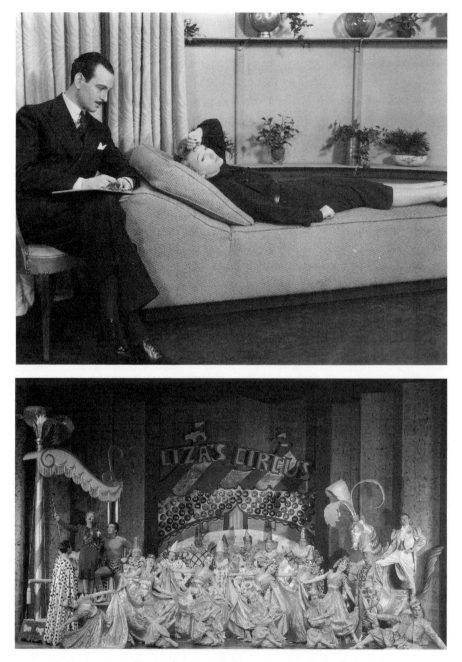

Scenes from *Lady in the Dark*, 1941. *The New York Public Library.*

Ira Gershwin and
Jerome Kern at work
on *Cover Girl* at the
Kern home on
Whittier Drive in
Beverly Hills, 1943.
The Gershwin Trusts.

Vincente Minnelli, Ira Gershwin, Gene Kelly, and producer Arthur Freed,
1950. *Museum of the City of New York.*

Judy Garland singing "The Man That Got Away" in *A Star Is Born*, 1954.
The Gershwin Trusts.

Leonore and Ira Gershwin at home, June 14, 1959, Beverly Hills.
The Gershwin Trusts.

A rarely seen photo of Ira Gershwin at the Goldwyn Studios
during the filming of *Porgy and Bess, 1958. The Gershwin Trusts.*

Porter's list songs had audiences applauding for more encores than he could supply, Ira's parody imagines audience begging for the list to end.

Such parodic catalogue songs call so much attention to their item-ized lists that romantic sentiment evaporates, but Ira and Vernon Duke wrote one that perfectly balances wit and passion. Duke had composed the melody for another song, "Face the Music with Me," but "since nothing had happened to that version" he told Ira "the tune was free" and he "could write it up."[13] Ira did—into the classic standard "I Can't Get Started." He also wrote the skit in which Bob Hope, a new comedian already playing the self-smitten egotist that became his trademark, vainly beseeches Eve Arden for a good-night kiss, but she spurns him and tries to hail a taxi. As cabs pass her by, Hope plies her with song, nonchalantly listing his phenomenal accomplishments:

> I've flown around the world in a plane
> I've settled revolutions in Spain . . .
> When J.P. Morgan bows, I just nod,
> *Green Pastures* wanted me to play God.

He then expresses his astonishment that, in spite of all his glories, Arden can withstand his charms:

> I've got a house—a show-place—
> but I get no place with you.

In the release, the only part of the song where Hope sings about *her* instead of himself, with its persistent return to the same whole note, Duke's music itself can't get started, and Ira uses inverted diction and sputtering rhymes to register the same frustration:

> You're so supreme,
> lyrics I write of you; scheme—
> just for a sight of you; dream—
> both day and night of you.

The melody then rises in a sequence of accented notes and rests, and Ira matches that musical exasperation with the perfect catch-phrase:

> and—what—good does it do?

In the face of such misery, Eve Arden finally relents and offers Hope a peck on the cheek; instead he embraces her in a long and passionate kiss. As she "comes up, gasping for air," Arden exclaims, "Heavens! You're wonderful! Just marvelous! Marvelous!" "That's all I wanted to know," Hope replies and cavalierly strolls away.[14]

Already lengthy even for a list song, "I Can't Get Started" grew longer still when radio stations requested that Ira write new lyrics, eliminating proper names, so that they could play recordings of it without fear of libel suits. Then, when female vocalists wanted to record it, he supplied still another set of lyrics:

> Beauty columns ask my advice,
> I was "Miss America" twice . . .
> with kings I've à la-carted . . .
> the Siamese Twins I've parted—.

In this version, too, he juxtaposed the elegance of inverted diction and abrupt colloquial exclamation:

> The upper crust I visit—
> but say—what *is* it with you?

Thus a song that started out as a parody of endless catalogue lyrics grew to be one of the longest of the breed.

"I Can't Get Started" was the only song from *The Ziegfeld Follies of 1936* to achieve any kind of popularity, reaffirming to Ira once more how difficult it was for songs tailored to satirical sketches to achieve independent success. He modestly attributed the good fortune of "I Can't Get Started" to an "early recording by Bunny Berigan—considered by jazz devotees a sort of classic in its field," which "may have been a challenge (or incentive) for the great number of recordings that have followed."[15]

If there was one other song from *The Ziegfeld Follies of 1936* that deserved to become a classic standard, it was "Words Without Music." Ira immediately recognized the music's extraordinary power:

> You can count on the fingers of one hand, and perhaps the thumb and index finger of the other, the number of our theater composers whose melodic line and harmonies are highly individual. There is no question but that Vernon Duke must be considered one of these. Although "Words Without Music" is scarcely known—and therefore not in the class of "April in Paris," "Autumn in New York," "I Can't Get Started," "What Is There To Say?" and many others—it is an excellent example of Duke's distinctive style.[16]

With his gift for "hearing" the emotional meaning latent in a musical pattern, Ira discerned in the brief musical phrases overtones of incompleteness and unfulfillment, which he then made articulate in hauntingly nostalgic images:

> Words without music,
> smoke without flame . . .
> nights without magic,
> days without end. . . .

The fact that "music" and "magic" never are given rhymes adds to the sense of incompleteness that runs through the chorus, undercutting the singer's hope that "words without music . . . will turn to song."

The verse is as richly simple as the chorus. When Duke opens with a phrase of three repeated notes, Ira matches it with three repeated words:

> It's an *old, old, old,* variation.

When Duke repeats the three-note phrase, Ira adroitly follows but with his own variation:

> on the *ve-ry old*-est of themes.

Although in both lines the word *old* occurs within, rather than at the end of the line, Ira makes it resound with rhymes throughout the verse, from

> when he en*fold*s you

to the final line where the verse leads into the chorus:

> you're in love and you *hold* on.

Given that George Gershwin's music seldom resonated with such world-weary heartache, Ira's ability to adapt his lyric to Duke's cosmopolitan, melancholy style is another tribute to his collaborative powers.

With such songs, *The Ziegfeld Follies of 1936* should have been an enormous success. "The problem," as Ira saw it, "was one of wealth of material rather than lack."[17] With so many comic stars, and Balanchine and Baker to boot, "we had too much show with too many elaborate production numbers." He and Duke had written twenty-eight numbers, "plenty of stageable songs and special material," only to see nearly half of them cut. For Duke, an indefatigable worker, the sheer volume of composition posed no problem; for Ira, The Jeweller, seeing so many of his gems discarded left him permanently disenchanted with the revue format. Particularly exasperating for Ira was the loss of a "stunner," "The Ballad of Baby-Face McGinty," aimed at the 1930s "folk ballads" that celebrated such gangsters as "Baby-Face Nelson" and "Ma Barker." In the sketch Judy Canova played a hillbilly "Maw" who used

the saga of McGinty to warn her three bearded sons about the perils
of a gangster's life:

> "Get Baby Face McGinty!" ·
> said Mr. Morgenthau.
> "He cheated on taxes, di'n't he?
> That's one thing we can't allow!"
> They got, they shot McGinty;
> they never gave a damn.
> For you're up against true ma-ni-acs,
> when you don't pay your income tax.

Even though audiences loved the number at the Boston tryout, the
show was running long so both skit and song were axed on the principle
that, as Ira put it, "The Show Must Go On—but not too long after
eleven p.m."[18]

Writing for revues also meant tailoring songs and sketches much
more closely to the talents of particular stars—a dangerous undertaking, as was proved when, shortly after *The Ziegfeld Follies of 1936*
opened in January, Fanny Brice took ill and was out for an extended
period. Although she ultimately returned, her loss took its toll; a revue
whose stars had seemed to guarantee a long run closed after barely
one hundred performances. A second edition, mounted later in the
year and sporting Gypsy Rose Lee in the cast, had an even shorter run.
Worn out after working with the "kinetic" Vernon Duke, now it was
Ira who needed a restful cruise.

While Ira basked in the Caribbean, George returned from Mexico,
refreshed and eager to work. So eager, in fact, he plunged back into
songwriting without Ira. A friend introduced George to a young lyricist
named Albert Stillman, and they wrote several songs together. While
Stillman would go on in the 1950s to write the lyrics for such successful
ballads as "Chances Are," "It's Not for Me To Say," and "Moments To
Remember," in 1936 he was still very much a novice, and only one of
his songs with George Gershwin, "The King of Swing," enjoyed any
measure of success. The short-lived collaboration was an erratic move
on George Gershwin's part. Ever since he and Ira had joined forces
on *Lady, Be Good!*, George had worked almost exclusively with his
brother. Ira had continued to write an occasional song with other
composers—Phil Charig, Vincent Youmans, Harry Warren, and others—but, except for the portions of *Porgy and Bess* with lyrics by Du-
Bose Heyward, every song with music by George Gershwin had had
for more than ten years a lyric by his brother.[19]

When Ira returned in February of 1936, he and George settled back into their songwriting partnership, but were at a loss for a project. Of the nearly dozen musicals offered to the Gershwin brothers in 1936, the books, Ira found, were "at best, fair." After his experience with *The Ziegfeld Follies*, Ira was adamant about one thing: "Revues we no want!" A decade that had begun with the promise of a new age of comic operetta now found the Broadway theater at a seeming dead end. While Ira could still believe that "given a cast, there's still a good chance" for musical comedy, he felt the Gershwins could no longer be pioneers: "for the time being, let others test." The culprit behind the miserable state of musical theater, he believed, was not just the Depression but the rise of the Hollywood musical, which had steadily been luring songwriters—and audiences—away from Broadway. "Boy!" he exclaimed, "what the pix have done to the legit."[20] Little did he realize that in a few months Hollywood would provide the Gershwins with the opportunity to write some of their greatest songs.

8

HERE TO STAY
1936–1938

It was touching to see how Ira, while singing, would become
so overwhelmed with admiration for his brother that he
would look from him to me with half-open eyes and panto-
mime with a soft gesture of his hand, as if saying, "He did
it. Isn't it wonderful? Isn't HE wonderful?"
—Rouben Mamoulian

ONCE Al Jolson belted out Irving Berlin's "Blue
Skies" from the hitherto silent screen in the
1927 "talkie" *The Jazz Singer*, Hollywood stu-
dios clamored for the wares of Tin Pan Alley. A hit song, producers
realized, could help boost a film at the box office, while a film, in turn,
was a wonderful showcase for "plugging" a song. From the earliest
days of the nickelodeon, when piano players covered up the noise of
the projector and entertained audiences by playing the latest hits during
reel changes, there had always been a link between the movies and
popular music. Now that songs could be sung on the screen, the two
industries merged. Film companies such as Warner Brothers (whose
lone "star" before the advent of sound had been Rin Tin Tin) began
buying up entire catalogues of Tin Pan Alley sheet-music publishing
firms and moving the songwriters themselves out to the West Coast.
By the 1930s the New York publishers, who had once produced and
marketed their own songs, complained they now did little more than
"collect royalties."

   The Jazz Singer also revealed the severe restrictions films imposed
upon song. In the musical theater, audiences accepted the convention
that characters not only talked but sang, and applause cushioned the

transition from singing back into dialogue. On the screen, however, what could possibly account for characters suddenly bursting into— and backing out of—song? The producers of the first musical films decided that a song could be sung on screen only as a "performance" by an actor playing the part of a singer (hence *The Jazz Singer*).[1] The first wave of film musicals, therefore, included a plethora of "back-stagers," such as *The Broadway Melody*, where singers and dancers rehearse and perform songs and dances as they struggle to "put on a show."

All that was needed for such flimsy musicals was an endless supply of standard Tin Pan Alley fare—"gotta dance" numbers, pollyanna weather songs (*The Hollywood Revue of 1929* featured "Singin' in the Rain"), and, of course, ballads that said "I love you" in thirty-two bars. Even a straight dramatic film could use such a ballad for its "theme" song, sung during the credits then played incessantly in the background. Such theme songs were the ultimate weapon in plugging both a film and a song, as the coast-to-coast radio broadcast of "Ramona" had proved, making the song a smash hit even before the film was released. Hollywood's demand for formulaic ballads, turned out cookie-cutter fashion, lured a stream of songwriters to the West Coast. Even Dorothy Parker came out and was put to work on the theme song for a picture called *Dynamite*. Quickly realizing she was in under her head, the light-verse wag submitted "Dynamite, I Love You," then caught a train back to the Algonquin Round Table. (The studio rejected it in favor of "Dynamite, Dynamite, Blow Back My Sweetie to Me.")

Most of the lyricists transplanted from Tin Pan Alley to Hollywood, such as Gus Kahn and Buddy DeSylva, were content to crank out the same formulas on the West Coast as they had back East. When more sophisticated theater composers and lyricists arrived from Broadway, they found film musicals a vastly different enterprise. In musical theater, songwriters were involved in a show from its inception through the extensive doctoring that could run up to and even beyond opening night. In Hollywood, however, songwriters wrote songs—period. They were seldom consulted about where their songs would go in the movie or how they would be staged. Rodgers and Hart went off to Hollywood in 1932 believing that films offered a unique opportunity for musicals, where characters could move from ordinary conversation, into rhymed dialogue, and then song. After a few years of frustration, culminating in their disastrous effort to musicalize the Depression in *Hallelujah, I'm a Bum!*, they returned to Broadway for good.

In 1930, George and Ira Gershwin boarded a plush private railroad car and headed west, too, but with no such high expectations. With *Girl Crazy* and *Strike Up the Band* running successfully on Broadway, and plans for *Of Thee I Sing* already in the works, they looked upon writing for films as a diversion. For $100,000, Fox Films put them to work on *Delicious*, a romantic comedy about a Scottish immigrant, played by Janet Gaynor, who falls in love with a wealthy American but spends much of the film dodging the assorted dangers of life in New York. Probably in deference to their stature, the Gershwins were allowed to write something other than straightforward love songs. George was invited to compose a concert piece, *Rhapsody in Rivets*, heard as background music while Gaynor flees through the city to escape deportation. He and Ira were also assigned to write a plot-carrying stretch of song, similar to the lyrical pastiche they had created for *Strike Up the Band*. Because "Welcome to the Melting Pot" occurs in Gaynor's dream about her arrival in America, it needed no realistic explanation for song; Uncle Sam, the Statue of Liberty, the Mayor of New York, and the usual cast of thousands unabashedly sing and dance for eight minutes in a "miniature musical."[2]

The Gershwins were even permitted to parody the tepid fare of film songs. When Gaynor mispronounces "delicious" as "delishious" (in the manner of Ira's father-in-law pronouncing upon every meal he ate at their house), the film acquires its "theme" song, replete with such tortured rhymes as "caprishious," "ambishious," and "repetishious." An even wittier spoof of the formulaic reductions of Hollywood came at the expense of one of George's loveliest melodies. Back in 1928 George had written "Lady of the Moon" for the aborted Ziegfeld operetta *East Is West*. Ira tried to salvage the melody with a new lyric, "I Just Looked At You," for *Show Girl*, but the song was cut during rehearsals. Finally, out in Hollywood, Ira picked up what he had come to call a "palimpsest" song[3] (where the same melody, over time, had received several sets of different lyrics) and added yet another lyrical layer by fitting the five-note title phrase to the *reductio ad absurdum* of romantic ballads—"Blah, Blah, Blah, Blah, Love." In the film, a young Russian composer affirms he has learned all about writing songs from the movies; what he has learned, it turns out, are the well-worn rhymes of Tin Pan Alley that had found a new home on the silver screen:

> Blah, blah, blah your hair
> Blah, blah, blah, your eyes;
> Blah, blah, blah, blah, care,
> Blah, blah, blah, blah, skies.

Ira had added a "Russian Refrain" for the scene, where the composer, backed by a chorus of compatriots, chants:

> Tolstoy, Pushkin—love
> Lenin, Trotsky—croon.
> Chaliapin—above
> Volga boatmen—moon.

But the studios decided a little parody had already gone a long way and cut the additional refrain. The Gershwins did not complain. As Ira put it at the time,

> My brother and I had a pretty good time writing for the movies . . . Of course working for the movie audience is a little different. But we managed to slip in a few of the things that theatre-goers like.[4]

With their sights set on satirical operetta and songs that went far beyond the bounds of thirty-two bars, the Gershwins clearly did not regard the Hollywood musical as a major vehicle for their work.

By 1936, when the Gershwins again looked to Hollywood, the film musical had changed significantly. The initial rash of addle-brained back-stagers had run its course, and audiences no longer flocked to the novelty of sound pictures. The Warner Brothers 1932 production of *Forty-Second Street* redefined the film musical. Although cast in the mold of the backstager, *Forty-Second Street* combined the jazzy rhythms of Harry Warren's music, the vernacular grit of Al Dubin's lyrics, and the innovative choreography of Busby Berkeley into a cohesive and spirited production. In the following year Fred Astaire and Ginger Rogers radiated a similar rhythmic energy in a brief but electrifying dance sequence in *Flying Down to Rio*. Their performance inspired RKO to pair them in a smartly slick film adaptation of Cole Porter's *Gay Divorce* (its title cleansed to *The Gay Divorcee*). Not only did the dancing of Astaire and Rogers embody the elegant sensuality of Porter's "Night and Day," they were permitted to violate the maxim that film songs had to be done as performances only. The very personification of the casual sophistication that marked the best lyrics of the era, it seemed as natural for Astaire to shift from talking to singing as from walking to dancing. He also had the "unheard-of privilege" of working as "closely with his scriptwriters, composers, and lyricists"[5] as he would have on a Broadway show. He even edited the dance sequences himself. With their integration of song and story and their emphasis on a unifying rhythmic flow, the Astaire-Rogers films continued in Hollywood the tradition of the Princess Shows.

"There is no set-up in Hollywood that can compare with doing an Astaire picture,"[6] Irving Berlin told the Gershwins, and the songs Berlin supplied for *Top Hat* in 1935 proved his point. Not only were they as good as anything Berlin had written for Broadway, songs like "Isn't This a Lovely Day" were integrated dramatically into the story line. Special effects and dramatic camera angles, moreover, made production numbers like "Top Hat, White Tie and Tails" more dazzling, while closeups and soft lighting made a romantic ballad such as "Cheek to Cheek" more intimate than it ever could be on the stage. Along with Irving Berlin, other songwriters, such as Jerome Kern and Oscar Hammerstein, Yip Harburg and Harold Arlen, headed west. At first, Harburg regarded the move as pure economic necessity: to earn royalties from sheet-music and recordings a songwriter had to have a certain number of hits, and "for that, chances were much better in films. The New York critics looked down on them. Broadway was the snob literary Park Avenue and Hollywood, skid row." What he found, however, was that "for a while, especially during the Astaire/Rogers period, Hollywood was making some great pictures with a wealth of great songs."[7]

Soon Harburg was receiving letters from Ira Gershwin, first asking, "Do they work you hard?" and "Is it fun?" "Write me reams," Ira begged. "Well, two pages, anyway—but single space."[8] Ira's wariness about the studios was well-founded. Despite their recent failures and disappointments, as well as the lack of vitality in the Broadway theater, the Gershwins still sought to write shows where there was full integration of songs and drama. In Hollywood, not only had they little hope for such integration, they would have to forgo the artistic control Broadway gave them over how their songs were placed and performed. Cranking out "I love you" in thirty-two bars for Hollywood studios might be no better than the piece-work of Tin Pan Alley the brothers had long since put behind them.

It was the prospect of doing an Astaire-Rogers picture that finally lured the Gershwin brothers back to Hollywood, but it took months of negotiations on a contract. Hollywood, as it turned out, now was wary of the Gershwins. After all, the studio moguls reasoned, they had had some flops in recent years, and their last collaboration had been an opera (an *opera*!). How could the Gershwins be counted on to turn out hit songs? A Hollywood agent cabled the brothers about studio concerns: "They are afraid you will only do highbrow songs, so wire me on this score so I can reassure them."[9] George fired back a telegram that had the terse poetry of one of Ira's lyrics:

RUMORS ABOUT HIGHBROW MUSIC RIDICULOUS STOP
AM OUT TO WRITE HITS

RKO sent the contract. It called for them to do an Astaire-Rogers film, and provided an option on a second picture, and a third for Sam Goldwyn. Ira and George again headed west in August of 1936—not, as they and other songwriters had come, by train, but this time on a transcontinental airplane.

Such New York speed and urgency quickly ran up against the slow pace of California life. While George initially chafed amid the palm trees and tennis courts, he wryly observed "Ira, of course, loves it out here . . . He can relax much more than in the East—and you know how Ira loves his relaxation."[10] It is regrettable that for a long while after their arrival, the brothers did little songwriting. On the other hand, the long respite from work, amid the "languid day-to-day (and night) of writing letters, tennis games, meeting friends,"[11] may have nurtured the subtle change in the way the brothers worked once they did resume songwriting. Reunited as sole collaborators for the first time in the nearly three years since *Let 'Em Eat Cake*, the brothers took up their old craft of "writing hits" in new ways. Having worked in satirical operetta and even opera, their return to thirty-two-bar romantic ballads was a little as if Shakespeare, after completing his great tragedies and comedies, had returned to the comparative simplicities of the sonnet, now infusing that form, however, with all of his experience in drama.

One of their closest friends in California, the pianist Oscar Levant, observed that for George, there was "a considerable problem of adjustment, after the freedom of *Porgy*, to the more precise definitions of the popular song."[12] Nonetheless, according to Alec Wilder, "the writing of his more ambitious compositions did not cause his songs to become too complex for popular appeal. Paradoxically, his last songs became *less* rather than more complex."[13] Deena Rosenberg, too, finds "less repetition of melodic fragments" in these last Hollywood songs and closer integration with the lyric: "one melodic motif follows a lyric's thought to its conclusion and is followed by a different motif coming in when the thought changes."[14] With this new "unselfconscious, almost conversational flow," George's music moved even closer to Ira's lyrics, and the songs that emerged from that coalescence of music and words were perfect for the casual elegance that had become Fred Astaire's stylistic trademark.

Before their new style emerged to produce the great standards they would write, the Gershwins wrote several songs that mark the transition from their recent work on Broadway. At first, the brothers were surprised at how little they were told about the film, initially called *Watch Your Step*. One thing they did know was that the opening scene was set in Paris, where Fred Astaire, playing a ballet dancer, wanders around town seeing posters featuring the face of Ginger Rogers as a popular dance star. Here, the Gershwins thought, was a spot for one of their classic "euphoria" songs, as Fred falls in love with the picture of a girl he's never met. Eagerly the brothers set to work on "Hi! Ho! At Last," a song which, with its intricate melodic line and such equally intricate rhymes as "*mock you*" and "*occu*py," indicates that they were still thinking in terms of sophisticated theater songs. When director Mark Sandrich praised "Hi! Ho! At Last" as "real $4.40 stuff" (an allusion to the going price of Broadway tickets), he may also have been subtly criticizing the Gershwins for continuing their "highbrow" theatrical ways. In typical Hollywood fashion, "Hi! Ho! At Last," along with the entire opening scene, was scrapped even before filming began, because the studio decided the set it would require would be too expensive. The loss of a good song, not through the painful process of doctoring that streamlined a theatrical musical, but out of Hollywood's seemingly whimsical lack of foresight, must have irked the Gershwins, and they probably welcomed the chance to write their next song for Broadway. Vincente Minnelli telegraphed from New York asking for a satirical number for his new show. Minnelli remembered that before the brothers headed west George had been "musically kidding around by exaggerating the lifts and plunges and *Luftpauses* of the Viennese waltz." Now that the producer was putting together a revue called *The Show Is On*, which would feature a potpourri of songs by Rodgers and Hart, Harburg and Duke, Dietz and Schwartz, and other great Broadway songwriting teams, he wondered if the Gershwins could work on "the Straussian take-off."[15] The Gershwins, always thinking in terms of integration, seized upon the chance to do a witty send-up of the waltz—as well as of themselves and their peers:

> Away with the music of Broadway!
> Be off with your Irving Berlin!
> Oh, I'd give no quarter
> to Kern or Cole Porter,
> and Gershwin
> keeps pounding on tin!
> How *can* I be civil

when hearing this drivel?
It's only for nightclubbing souses.
Oh, give me the free'n'easy
waltz that is Viennesey.

"By Strauss" is played, as the sheet-music solemnly indicates, "*Tempo di Valse Viennoise*," and Ira used George's exaggerated musical thumps to underscore his multi-lingual play:

By Jo, by Jing,
by Strauss is the thing!
So I say to Ha-cha-cha:
Heraus!
Just give me an Oom-pah-pah
by Strauss!

With tongue firmly in cheek, the Gershwins sent "By Strauss" on its way to Minnelli, little realizing that they had written their last song for Broadway.

Returning to *Watch Your Step!*, they still lacked a script, but they knew that Astaire-Rogers films typically featured a quarrelsome "challenge song" between the stars. Perhaps thinking of his wife's penchant for saying "eyether," as opposed to his own more vernacular "eether," Ira took George's turnaround melodic phrases and gave expression to his love of expression:

You say eether and I say eyether,
you say neether and I say nyther;
eether, eyether, neether, nyther—.

A lyric about language, about talk, about conversation, in "Let's Call the Whole Thing Off" the verbal sparring goes on through "potato"/"po-tah-to" to "pajamas"/"pah-jah-mas," yet the playfulness never loses sight of the combative affection that characterized Astaire and Rogers in their films. Although "Let's Call the Whole Thing Off" has its roots in the patter songs of Gilbert and Sullivan, its American character was demonstrated in London, where, Ira learned, more than one singer completely missed the point that there were two pronunciations and adhered to "proper" British pronunciation throughout:

You say eyether and I say eyether,
You say nyther and I say nyther;
Eyether, eyether, nyther, nyther—
let's call the whole thing off!

With this song the Gershwins began collaborating even more intricately. While George would sometimes flippantly describe his method of songwriting as "writing music and letting my brother do the rest,"[16] in actuality, as he put it, "we work the thing out together." With DuBose Heyward on *Porgy and Bess*, moreover, George noted that "for the first time I set music to words," and that experience carried over to Hollywood, where, Ira found,

> we worked together much more . . . we would discuss an idea and I might have a title, and he would start setting and we'd say "Well, that's a very good start," and we'd work up the tune and lyrics together.[17]

Looking at the manuscript for "Let's Call the Whole Thing Off," Ira was astonished to find that even their handwritings were beginning to look alike.

Seemingly as a result of their new closeness, the Gershwin brothers quickly produced an array of classic standards. One day George played a characteristic musical phrase—a single note repeated four times but in an unusual rhythmic pattern of three eighth-notes followed by a quarter-note. Ira listened, then asked for two additional notes so that he could use the six-syllable line, "The way you wear your hat." Not only did George comply, he took his inspiration for the additional two notes from the lyric: the first repeats the same note but the second new note leaps up three intervals in the scale and is set, appropriately enough, on the word "hat." For his next phrase, George made the final note drop three intervals, and Ira, in turn, came downward in his lyrical imagery:

> the way you sip your tea.

"They Can't Take That Away from Me" was one of Ira's rare forays into the formula of romantic loss, yet, typically, he makes the loss of love almost as moving as its discovery. Where a lyricist such as Oscar Hammerstein might have strained for soaring poetry to catalogue "all the things you are," Ira Gershwin opts for utterly prosaic items, from "the way you hold your knife" to "the way you sing off key." The lover who notes such trivial details, however, registers a greater, though understated, passion than one who celebrates only the grander features of his beloved.

For all of the clever imagery, however, the key word of the lyric is the utterly simple *that*, which Ira weaves through conversational lines:

> the memory of all *that*—
> no, no! they can't take *that* away from me!

On the one hand "that" seems to minimize the loss of "all *that*" yet at the same time to cherish the indefinable essence of character captured in the unbegrudging common place catch-phrase "they can't take *that* away from him."

Just as George's music flows in longer lines, Ira's lyric becomes more elastic, syntactically stretching beyond the contours of the musical phrases. The verse opens with an intricate sentence that nonetheless progresses as effortlessly as conversational chatter:

> Our romance won't end on a sorrowful note,
> though by tomorrow you're gone;
> the song is ended, but, as the songwriter wrote,
> "The melody lingers on."

Only the adroit alteration of long and short "o"s and the subtly memorable rhymes ("*Our ro*-mance/*sorrow*/tom*orrow*") lift the language from speech into song. Instead of dividing the two parts of the song, Ira's syntax spills over from the verse,

> though they take you from me,
> I'll still possess . . .

into the chorus:

> the way you wear your hat.

In the release, Ira's syntax again runs over the musical boundaries:

> We may never, never meet again
> on the bumpy road to love,
> still I'll always, always keep
> the mem'ry of . . .

Here, as the melodic phrase ends, the lyric's dangling "of" forms a suspended syntactic bridge into the final A-section:

> the way you hold your knife . . .

Years later, when he was collecting his songs for publication as *Lyrics on Several Occasions*, Ira looked at this release and thought it could have been improved by using some comically skewed negations:

> still I don't know when I won't
> be thinking of . . .

But after a few minutes' reflection he realized that the original "simple" release was better in contrasting "always, always" and "never, never," a perfect balance of syntactic and musical phrasing born of the mutuality of the brothers' newfound method of collaboration.[18]

One of the Gershwins' most intricate fits of words and music emerged during this period. In "They All Laughed" George starts out with a ten-note phrase, and Ira responds with a ten-syllable line:

> They all laughed at Christopher Columbus

Then George's melody shortens to seven syllables and Ira slightly truncates his lyric:

> when he said the world was round.

Now George repeats that same initial ten-note musical phrase and Ira follows with a new ten-syllable lyric:

> They all laughed when Edison recorded/

But where any other composer would then have given his lyricist another parallel seven-note line, George Gershwin abruptly stops short on one note—and Ira stops with him:

> sound!

Ira fitted the tiny musical space with as much inventiveness as the characters—Edison, Marconi, Fulton—he celebrates in his lyric.

Such variations on formulaic love songs were perfect for the urbane Astaire, but the Gershwins tailored their music and lyrics to the singer in even subtler ways. In writing for Astaire on Broadway they had provided him, as they did every singer, with long notes and open vowels, couched in soft consonants, so that he could project a song to the back of the balcony. Even though Astaire's voice was not strong, writing for him on Broadway was little different from writing for Ethel Merman. So ingrained was this principle of singability in stage musicals that Oscar Hammerstein once fretted over ending a song with the word "talk," since a singer's efforts to sustain the note would be cut off by the short vowel and the dental and guttural consonants of "talk."

With Fred Astaire in front of a microphone in Hollywood, however, the old rules for singability went out the sound-stage window. As in most musical films, all Astaire's songs were prerecorded to ensure perfect sound quality; then when the scene was shot, he would simply mime his own recording—with such effortlessness he barely seemed to have to breathe as he "sang." Given that Hollywood practice, lyricists could worry less about singers having to project open vowels and think more in terms of Astaire's skill at enunciating syllables and following

the trickiest of rhythms. Using shorter vowels and more clipped conso-
nants, Astaire singing could now sound more like Astaire talking. Irving
Berlin had given him the crisp syllables of "Top Hat, White Tie and
Tails" and Jerome Kern and Dorothy Fields provided phrases such as
"I Won't Dance—Don't Ask Me," whose sharp accents could be tapped
out as sharply by his voice as by his shoes.

Such consonants and stresses are so native to English that the
earliest poetry in the language was created not with rhyme and meter
but alliteration and accent. From Anglo-Saxon verse ("Bitter breast
cares have I abided") through Shakespeare ("I had rather hear a brazen
candlestick turned or a dry wheel grate on the axletree") down to
modern advertising slogans ("When Better Cars Are Built, Buick Will
Build Them"), the deepest music of English lies in its hard accents and
rough consonants. Ira, more than any other lyricist who wrote for
Astaire in Hollywood, revelled in the freedom to use these resources
of the language. "Let's Call the Whole Thing Off" ends not in an open
vowel but a barrage of gutturals and fricatives: "let's call the calling
off *off*!" In "They Can't Take That Away from Me," his inspired opening line ended with an even sharper bite—"The way you wear your
hat." In all the songs the Gershwins wrote for Astaire during their
year in Hollywood—"Nice Work If You Can Get It," "(I've Got) Beginner's Luck," "Things Are Looking Up," "They All Laughed," "Stiff Upper Lip"—Ira's consonants shook English right down to its Anglo-
Saxon roots.

As those titles also indicate, Ira Gershwin's lyrics, even though
their subject was romance, still managed to reflect their times in an
oblique way. Where his songs of the 1920s reflected the linguistic intoxi-
cation of the Jazz Age, these songs of the late 1930s resonate with the
Depression. With its catalogue of Americans who overcame failure
and derision ("Fulton and his steamboat," "Wilbur and his brother,"
"Whitney and his cotton gin"), "They All Laughed" can be heard as an
anthem of faith in American resiliency. Similarly, "Nice Work If You
Can Get It" and "Stiff Upper Lip" capture stoical sentiments of the era,
and even a euphoric song of first love, "Beginner's Luck," invokes what
was for many the necessity of beginning over. Nor was the Depression
the only bleak cloud in Hollywood. With so many European expatriates
in California, the Gershwins experienced "depressing moments" as they
heard "talk of Hitler and his gang creep into the conversation"[19] far
more frequently than in New York. In a purely rhythmic number, "Slap
That Bass," Ira's lyric takes note of "dictators" and laments "the world
is in a mess."

The most somber sentiments actually manifest themselves in the title song for the film, now called *Shall We Dance,* which normally was an ecstatic upbeat number. As they worked on the title song, however, Ira felt that George's music had an "overtone of moody and urgent solicitude." Seizing upon the rhetorical question in the film's new title, he followed it with others that reflected the uncertain times:

> Shall we dance or keep on moping . . .
> Shall we give in to despair?
> Or shall we dance with never a care?

The lyric then answers those questions with a somber resolution to seize the day:

> Life is short, we're growing older.
> Don't you be an also-ran!
> You'd better dance, little lady
> dance, little man,
> dance whenever you can!

While Ira modestly insisted this lyric was hardly "an emanation of the 'time's a-fleeting' boys from Horace to Herrick,"[20] "Shall We Dance" was a dark *carpe diem* imperative, unusual for an Astaire-Rogers musical.

With the score of *Shall We Dance* completed, the Gershwins sat back for filming and waited for the Astaire-Rogers magic. "George and I were pretty proud of *Shall We Dance,*" Ira affirmed, but he was concerned that perhaps the songs were *too* good:

> We thought it had a smart score. It had a lot of hits. But *all* the songs were smart, a little sophisticated. Maybe that was a mistake, to put so many smart songs in one picture.[21]

Normally such casually sophisticated songs would have been perfect for Astaire and Rogers, but the pair's elegant lustre had begun to fade. From the very beginning of their success Astaire and Rogers "wondered how long it would be safe to carry on this cycle of team pictures. We didn't want to run it into the ground and we discussed the situation with each other frequently." As early as 1935, Astaire began "to wait for some small clue from the public as to whether or not they had had enough." Finally, amid the usual rave reviews for *Swing Time,* it came. One critic wrote:

THE SINGING AND DANCING LIMIT
Ginger and Fred are at it again in "Swing Time," singing and dancing like anything. One begins to wonder how many more of that type of film

the public is prepared to enjoy. I know of at least one member of it who has reached the limit.[22]

"Well, there it was," Astaire said to himself. The filming on *Shall We Dance* had just begun.

With similar concerns that the Astaire-Rogers formula was wearing thin, the studio tried to stave off audience ennui in *Shall We Dance* by subverting expectations: Astaire and Rodgers do almost anything *but* dance together. While this enlivened the formula, it diminished the work of the Gershwins. Instead of the sumptuous dance sequences that glorified songs such as "Night and Day" or "Cheek to Cheek," Astaire and Rogers walk dogs or roller skate as they perform the Gershwin songs. *Shall We Dance* "does not take advantage of the songs as it should," George complained. "They literally throw one or two songs away without any kind of plug." He was especially irked at the treatment of "They Can't Take That Away from Me": Astaire and Rogers don't even dance a step, merely sit on a car ferry from Hoboken to Manhattan. Ira's disappointment was equally intense, but more for his brother than for himself:

> In New York, George had always been consulted as to how the numbers should be done . . . They always took his suggestions as to the production of the numbers. Here it seemed the moment your contract was ended, and the director and producer had the number of songs required, you were through. Then everything was left to the studio, to do whatever they wanted with the songs.[23]

The cursory presentation of "They Can't Take That Away from Me," one of the greatest of Gershwin songs, worsened the ignominy of its loss, in the Academy Award competition, to "Sweet Leilani."

The Gershwins' next picture, *Damsel in Distress*, however, seemed to promise them everything songwriters could ask for: a witty and literate story by P. G. Wodehouse; George Stevens as director; choreography by Hermes Pan; and the vaudeville team of George Burns and Gracie Allen—everything except Fred Astaire and Ginger Rogers. As Astaire had feared, reviews of *Shall We Dance* reflected what he termed the "Well—here we go again attitude."[24] The pair decided to split; Fred stayed with the *Damsel in Distress* but Ginger was assigned to another movie. Fearing comparisons with any dancer who might replace Ginger, the studio teamed Fred with Joan Fontaine, who could not dance or even sing. While those inabilities, along with her delicate beauty and elegant British accent, distanced her from Rogers, they restricted the way songs could be presented. Astaire could sing to Fontaine, but he could hardly *dance* "to" her, and thus the Astaire-Rogers magic that enabled songs to emerge from dramatic situations, rather than be done as performances, was missing.

In only one number, "Things Are Looking Up," did *Damsel in Distress* try to re-create that magic with Hollywood smoke and mirrors. Astaire, playing his usual role of an American celebrity abroad, falls in love with Fontaine, in the role of a wealthy British heiress. As he pursues her across a meadow toward her castle, he deftly stumbles from befuddled speech into a song of romantic euphoria, and Ira provides a verse that neatly announces the transition from dialogue into sung speech:

> If I should suddenly start to sing
> or stand on my head
> or anything,
> please don't think that I've lost my senses.

In what Ira referred to as the "vest" of a song, a two-line segment where verse turns into refrain, Astaire progresses further from speaking to singing:

> And it seems that suddenly I've
> become the happiest man alive.

Ira here crafted what he called a "run-on" line, where the syntax of "I've . . . become" spills over the break between the two musical phrases. With his impeccable sense of rhythm and enunciation, Astaire observes the contour of that run-on line in a way that registers the momentum of his growing euphoria. Other singers, to Ira's consternation, ignored the principle that "rhyme, even in a run-on couplet, ought to be observed—or at least not negated—especially when the music calls for pause or breath."[25] Such singers instead sustained the long vowel at the end of "sudden*ly*" and thus delivered the vest more "singably" as

> for it seems that suddenly
> I've become the happiest man alive.

As Astaire singingly talks (and dancingly walks), choreography, lighting, and camera-work take their cues from the lyric. The lovers move toward the castle, Astaire's stroll becoming more sprightly, and at the phrase "I've been looking the landscape over" the camera seems to move with him by panning over the rolling meadow, which, in turn, dances with a very un-English brilliance. Then, when he exults "things are looking up since love looked up at me," the angle shifts, and the lovers now gaze up at the viewers as if the camera itself were the source of the sunlight. Even in this sparkling lyric, Ira took sidelong glances at the dark times with phrases such as "the long, long ages of dull despair are turning into thin air," "my depression is unmistakably through" and, echoing Hoover's by-then-comic prediction about prosperity, "for I've certainly turned the corner." These darker intrusions are also reflected visually in the massive trees and shadows that suddenly loom into view (trees and shadows that also conveniently obscure Fontaine's movements when Astaire starts to dance). Before he hits full stride, however, he gallantly sets Fontaine beneath a tree, and instructs her only to "see the sunbeams—every one beams just because of you," as the camera cuts between her radiant face and his solo dance. Near the end of the number Fontaine gamely has a go at dancing herself and joins him for a few steps. Although Astaire maintained "she handled it beautifully,"[26] about the best one can say of her performance is that Astaire could make any partner look good.

Whether or not Fontaine's failure to dance was the scene's Achilles heel, "Things Are Looking Up," for all of the attention the film lavished on it, did not become the hit the Gershwins hoped for. In *Lyrics on Several Occasions*, Ira confessed his puzzlement that "Things Are Looking Up" "never reached near as many ears"[27] as the other ballad in the film, "A Foggy Day (in London Town)." The Gershwins wrote "A Foggy Day" well before they had seen a script for *A Damsel in Distress*; thinking that the initial meeting between Fontaine and Astaire would take place in London, Ira suggested a "fog" song. As sometimes now happened in their collaborations, it was Ira who led off, proposing, as a working title, "A Foggy Day in London," then suggested adding another syllable, "Town," perhaps because it gave the line a quaint touch. George liked the addition because he could set the eight syllables with two parallel four-note phrases:

> A foggy day
> in London Town.

Characteristically, he didn't stay parallel for very long, mixing in three- and five-note lines, but Ira, like a skilled dancing partner, effortlessly followed step:

> Had me low
> and had me down.
> I viewed the morning
> with alarm.

Even when George threw in a six-note phrase, Ira used it to underscore ennui by drawing out the plaintive vowels of "The British Mu-se-um," before returning to a four-syllable kicker: "had lost its charm."

The increased interplay between the brothers in their Hollywood collaborations produced perfect fusions of words and music more efficiently: the entire chorus of "A Foggy Day" was completed in less than an hour. The verse, however, took up all of the next day. Again, Ira took the lead by asking George "for an Irish verse," and, he marvelled, George "sensed instantly the degree of wistful loneliness I meant":

> Generally, whatever mood I thought was required he, through his instinct and inventiveness, could bring my hazy musical vision into focus. Needless, to say, this sort of affinity between composer and lyricist comes only after long association between the two.[28]

In a few bars, Ira's lyric runs with George's music in an emotional gamut, ranging from casual self-deprecation,

> I had that feeling of self-pity,

through nervous irritation,

> what to do? what to do? what to do?

to an urbane resignation punctuated by a most British adverb modifying a thoroughly American adjective:

> the outlook was decidedly blue.

"A Foggy Day" is the most sophisticated of the Gershwins' songs in the pollyanna weather genre, a far cry from their fledgling effort of 1920, "Waiting For the Sun To Come Out."

Despite its London setting, "A Foggy Day" was filmed as a night scene in the countryside, where it comes off as the darkly wistful follow-up to "Things Are Looking Up." After Astaire and Fontaine finish that sun-drenched number, she invites him to an evening party, but in the intervening hours the inevitable complication arises, and, as darkness falls, she sadly sits at her window, listening to him blithely singing on his way to her. The camera then picks up Astaire, in tuxedo and cape, as he traverses the same path he and Fontaine had strolled across in the afternoon—now, however, shrouded in darkness and mist. The lighting, as well as the camera-cuts between his jaunty progress and Fontaine's sad demeanor, underscores the brooding character of lyric and music. Only when Astaire concludes with "through foggy London Town the sun was shining ev'rywhere," does the fog suddenly dissipate and moonlight pour down in a dramatic foreshadowing of their reconciliation.

Just as Hollywood could provide such lavish effects to highlight romantic ballads, the cameras could stage production numbers more imaginatively than even the most technologically endowed Broadway stage. "I Can't Be Bothered Now," for example, is done as Fred dances his escape from a London bobby through traffic, and "Stiff Upper Lip" has him tap dancing and tumbling through an amusement park with George Burns and Gracie Allen, at one point dancing with their reflections in the distorting mirrors of the fun-house. For that scene Ira wrote a transatlantic version of a "seeing depression through" lyric, lacing its infectious optimism with the gutturals, fricatives, and plosives native to British speech:

> Stiff upper lip! Stout fella!
> Carry on, old fluff!
> Chin up! Keep muddling through . . .
> quite, quite, quite, quite, quite . . .
> Sober or blotto, this is your motto:
> keep muddling through!

Always the meticulous scholar, Ira Gershwin was surprised to find, when he checked through his reference library some years later, that while "muddle through" was a British concoction, "stiff upper lip" was an Americanism that was only adopted by the English after 1880. Just the reverse had happened with "Nice Work If You Can Get It." While it served as an American slogan in the Depression, the catch-phrase, Ira knew, had its roots firmly in England. He recalled a *Punch* cartoon where two London charwomen discuss the daughter of a third, who, according to the first charwoman "as become an 'ore," to which the second replies, "Nice work if you can get it."[29] Ira's use of this slangy title-phrase is yet another instance of how adroitly he fitted his words to George's music. In the first half of the first A-section, George's melody is a smooth and straightforward progression of quarter-, half-, and whole notes, and Ira sets it with equally simple romantic phrases:

> Holding hands at midnight
> 'neath a starry sky.

But in the next four bars the music turns sharply syncopated as dotted eighth- and sixteenth-notes leap up and down the scale, and Ira gives an equally bumptious turnaround to his title phrase:

> —nice work if you can get it!
> —and you can get it if you try!

The film accentuates the stylistic difference by having English madrigal singers warble the traditional phrasing, while Fred Astaire takes the upbeat, colloquial lines. The same contrast of musical and verbal phrases operates in the other A-sections, as well as in the release, where an almost cloying progression of romantic images—

> Just imagine someone
> waiting at the cottage door,
> where two hearts become one—

is capped by a brassily direct catch-phrase:

> who could ask for anything more!

Clearly, Ira had a special fondness for this catch-phrase, having used it earlier in "I Got Rhythm," though in that song it concludes the A-sections, while in "Nice Work If You Can Get It" it concludes the release. Once again, the staging and filming of this number wonderfully showcased the Gershwins' artistry, with the camera zooming in on close-ups of Fred Astaire—singing, dancing, and playing the drums with his hands and feet!

While it lacked the Astaire-Rogers magic, *Damsel in Distress* demonstrated how superbly Hollywood could present the Gershwins' songs; reviewers praised virtually every aspect of the film, from the songs to the photography, but the public did not warm to Astaire without Rogers. By contrast, the Gershwins' next assignment, *The Goldwyn Follies of 1938*, showed how badly a film could present their best—and last—work. Early in 1937, as he was working on *The Goldwyn Follies*, George began to experience severe headaches, bouts of dizziness, and blackouts. Tests and specialists could find nothing, however, and his symptoms were attributed to nervousness and overwork. Sam Goldwyn, nonetheless, held the Gershwins to their contract and insisted they start work immediately. Eager to assume the mantle of Ziegfeld, Goldwyn had assembled a star-studded cast—Adolph Menjou, Ella Logan, the Ritz Brothers, Edgar Bergen and Charlie McCarthy, and, of course, the "Goldwyn Girls." For cultural good measure, Metropolitan opera singers would boom out a chunk of *La Traviata*, and ballerina Vera Zorina would dance to a Gershwin "swing" symphony.

At times, George could laugh at "the Great Goldwyn" and his "super, super, stupendous, colossal moving picture extravaganza."[30] As his symptoms worsened, however, he was outraged at the producer's imperious condescension, such as summoning the brothers to his office to perform what they had written thus far. Not only did Goldwyn make the brothers "put over" their work, like Tin Pan Alley hacks, he had the audacity to advise George that he should try to write more like Irving Berlin. The only one of their songs Goldwyn liked was "I Was Doing All Right," and then only for its release:

> whenever you're away,
> can't sleep nights and suffer all the day;
> I just sit and wonder
> if love isn't one
> big blunder

Ira also had to write an additional refrain for Charlie McCarthy to sing to Edgar Bergen ("I was a tree—oh, me oh my! I was doing all right till you came by"), a segment which was mercifully cut from the film. Even as used, "I Was Doing All Right" is barely heard, sung as a mere background to dialogue. Still, the song fared better than "I Love To Rhyme," which was interrupted and finally cut off at mid-point by Charlie McCarthy's wisecracking.

At least these songs made it to the screen; "Just Another Rhumba," one of Ira's finest comic lyrics, was cut out of the film entirely. Taking the ordinarily dismissive catch-phrase, "just another . . . ," Ira applies it to something the singer can hardly dismiss—a rhumba that has transformed him into a hopeless addict of the Latin beat (the "fascinating rhythm" of the 1930s). With characteristic playfulness, Ira makes fun as well of the oddities of English; in this case his target is the letter *b*, pronounced in "rhumba" but silent in other words. Thus when the singer asks, of his rhumba-addiction,

> Can you imagine anything dum-bah?

he could also be complaining about English spelling conventions, which include such oddities as

> Why did I have to succum-bah?
> it certainly has my num-bah?
> so much so I can't even slum-bah?
> . . . it has me under its thum-bah?

Each time the song seems to end, George's music suddenly starts up again in teasing imitation of songs that fueled the Latin craze.

The only song the film did justice to was one in which Ira felt his lyric was flawed—and George's music less than splendid. The brothers had one of their characteristic arguments over the number, as Yip Harburg recalled:

> One midnight in Beverly Hills I received a phone call from George. I hurried over to find him in rebellion against his brother Ira the scholar.

> They were working on *The Goldwyn Follies*. George had a tune which
> Ira rejected because it was "too pop" . . . "What's wrong with a pop song?"
> George argued. "This is a movie and it should have a pop song."

The short twenty-four-measure melody had been one of George's favor-
ites—what he dubbed his "Brahmsian" theme—saved from his tunebooks for *Girl Crazy*.

> George played the tune for me. It did not have the blaze of the Gershwin
> hallmark, but it was a brave sweep of melody, effective and appropriate.
> Unfortunately, it cried out for that sentimental love lyric, a theme that
> always sent Ira scurrying. The love song was his *bête noire*.

Ira also protested that its very brevity posed special problems for lyrical
development; plus, "there was no special plot situation" in the script
for the lyric, thus leaving him "wallowing in a swamp of vague gen-
eralities":

> We argued, until like Shakespeare's whining schoolboy, creeping like
> snail unwillingly—Ira murmured "All right—I'll write it, but the song
> will be Goldwyn not Gershwin." Before dawn, he had bitten into half of
> the lyric of the memorable "Love Walked In."

As Ira recalled his work on "Love Walked In," it was only "after a long
struggle (two weeks? three weeks?)" that he completed it and "was
certainly not too proud of it." "Finding myself endowing love with an
ambulatory ability was more than a bit much":

> Love walked right in
> and drove the shadows away;
> love walked right in
> and brought my sunniest day.

What irked Ira even more was that he felt he had not set the opening
four-note phrase properly: "Love walked *right* in" (the "right," he chided
himself was "obviously a padding word").[31] When it came time to pub-
lish the sheet-music, the frustrated lyricist scratched "Right" from the
title of the song.

In the film, "Love Walked In" gets lavish attention, first sung by
the hero as he cooks hamburgers in a restaurant (unaware, of course,
that the heroine has just walked in), then reprised several times
throughout the picture. With such exposure, "Love Walked In" made
it to the top of radio's *Your Hit Parade*, as Ira and Leonore discovered
one night as they listened to the car radio while stranded atop Donner
Pass waiting for a tow truck. Although Ira was pleased at the success
of a tune he always felt was too "churchy," he was concerned about

such "hit" programs in that they placed a premium on a song's popularity rather than its quality. Overexposure by radio play, he foresaw, could quickly exhaust a song's endurance, leading to increasingly rapid turnover of songs and a falling off in craftsmanship.

Ira's perfectionist criticisms of "Love Walked In" may reflect the fact that it was the last song he and George completed together. He had no such self-recriminations, however, about his lyric for the song they were working on when George died, "Love Is Here To Stay," perhaps his greatest "simple" lyric. In it, he combines his earliest lessons in "singability" with the intricate faceting of consonants he had recently mastered in writing for Fred Astaire in Hollywood. The seemingly artless lines bristle with *r*'s and *v*'s, *t*'s and *d*'s, but then glide into long open vowels:

> It's very clear our love is here to stay
> Not for a year, but ever and a day.

With their ease of collaborative give-and-take, Ira asked George to provide him with some additional notes at key points of the melody so that he could work in a single word that would give the song its "kick." George complied, and Ira set the notes with the simplest of words—"and":

> the radio *and*
> the telephone *and*
> the movies that we know
> may just be passing fancies—
> *and* in time may go.

That "and," ironically, was their last word as songwriters together. Over the course of work on the film George's condition worsened. He would display lack of coordination at the dinner table, collapse suddenly on the stairs or on the street, and, most alarmingly for him, experience partial paralysis of his hands while playing the piano. Frequently, too, he would complain of the smell of burning rubber in his head. On July 9, 1937, he lapsed into a coma and was rushed to the hospital. Only there did doctors discover a massive brain tumor; they operated but two days later George Gershwin, only thirty-eight years old, was dead. Such a sudden and untimely death was a particularly tragic instance of the universal mutability figured in the imagery of the lyric:

> In time the Rockies may crumble,
> Gibraltar may tumble,
> they're only made of clay.

Although the lyric concludes with the affirmation, "but—our love is here to stay," Ira Gershwin sadly altered the song's title before it went to publication. Their working title had been "Our Love Is Here To Stay," but Ira scratched out the "Our," leaving it, simply, "Love Is Here To Stay."

Despite the loss of George, Ira was still expected by Goldwyn to furnish the songs under contract. Devastated as he was, he asked Vernon Duke to help him complete the additional songs, "I'm Not Complaining" and "Spring Again." Duke also took down a melody Ira sang for a verse for "Love Is Here To Stay"; Ira's lyric registers his own distraught state of mind:

> The more I read the papers,
> the less I comprehend
> the world and all its capers
> and how it all will end.
> Nothing seems to be lasting . . .

Ira's list of ephemeral things might well have included "Love Is Here To Stay," which seemed destined for oblivion. In *The Goldwyn Follies* the song received "so little footage," he complained, "that it meant little."[32] Sung by a young hopeful on a radio talent show, the other stars listen to it for a moment, then begin talking again as "Love Is Here To Stay" fades into the background.

Once that frenetic work was completed for Goldwyn, Ira lapsed into a prolonged period of despair when, as he recalled it later, "days and nights passed in a blur."[33] Compounding his profound sense of loss, according to Gershwin biographer Edward Jablonski, was guilt: "like everyone else, including batteries of doctors, he had believed, perhaps fervently wanted to believe, that his brother's illness was psychosomatic [in origin]."[34] As the person who had always been closest to his brother, Ira felt the most responsible for George's death. Reassurances from doctors that earlier treatment would not have saved George's life failed to assuage Ira's anguish. Only love and companionship sustained him. Fortunately, the home in Beverly Hills where he and Leonore and George lived, had become the social center for many of the songwriters—Jerome Kern, Harold Arlen, Yip Harburg—who had come to Hollywood from New York. Surrounded by friends, his dazed sense of loss began to abate, and he recalled one afternoon in particular, when he

> got to the record player and somehow found myself putting on the Fred Astaire—Johnny Green recordings of the "Shall We Dance" score, most of which had been written in that very room less than a year before. In

a few moments the room was filled with gaiety and rhythm, and I felt
that George, smiling and approving, was there listening with me—and
grief vanished.[35]

Though grief may have vanished, it took longer for Ira to return
to his craft. While his many previous collaborations enabled him to
dismiss the public myth that his talent had been totally dependent on
that of his brother, the closeness of their work together in the months
before George died may have made Ira wonder whether he could ever
collaborate fully and successfully with another composer. Here, too,
his old friends helped. Gradually Kern and Arlen got Ira back into
writing songs between poker games and pool at the Gershwin household. Not meant for any shows, most of these were simply friendly
exercises that were not even published at the time. Even the titles seem
to carry references to the loss of George—"Something's Wrong," "Hard
To Replace," "I'll Supply the Title (You'll Supply the Tune)," and, most
poignantly, a pair of songs—"Once There Were Two of Us" and "Now
That We Are One." While all that Ira wrote for nearly two years were
these few private collaborations with friends, such songs kept him from
total inactivity.

Another force that kept him active was his wife Leonore. She
herself once said, "If I hadn't been Ira's wife, I wouldn't have been in
George's crowd at all." Being there, as Ira's wife, now, after George's
death, meant assuming something of their mother's "insistent authority, energy at its most direct and fundamental." As Gershwin biogra-
phers and family friends, Edward Jablonski and Lawrence Stewart
recount it:

> Leonore, by an extraordinary act of will, assumed command, forbade
> public tears—even at 1019 North Roxbury—and turned the spotlight
> upon Ira. He was the remaining Gershwin: insofar as Ira was a visible
> presence, then so far would Gershwin live. It was not a role for which
> life had prepared Ira. He had always been one to put himself just beyond
> the spotlight, in that most intense darkness where the viewer's eye,
> blinded by incandescence, cannot see or focus—but where he, on the
> edge of light, could watch all with protected clarity. Ira had always made
> his being felt through his lyrics, through the rhetorical assumption of
> personality. But now, in Lee's phrase, "he must take his place"—and that
> meant being bodily evident.[36]

As Ira later put it, with characteristic understatement, "The name
Gershwin means far more to Lee than it ever did to me." With such
friends, and such a wife, Ira was ready, even without George, when
his greatest theatrical opportunity presented itself.

9

This Is New
1939–1941

Kurt Weill and I sat at a table in a little midtown restaurant and told each other vehemently why we would not write a musical comedy . . . We were both completely uninterested in doing a show for the sake of doing a show, in Broadway parlance, and the tight little formula of the musical comedy stage held no interest for either of us . . we discovered the kind of show we both definitely *did* want to do . . . a show in which the music carried forward the essential story and was not imposed upon the architecture of the play.

—Moss Hart

B Y 1939, Moss Hart had had enough of collaboration. Throughout the decade, he and George S. Kaufman had co-authored such plays as *You Can't Take It with You* and *The Man Who Came to Dinner*, and Hart had written the books for Irving Berlin's *Face the Music* and *As Thousands Cheer*, as well as the book for Cole Porter's *Jubilee*. Now, however, he was determined to go it alone. Finding that he had an increasing lack of interest "for plays with plots, for what is known as the well-made play," Hart wanted to write a play that reflected his new interest "in characters rather than stories."[1] With that resolve he started in on *I Am Listening*, a play about a successful career woman, the editor of a fashion magazine, who seeks out psychiatric treatment for traumatic depression. Moss Hart had himself been a patient of the noted analyst Doctor Gregory Zilboorg (who had also treated George Gershwin), and he felt he could handle the subject of psychoanalysis without resorting to the lame "sex" jokes that had marred the efforts of other playwrights.

As the work developed, however, Hart sensed that it could incorporate extended musical sequences: the scenes in the psychiatrist's office, as well as those set in the editorial offices of the fashion magazine, would consist of straightforward dialogue; once on the psychoanalyst's couch, however, the heroine would recount her dreams and fantasies, and these, with the help of blackouts and a revolving stage, could be presented in song.

At that point Hart was approached by composer Kurt Weill. World-famous for his work with Bertolt Brecht, Weill, along with his wife Lotte Lenya, had fled Nazi Germany in 1935. In America, he was determined to establish himself on Broadway but insisted upon working only with the finest playwrights. In 1938, he and Maxwell Anderson adapted Washington Irving's whimsical history of Dutch New York into *Knickerbocker Holiday*, a musical satire of fascism. Now he sought out Moss Hart to work on a musical project called *The Funnies*. Finding that Weill shared his own distaste for formulaic musical comedies, Hart instead proposed that Weill help him transform his psychoanalytic play into not a traditional musical but something else—a "play with music." Weill agreed enthusiastically but saw an immediate problem: music and story they could do—but who would write the lyrics? Hart was accustomed to working with composers like Porter and Berlin, who wrote their own lyrics. Weill—though his thick accent belied the fact that, as Ogden Nash noted, his "English was perfect"[2]—had never put words to his own music.

Both men's thoughts then turned to Ira Gershwin. Moss Hart had long been a close friend of the Gershwins, and Weill had admired Ira ever since meeting the Gershwin brothers in Berlin in 1928. When they met again, in 1935, Ira was taken aback when "out of the blue Kurt said he would like to collaborate with me."[3] Weill had just seen the premiere of *Porgy and Bess* and recognized in Ira a lyricist who could carry on the tradition of *Zeitopera*—opera that was set in contemporary times and drew on popular musical idioms—which he had initiated with Bertolt Brecht in *The Threepenny Opera*.

Hart sent a telegram to Ira, appropriately enough for such a revolutionary project, on New Year's Day of 1940. Although he had been setting words to melodies by Jerome Kern, Harold Arlen, and other friends for the private consumption of the Hollywood coterie of songwriters, what Ira's imagination craved was inspiration from a dramatic context. As Hart outlined his idea for the "play with music," eventually entitled *Lady in the Dark*, Ira could see that it offered unique opportunities for lyrical integration. So eager was he to return to work that the usually phlegmatic Ira Gershwin surprised Hart by quickly agreeing to the project. When Hart told Weill, the bemused composer observed that Hart had started out determined to work alone; now he had not one collaborator, but two.

Ira's eagerness is all the more puzzling given his initial antipathy toward psychoanalysis as a theme for a musical, and the ensuing debacle of *Pardon My English*. If his willingness was based on faith in the dramatic talents of Moss Hart, Ira was rewarded with the best "book" he ever had to work with, one that enabled him to draw upon all of the resources of poetic tradition in anchoring lyrics firmly and deeply into character and dramatic situation. From the moment the curtain went up (*without* the traditional overture to precede it), Hart's script astutely avoided all the clichés of psychoanalysis. The psychiatrist's office is bright and cheery and, except for the couch, lacks any accouterments of the analyst's trade. Dr. Brooks himself is agreeably good-looking and clean-shaven, "decidedly un-Viennese," in Hart's stage directions. When the heroine, Liza Elliott, enters, she is disarmed by the atmosphere of sunlight and flowers yet voices her skepticism about psychoanalysis. Her business-like clothing and demeanor are evidence of her claim that she is successful and well-adjusted, and she expresses only "contempt for women who spend their days pouring out their frustrations at so much per hour."[4] Her brittle façade crumbles, however, when she suddenly blurts out that she is "going to pieces" for "no reason—no reason at all."

As the doctor presses her about her symptoms, Liza hesitantly describes a constant state of anxiety and increasingly longer bouts of overwhelming depression. When she confesses that recently she has had seizures of absolute panic, the doctor gently insists that she begin therapy immediately. Reluctant, but helpless, Liza takes off her hat and lies down on the couch; when the doctor asks her to talk about whatever comes into her mind, she complains that the only thing on her mind at that moment—and at her moments of panic—is a song, a song she remembers from childhood. When he asks, "What are the words of the song?" she replies, "I don't even remember them."[5]

Thus, within one deft scene, Moss Hart focused the entire story upon song, providing Ira Gershwin and Kurt Weill with an extraordinary opportunity to integrate lyric and music with drama. As Liza strives to recall the song, Weill's "haunting melody," as Ira described it, wafts up from the orchestra. In the course of the play it became a leitmotif, "brilliantly orchestrated" by Weill "to sound sweet and simple at times, mysterious and menacing at others."[6] Only at the very end of the play, however, do we hear Ira's lyric for the melody, for Liza's cure comes only when she finally recalls the words to that childhood song. Thus Ira was given a dramatic context where his lyric would be absolutely central. If the goal of psychoanalysis, the "talking cure," is to bring the deepest layers of the unconscious to consciousness through verbal expression, it closely parallels the art of the lyricist, who struggles to find the words that will articulate the emotional significance of an abstract musical pattern.

As the doctor and Liza struggle to put words to the fragmentary melody, they could be not analyst and patient, but lyricist and composer. A skilled collaborator, Doctor Brooks suggests that Liza recount a recurrent dream in which the song, with its elusive words, figures over and over:

> Hum what you remember of the song. It doesn't matter about the words. Just hum the music.[7]

Although he knows full well that the words are indeed what will matter, for now he has Liza only hum the melody; as she does, the lights dim, music swells from the orchestra pit, and, as the stage revolves, we enter the musical world of Liza's mind.

For those fantasy sequences of the play, Moss Hart and Kurt Weill blocked out several "little one-act operas" in the spring of 1940; then Ira Gershwin took the train to New York to join his collaborators for a summer of intense work. He had forgotten how gruelling putting together a Broadway show was—"long hours, long discussions, and extensive cuts"—particularly "during the hottest spell" of a New York summer:

> I used to work until 4 or 5 in the morning and then try to sleep in a half-filled bathtub for a few hours, then go back to the grind again to find a new rhyme.[8]

The score that resulted was well worth it—a "combination of light opera, musical comedy, and choral pieces—something which had never been done in this country before." He found Weill a "receptive and responsive" collaborator, one who "came up with excellent suggestions for lyrics."[9] The composer was even willing to let Ira's words come first for much of the score, and that freedom gave Ira license for poetic flights greater than he had ever taken. In the first dream sequence, for example, Liza imagines herself not as the prim businesswoman marketing glamour to others but as a beautiful woman adored by all the world. A dozen men, attired in evening clothes and carrying lyres, march on stage under the banner "New York Chapter—Liza Elliott Admirers" and, standing beneath her penthouse window, serenade her in terms drawn from poetic tradition:

> Oh, Fabulous One in your ivory tower—
> Your radiance I fain would see . . .
> What Beatrice was to Dante
> are you to me!

The list of famous lovers ranges from Guinevere and Lancelot through Brunhilde and Siegfried, and in his manuscript versions of this song Ira seemed to be leafing through dozens of poetry anthologies as he sketched other literary couples—Petrarch and Laura, Keats and Fanny Brawne, Tasso and Leonora, Byron and Theresa, Mary Godwin and Shelley, Swift and Vanessa, Mary Devereaux and Poe, even Sappho and Plaon. Even though he also threw in homegrown, prosaic matches, from Pocahontas and Captain Smith to Calamity Jane and Buffalo Bill, he had the serenaders insist:

> Oh, Sweet! This is no potpourri!
> What Mélisande was to Pelléas
> are you to me!

As Liza's praises are picked up by her maid and chauffeur, Ira delves further into literary tradition, to the seventeenth-century poets, lifting Robert Herrick's "Upon Julia's Clothes" and recasting it as a paean to Liza:

> When as in silks our Liza goes
> then, then, methinks how sweetly flows
> the liquefaction of her clothes.

From such urbane praise, Ira's lyric clunkingly returns to the modern world of machinery and big-city hardware stores:

> A delicate poem by Herrick—
> but, surely, heavier than a derrick
> compared to our Miss Liza—she's so glamorous
> she makes all other women appear Hammacher Schlammorous.

Not only did such surrealistic juxtapositions reflect the discordant logic of dreams, Liza's fantasies also licensed Ira's verbal playfulness, a playfulness reflected in Hart's stage directions, which at one point, have a florist deliver a gigantic tulip from one of Liza's admirers.

When Liza enters, her red hair elegantly coiffed, and attired in a gorgeous blue gown, she is a striking contrast to the unassuming figure she cuts in real life. With her maid she blithely sorts through a pile of telegrams that continue the adulation:

> Huxley wants to dedicate his book to you
> and Stravinsky his latest sonata . . .
> Epstein says I simply have to pose for him . . .
> no refusing these artistic ultimata!

Then, in another burst of uncharacteristic abandon, Liza takes a limousine to Columbus Circle, climbs on a soapbox, and delivers a speech denouncing the notion of reincarnation, affirming instead, like Herrick, the philosophy of *carpe diem* in "One Life to Live":

> I believe I'll only live once
> and I want to make the most of it;
> if there's a party, I want to be the host of it;
> if there's a haunted house, I want to be the ghost of it,
> if I'm in town, I want to be the toast of it.

To underscore the fleetingness of time, Ira employs his penchant for clipping syllables:

> No time like Now-time
> for that big Wow-time
> and gloom can jump in the riv'!

For all of its verbal playfulness, the image of gloom's suicidal leap hints at Liza's underlying despair.

Those darker elements of her fantasy emerge when the audience celebrates her speech with more adulation, serenading her as the "Girl of the Moment." At first, the word "moment" seems to mean "momentous":

> Oh, girl of the moment
> with the smile of the day
> and the charm of the week
> and the grace of the month
> and the looks of the year.

That meaning shifts, however, just as Liza is about to be accorded the ultimate honor—having her portrait painted, by order of the President, for a new postage stamp. While Liza poses before the artist, the crowd chants its sophisticated curiosity:

> Is it Impressionistic?
> Or is it American primitive . . .
> Is it Pointillistic?
> Is it Surrealistic?

However when the portrait is completed, it is harshly realistic, portraying Liza as her everyday, unglamourous self. Recognizing it, Liza screams and hides her face, while the crowd turns cynical, reprising "Girl of the Moment" but now as a "wild bolero" in which "moment" means not "momentous" but ephemerally "momentary":

> Oh, girl of the moment,
> ev'ry moment
> was a waste of precious time!

With this bitter accusation that Liza, in real life, has failed to seize the day, the first musical sequence comes to a raucous close. The lights go out, the stage revolves, and Liza, once again attired in her plain business suit, is back on the analyst's couch.

Such a role would be a demanding one for any actress, but given the singing and dancing called for in the musical dream-sequences, it required an extraordinary talent. As Hart worked on the script, he realized that one of the few people who could handle the part of Liza Elliott was the mercurial Gertrude Lawrence. The emotional range she had first brought to the American stage in *Oh, Kay!* would be stretched even farther in *Lady in the Dark*, which, as one reviewer put it, let her "make use of all that she knows," from "pathos" to "lowdown shenanigans . . . all with unerring authority." When Hart read the first act to her, she recognized it "as an adventure in the theatre and something she had always hoped for as an actress."[10] Before she agreed to do it, however, Lawrence had to consult her lawyer, her friend Noel Coward, and, most important, her astrologer.

Lawrence's versatile talents unfolded in the ensuing scenes, as the doctor traced Liza's confusion back through her adolescence into her childhood, a journey that gave Gershwin and Weill the opportunity to write songs in a variety of historical styles. In a flashback to her school days at the beginning of the century, Liza sings a fairy-tale ballad, "The Princess of Pure Delight," which turns on the riddle, "What word of five letters is never spelled wrong" (the answer being, of course, "r-i-g-h-t"). Ira had written it as a poem, with "regular, confining stanzas," and when he gave it to Weill was concerned that the metrical pattern "might make for musical monotony"; but Weill's musical setting of Ira's lines was delightfully "cohesive."[11] For her high school days, they wrote "Unforgettable" and "Bats About You," both deft—and daft—parodies of 1920s Tin Pan Alley ballads. Though cut from the show before opening night, they were not only funny but integral to the play's psychological themes of memory and madness.

Amid all the comic pastiche and parodies is a beautifully simple ballad, "This Is New," originally written for the character Randy Curtis, a Hollywood movie star who falls in love with Liza. A real-life movie star, Victor Mature, was cast in the role, but, to Ira's dismay, "when handsome 'hunk of man' Mature sang, his heart and the correct key weren't in it."[12] Therefore the verse had to be cut and "Gertie" had to sing the chorus to Mature. One of Ira's best variations on the theme of romantic euphoria, the verse of "This Is New" reaches into the poetic tradition once more but this time not to the seventeenth-century Cavalier poets but to Coleridge and the Romantics:

> With you I used to roam
> through the Pleasure dome
> of Kubla Khan.
> I held you tight, my love,
> in the gardens of Old Babylon.

Taking Coleridge's theme of lost vision, Ira ties it to the motif of reincarnation by making the euphoria of love at first sight an instance of *déjà vu*:

> I lost you through the centuries,
> I find you once again

That paradoxical blend of repetition and newness is captured at the opening of the chorus, where the first two notes are repeated *F*'s, but Weill makes the second an *F#*. Ira's words subtly parallel this musical repetition and chromatic variation:

> This is new—.

The word "is" repeats the *is* of "This" but voices the sound, so that the oral progression is from an *s* to a *z* sound, the linguistic equivalent of a musical progression from a note to its sharp:

> Th*is is* new.

Ira then weaves those verbal chromatics throughout the song as deftly as Weill handles the haunting musical intervals, from

> I wa*s* merely e*x*isting,

through

> *is* it Ven*us* in*s*isting,

to the final alternations of:

> life *is* bl*iss*
> and th*is*
> *is* new.

Thus with the simplest of syllables Ira created a pattern of shifting sounds that enhances the eerie sensation of newness yet sameness.

From such elegant simplicity, Ira could turn to comic lyrics that carried plot for extended stretches. The most brilliant of these occurs in the trial scene that concludes the fantasy portion of the play. A blatant throwback to Gilbert and Sullivan, the trial centers on Liza's inability to make up her mind. As editor, she cannot decide between two possible covers for the new issue of *Allure*, a situation that brings her in conflict with her longtime advertising manager, Charley Johnson. In her personal life Liza is confronted with another quandary when Kendall Nesbitt, her longtime lover, divorces his wife and offers to marry her. Hart originally planned to stage the trial in the midst of a minstrel show, affording Weill and Gershwin an opportunity for songs and dances and providing a metaphor for mental anguish (as John Berryman would later find when he cast his *Dream Songs* in minstrel banter).

It was the production designer, Hassard Short, who thought there could be more "riotous color and regalia" if the sequence were staged as a circus performance—even though the minstrel numbers were "practically completed." Hart quickly took to the idea and rewrote the scene so that Liza's bewildered mind becomes a three-ring circus. The change probably enabled Kurt Weill to draw upon a more familiar musical idiom; while the circus is a European genre, the minstrel show would have required the kind of familiarity with American music that George Gershwin had acquired in his frequent treks to Harlem.

Ira, as always, was able to match his collaborator's music as well as provide the "very operatic" recitative the playwright called for to make the metaphoric link between the circus and the subconscious. The ringmaster, played by newcomer Danny Kaye, announces:

> The greatest show on earth!
> Liza Elliott's Gargantuan Three-Ring Circus
> featuring for the First Time
> the Captivating and Tantalizing Liza Elliott . . .
> the Woman Who Cannot Make up Her Mind!
> In addition We Bring You an Assortment
> Of Other Scintillating Stars of the Tanbark Ring
> And a Galaxy of Clowns and Neuroses
> In a Modern Miracle of Melodramatic Buffoonery
> And Mental Tightrope Walking!

The stellar imagery linked the circus to the motif of astrology, which Hart, inspired by Gertrude Lawrence's reliance upon her horoscope, portrayed as an ancient form of divination that was a harbinger of psychoanalysis. The centerpiece of the trial was to have been "The Song of the Zodiac," which Liza sings from the witness stand, blaming her failure to make up her mind on the stars. The lyric consisted of a dozen couplets, one for each constellation, illustrating how fate controls everyone. The first problem with "The Song of the Zodiac" was that Ira had to rhyme each astrological sign, and his couplets, laden with padded and inverted words, show the strain:

> To be born under Leo
> is no panaceo;
> Libra's progeny
> make for misogyny;
> Scorpio's litter
> must turn out bitter.

Secondly, producer Sam Harris wanted his star to have a lively, rousing song at this point, rather than a fatalistic, philosophical number. Worst of all, "The Song of the Zodiac" slowed the pace of what had been a frenetic trial scene as twelve chorus girls enter, one by one, each dressed in a costume symbolizing a constellation. Since it couldn't be shortened without losing the point of universal fate, "The Song of the Zodiac" was cut, and Ira, who had returned to California, once again had to board the train to come back east for some old-fashioned doctoring.

The "Song of the Zodiac" was replaced by two shorter and fast-paced songs, the first of which, "Tchaikowsky," on its surface seemed to bear no relation whatsoever to the scene. It was introduced abruptly by Danny Kaye, now in the role of the judge at Liza's trial, who, upon hearing the chorus sing a charming number, mildly inquires, "Who wrote that music?" When told it was composed by Tchaikowsky, he roars, "Tchaikowsky! I love Russian composers!" then tears into the lyric. The "lyric," in fact, was a "poem" Ira had written back in 1924 as "The Music Hour," which he published in *Life* magazine (the original *Life*, which featured light verse rather than photographs). He had been browsing through George's sheet-music, and, bemused by the many advertisements for works by Russian composers, he penned a witty collage of their names in dipodic verse (where strong and moderately strong beats alternate with weaker ones):

> There's Malichevsky, Rubinstein, Arensky and Tchaikowsky,
> Sapelnikoff, Dimitrieff, Tscherepnin, Kryjanowsky,
> Godowsky, Arteiboucheff, Moniuszko, Akimenko,
> Solovieff, Prokofieff, Tiomkin, Korestchenko . . .

On one level, the poem had none of the close relation to plot and character of "The Song of the Zodiac"; yet, in a deeper sense, its sudden, irrelevant intrusion into the action has precisely the absurd illogic of dream.

Just as Sullivan deftly managed to set such unsingable patter by Gilbert to music, Weill created a melody, marked "allegro barbaro," that transformed Ira's poem into a mad sword dance:

> There's Liadoff and Karganoff, Markievitch, Pantschenko
> and Dargomyzski, Stcherbatcheff, Scriabine, Vassilenko,
> Stravinsky, Rimsky-Korsakoff, Mussorgsky and Gretchaninoff,
> and Glazounoff and Caesar Cui, Kalinikoff, Rachmaninoff,

Danny Kaye delivered the catalogue with impeccable ferocity, sometimes rattling the entire forty-nine names in thirty-nine seconds, culminating in his final outburst: "I really have to stop/the subject has been dwelt upon enough!"

That ending, abrupt as the seemingly "unintegral" opening of "Tchaikowsky," was in keeping with the surrealistic progression of the fantasy and inevitably elicited "thunderous applause" from the shocked audience. On opening night, Ira recalled, such applause "rocked the theater for at least a solid minute." His delight was short-lived, however, when he heard a staff member exclaim "Christ, we've lost our star!" It was then that Ira realized that the next number was a solo for Gertrude Lawrence, and Lawrence was hardly the star to allow anyone, least of all a newcomer, to steal her limelight. "Either Miss Lawrence would leave the show," Ira reflected, or "Danny Kaye would have to be cut down to size."[13]

The heavens, however, smiled on *Lady in the Dark*: Kaye's performance only spurred Lawrence to new heights. "The Ballad of Jenny," which Ira and Weill had written for her in place of "The Song of the Zodiac" was another catalogue lyric, but one that wittily illustrated the dangers of a woman's making up her mind:

> Jenny made her mind up when she was three,
> she, herself, was going to trim the Christmas tree.
> Christmas Eve she lit the candles—tossed the taper away.
> Little Jenny was an orphan on Christmas Day.

The lyric traces the course of Jenny's life, through Vassar, where she majored in foreign languages but,

> in twenty-seven languages
> she couldn't say no.

Then, at twenty-two, determined to get a husband, Jenny

> got herself all dolled up in her satins and furs
> and she got herself a husband—but he wasn't hers.

Finally, at the age of seventy-five she makes up her mind to be the oldest woman alive, but

> gin and rum and destiny play funny tricks
> and poor Jenny kicked the bucket at seventy-six.

In rehearsals Lawrence had delivered the song as a straightforward narrative, but after the show-stopping applause for Kaye's "Tchaikowsky" she further shocked the opening-night audience, as well as cast, crew—and lyricist—with an impromptu rendition:

> Not only were there new nuances and approaches, but on top of this she "bumped" it and "ground" it, to the complete devastation of the audience. At the conclusion there was an ovation which lasted twice as long as that for "Tchaikowsky."[14]

In emphasizing Jenny's aggressive sexuality, Lawrence's burlesque version was, like "Tchaikowsky," more in keeping with the psychic abandon of dream. Thus the two numbers that replaced the slow-paced "Song of the Zodiac" were not only more dynamic but also more profoundly integral to the setting of Liza's mind as a three-ring circus.

As the circus trial progresses, Ira's lyrical juxtaposition of legalistic logic with linguistic absurdity rivals that of Gilbert and Sullivan at their best. Revelling in the opportunity Weill gave him to write words first, like Gilbert, Ira slyly alludes to his newfound freedom as he has the jury intone:

> let the melody fit the rhyme—
> the melody fit the rhyme!

But the priority of words over music is immediately dismissed by Danny Kaye with a bang of his gavel:

> This is all immaterial and irrelevant—
> what do you think this is—Gilbert and Sellivant?

Writing words first certainly did not mean less work for Ira. His worksheets for *Lady in the Dark* run to almost forty single-spaced typed pages. It did, however, enable him to transform Moss Hart's dialogue into light verse, leaving Kurt Weill to set it all to music.

In one of the wittiest stretches of recitative, Charley Johnson, taking the role of prosecuting attorney, accuses Liza of victimizing her longtime lover, Kendall Nesbitt, by not agreeing to marry him. In a wonderful reversal of gender roles, Johnson appeals for sympathy for Nesbitt, who is finally divorcing his wife and offering to make Liza an "honest woman":

> He gave her the best years of his life.
> She was, shall we call it, his mistress?
> 'Twas only for her he's divorcing his wife
> and now the man's in *dis*tress.
> The mister who once was the master of two
> would make of his mistress his Mrs.
> But he's missed out on Mrs. for the mistress is through—
> what a mess of a mish mash this is!

The verbal dexterity continues with a lampoon of convoluted legalese that would have titillated that ex-barrister W. S. Gilbert. Springing to Liza's defense is the circus bareback rider, movie-star Randy Curtis, who now shows his skill at balancing the spirit and the letter of the law:

> She gave him her heart, but not her word—
> This case, therefore, is so much deadwood.
> Her promise to wed he never heard
> for she never promised she wed would.

Once again, the inanity of this verbal fencing—replete with convoluted syntax and inverted word order—only reflects the anguished confusion in Liza's mind. That confusion climaxes when the music of the song whose words Liza cannot remember suddenly intrudes amid all the comic banter of the trial. Liza pleads "Don't! Don't! Don't sing that!" while the chorus taunts and threatens her until the stage darkens and revolves, and Liza is back on the couch in the psychoanalyst's office.

For the rest of the play there is no music except for that haunting refrain, and Liza struggles to resolve her mental despair by recalling its words. Her first step is to remember that she used to sing the song as a little girl, and next she recalls that it was associated with what she then called the "bad feeling"—a childhood sense of painful humiliation. Gently encouraged by Dr. Brooks, she then, in a flashback to childhood, envisions a group of people in evening clothes, one of them a red-haired woman of extraordinary beauty in a blue dress, who turns out to be Liza's mother. When her father enters carrying Liza as a small child, the people praise her, but the father sweetly calls Liza his "ugly duckling." Gazing adoringly at his wife, he says that not only is he reconciled to his child's plain looks but that he's "rather pleased," for "one beauty in the family is enough." Liza's mother agrees that her daughter will "never be a beauty" but tenderly vows "we shall make the most of your good points."[15] The father then insists that Liza sing her "little song" for the company before she goes to bed, but as the child tries to sing the words to that persistent melody she bursts into tears and runs out of the room.

The next memory Doctor Brooks elicits from Liza is of how, at age ten, when she learned of her mother's death, she could not cry. Instead, with a perverse delight, she steals into her mother's wardrobe, dons her evening cloak, and smiles at herself in the mirror. At that moment her father comes in and is horrified to see Liza apparently exulting in her mother's death. As the flood of memories continues through childhood and adolescence, Liza slowly comes to realize, with the help of Doctor Brooks, that her early feelings of ugliness led her to reject the role of attractive woman for herself, even as she devoted herself to a career of marketing *Allure* to other women. At last the words of the song come back to her, and Liza can sing them—"joyfully," in Hart's stage direction.

With so much of the play hinging on the lyric that finally emerges, Ira Gershwin struck upon an unusual strategy. Instead of trying to write the kind of dazzlingly witty and literate lyrics he had penned for the musical dream sequences, he used those previous verbal pyrotechnics as a foil to highlight an utterly simple lyric. Such a lyric would also fit the story, which called for the kind of turn-of-the-century song that would appeal to a child. Ira then concocted a child's version of his first truly superb simple lyric in the "lady-in-waiting" genre—"The Man I Love." Now, however, he transformed the singer into a little girl waiting for a magical vessel, "My Ship." The song has no verse, only a straightforward chorus that opens with a perfectly singable phrase of billowing sibilant and liquid consonants and open vowels that soar to the highest notes of the melody:

> My ship has sails
> that are made of silk.

For "memorability" Ira created faceted repetitions, barely heard, such as the *il* of "silk" that recurs in:

> My ship's aglow
> with a mi*ll*ion pearls
> and rubies f*ill*
> each bin.

Even fainter, but still subtly memorable, is the rhyme between "mill*ion*" and "b*in*."

For all of Ira's mastery of his "simple" craft, he could still make errors. One day in rehearsals Gertrude Lawrence, after singing the original release,

> I can wait for years
> till it appears,
> one fine day one spring,

suddenly stopped and, as Ira recalled with trepidation:

> fixed me with a look (I was in the fourth or fifth row) and demanded: "Why *four* years, why not five or six?" During the writing of a song, it is sung repeatedly, word by word and line by line, by lyricist and/or composer, be their voices fetching, raucous, or even nonexistent. This is done to keep testing the singability and clarity in sense and sound. Careful as one tries to be, however, occasionally an aural ambiguity is overlooked. . . . [Gertrude Lawrence] was quite right, and I quickly told her to change "*for* years" to "*the* years." Somehow neither Kurt nor I had noticed that preposition "for" received the same musical value as "wait" and "years."[16]

While "for" was indeed an error, what appears to be a blemish—the inverted word order that occasionally mars even Ira's best lyrics—turns out to be the most artful of artlessness:

> and of jam and spice
> there's a paradise
> in the hold.

Once the mark of his apprentice lyrics and a device he even had to resort to in his most masterful settings of his brother's music, Ira's awkward phrasing here beautifully registers a little girl's hesitant longing. The inversion is especially effective at the climactic turn from the second release into the final A-section of the refrain:

> But the pearls and such
> they won't mean much
> if there's missing just one thing.

Here the very misplaced word order underscores the plangency of a child's resolution.

The "missing thing" in the lyric is not just the conventional man of her dreams:

> If the ship I sing
> doesn't also bring
> my own true love to me.

In the dramatic context of Liza's recovery, the ship arrives carrying her newfound self-awareness. As she says before singing the song again at the end of the play,

I'm learning all about someone I don't think I ever really knew before—myself. It's frightening—and wonderful. Somehow, I'm going to find the courage to see it through.[17]

The word "sing," falling as it does on the very highest note of the melody, stresses that it is the *singing* that brings her ship in, a singing made possible because the melody now has words—a lyric—that express its latent significance.

Hart does give a romantic ending to the story, but one that emphasizes self-understanding more than love. Liza realizes that both her longtime lover Kendall Nesbitt and the newly smitten movie star Randy Curtis love her out of their own insecurity. What they both admire is her strength and look to her, unconsciously, for maternal protection. Her true love turns out be her longtime sparring partner, Charley Johnson, the advertising manager of the magazine, who has long resented her strength as a "Boss Lady," given his refusals to see women as little more than silly dolls whose fannies he can pat. By the end of the play, however, he grudgingly confesses his love for Liza and together they begin to work, as equals, on the design of the magazine.

As they work, Liza hums "My Ship" and, Charley, too, recalls the melody from childhood. When he asks her if she remembers the words, she happily and firmly announces, "Yes—I know all the words—now"[18] and together they sing them as the curtain descends. The reprise of the lyric makes "remembering the words" the key to both the art of the lyricist and that of the psychiatrist—probing emotional depths and bringing them to the surface of consciousness by giving them expression in language. In changing his original intent to write a play about the "talking cure," to a "play with music," Hart united with Ira Gershwin and Kurt Weill to produce a union of drama and song unique in American theatrical history.

On opening night, January 23 of 1941, Gertrude Lawrence sent Ira Gershwin a telegram that said, "I have a deep conviction which is very comforting—that our beloved George is watching over us both and is pleased with our success." Playing at the Alvin Theatre (where George and Ira's songs had once filled the frothy musicals of Aarons and Freedley), *Lady in the Dark* ran for a stunning 467 performances.

Reviewers lauded the show and several noted its significance in establishing Moss Hart "at last as something more than George Kaufman's junior partner" and showing that Ira Gershwin, "while he may never find anyone to whom he's so much attuned as he was with his brother," was nevertheless able "to write lyrics that rank with his very best. If *Lady in the Dark* had done nothing else, it would have done the theater an inestimable service merely by letting Moss Hart and Ira Gershwin extend their talents to new settings, and on their own."[19]

Its very uniqueness, however, made *Lady in the Dark* an isolated achievement. As Lehman Engel observes, *Lady in the Dark* is the *only* musical with an original book that has endured as a classic.[20] All other great musicals, from *Show Boat* and *Oklahoma!* to *My Fair Lady* and *West Side Story*, had books that were adaptations, usually made by the lyricist, of existing novels or plays. As a "play *with* music," *Lady in the Dark* sets itself further apart from such classic musicals by its sharp division between dramatic scenes and musical fantasies. Characters do not, as they do in other musicals, move from realistic dialogue into song and back again. Perhaps that very uniqueness helps account for the fact that *Lady in the Dark*, of all the great classics of American musical theater, is one of the least familiar to audiences of today.

What also contributes to that unfamiliarity, Engel argues, is *Lady in the Dark*'s lack of a "big ballad," the kind of standard, such as "Some

Enchanted Evening" or "They Say It's Wonderful," that identifies it in the minds of theatergoers and ensures successful revivals generation after generation. Even Rodgers and Hart's *Pal Joey*, another pioneering musical, from 1940, regularly lures audiences back to hear "Bewitched, Bothered, and Bewildered." With its thoroughgoing integration of song and story, *Lady in the Dark*, ironically, had no such set "showpiece." Given Ira Gershwin's insistence that integral lyrics take precedence over free-standing ballads that say "I love you" in thirty-two bars, "This Is New" and "My Ship," the songs that come closest to being "standards," are both so tailored to their dramatic context that neither became an independent hit. By choosing to forgo *all* the formulas of musical comedy, Moss Hart, Kurt Weill, and Ira Gershwin did indeed produce a unique "play with music" but one whose very transcendence of formula has limited its appeal. In more than fifty years, *Lady in the Dark*, one of Ira Gershwin's greatest contributions to the musical theater, has never had a major revival.

10

Sing Me Not a Ballad
1941–1945

Lyrics are written up to public taste, and that's a high target
... The words mustn't be precious or condescending ... A
writer can't get away with the "blue-you" sort of stuff any
longer ... A good lyric should be rhymed conversation.
                                                    —Ira Gershwin

HAD Moss Hart, Kurt Weill, and Ira Gershwin continued their collaboration, we might date the era of the integrated Broadway musical from 1941, with *Lady in the Dark*, rather than with the premiere of *Oklahoma!* two years later. The very success of *Lady in the Dark*, however, reinforced the rigorous standards of its creators in a way that inhibited this further collaboration. Just as Moss Hart and Kurt Weill had, from the outset, conceived of their "play with music" as a clean departure from traditional musical comedy, Ira Gershwin also now insisted that any future project must transcend theatrical convention. "Let's not do anything unless we feel it's something that *has* to be done," he wrote to Weill. "I have had three or four offers for shows but have turned them all down because they did not have to be done or somebody else could do that particular kind of show just as well as I could."[1]

Years earlier, Ira's high artistic standards had earned him the nickname of "The Jeweller," a sobriquet that reflected the exquisite care with which he set syllables, words, and phrases, "mosaically," to music. Now, after his work in political operetta, *Porgy and Bess*, and *Lady in the Dark*, the nickname revealed another facet of his artistry.

His longstanding antipathy to the free-standing "pop" ballads of thirty-two bars had evolved into his conception of lyrics as "lodgments," words not only fitted to music but tailored to a specific character and dramatic moment in a musical. In answer to the perennial question "Which comes first, the music or the words?" Ira would always respond "the contract." By which he meant, as his secretary, Lawrence Stewart, explained:

> A professional writes to specification, not on spec. For a musical-comedy lyricist—and Ira regards himself as such, not as a writer of popular songs—the song's situation is fundamental . . . Ira's working habits require a well-defined point of view.[2]

Although he frequently had to write to the flimsiest of specifications, as in the Aarons and Freedley musicals of the 1920s, by the 1940s he had arrived at a point where he would only consider scripts whose characters and story inspired integrated lyrics.

In that insistence, however, Ira Gershwin remained as dependent as ever upon a playwright to provide him with a dramatic setting. Other lyricists, such as Oscar Hammerstein and Yip Harburg, had gone on to create their own books, usually adapting a novel or play into a vehicle that could showcase their songs. Shortly after George Gershwin's death, his biographer Isaac Goldberg speculated about Ira's future in precisely these terms:

> It is quite like Ira's self-effacing nature to be thinking, even in these lonely days, more of George's future than his own—of the enshrining of George's memory. I have always had the feeling that Ira could, and should extend his activities from the writing of lyrics to the planning and execution of a "book," as the story of a musical show is known. His skepticism and his humor are rich enough to provide action as well as song.[3]

Yet, as Ira told an interviewer in 1946, having "become a successful lyricist," he "never has written a book, never tried his hand at a script, feels himself no expert at the other man's game."[4]

If ever Ira Gershwin should have tried his hand at creating his own dramatic setting for his lyrics, it was in 1942, when he and Kurt Weill discussed the possibility of an operetta about Nell Gwynne, the most flamboyant of King Charles II's mistresses. The Restoration setting had a special appeal for both composer and lyricist, for it evoked the world of John Gay's *The Beggar's Opera*. For Weill, Gay's score, based on popular songs of the day, had been the model for the *Zeitopera* he and Bertolt Brecht re-created as *The Threepenny Opera*. For Ira, the art of the lyric had fully emerged in the Restoration, John Gay was the first true lyricist. "The great art-song writers of the Elizabethan Age," as he pointed out, always wrote their lyrics as poems first, then set the words to "their own lute accompaniments":

> But already in that period were numerous instances where lyrics were fitted to music. This was done by satirists and parodists who, discarding the words of folk song and ballad, penned—quilled, if you like—new lyrics to traditional tunes—lyrics which politicized, thumbed the nose, eulogized, or went in for out-and-out bawdry.[5]

Out of that "practice of putting new words to pre-existent song" came "ballad opera," and "England's outstanding opus in this realm was Gay's *The Beggar's Opera*." Not only were Gay's words set "mosaically" to music, they were "lodgments" as well—tailored to specific characters and dramatic situations. For all of his scholarly knowledge of English poetic history, Ira was also a Broadway pragmatist, noting that Gay's opera "was so successful that it ran sixty-two nights, a new theatrical record that 'stood unchallenged for almost a century.'"[6]

One could add, however, that Gay not only set lyrics to numerous popular and traditional tunes, he wrote his own book as well. Ira Gershwin, however, remained exclusively a lyricist and, as such, collaborated with both playwrights and composers in plying his art. While he and Kurt Weill were enthusiastic about the Nell Gwynne operetta, they could not find a playwright to do the book. Moss Hart was a dramatist who worked strictly with contemporary settings, and he was soon engaged in a play about World War II, *Winged Victory*. Edwin Justus Mayer, a writer who had been successful with period dramas, discussed the idea with Weill and Gershwin, but no script emerged and plans for the operetta were shelved. Weill went to New York to work with Ogden Nash on *One Touch of Venus*, while Ira remained in Hollywood.

By anchoring himself in Hollywood, Ira Gershwin limited his opportunities to work on the new musical dramas that filled Broadway in the wake of *Oklahoma!* Travel between the coasts, always an arduous journey for him, was greatly restricted during wartime, but Ira would have been content to remain in California anyway. Although he considered himself "first and last—a New Yorker," California increasingly enchanted him:

> the sky was blue and cloudless, the days sunny and balmy, the nights cool. There was greenery everywhere; and if the luscious looking roses

gave no aroma (as we'd been forewarned) their lack of scent was more than made up for by orange blossoms, honeysuckle, and night-blooming jasmine. Too, we'd been continually vogue-phrased that the climate was enervating, but somehow we worked as well as ever . . . I never felt better and decided that the Charles Dudley Warner dictum, "Everybody talks about the weather but nobody does anything about it," could be refuted. Which I did by staying here for good.[7]

Ira and Leonore purchased a house in Beverly Hills soon after the completion of *Lady in the Dark*. After the ceaseless moves of the Gershwin household during his boyhood, Ira finally could settle into a home where he would spend most of the rest of his life. "As time went by, his excursions became fewer; he managed to run things nicely from where he was. The size and luxury of the house, and Ira's preference for staying close to home, inspired Harold Arlen to dub the new quarters the Gershwin Plantation."[8]

Thus during what we now recognize as the Broadway musical's greatest era, Ira Gershwin was rooted in California. Almost all of his work over the course of the next twenty years was done for Hollywood films, few of which provided the kind of script he longed for. While studio practices enabled him to collaborate with such talents as Aaron Copland, Jerome Kern, Kurt Weill, Harry Warren, Burton Lane, and Harold Arlen—virtually every major popular composer of his day—they also meant he would never work long enough with any one of them to establish the close coordination between words and music that he had with George Gershwin. With each new assignment, Ira had to adjust to a completely new musical style, which ran the gamut from the elevated idioms of Kern and Copland to the jazzy melodies of Warren and Arlen.

In the years after *Lady in the Dark*, Ira, by his own admission, did "little else but read, answer letters and turn down scripts."[9] One script that intrigued him, however, was by Lillian Hellman, for a 1943 Sam Goldwyn film, *The North Star*. Fired by the wartime alliance between America and his ancestral homeland, the producer envisioned an epic set in a Russian village. In typical fashion, he gathered a galaxy of stars, from Dana Andrews and Anne Baxter to Walter Huston and Eric von Stroheim. Then the producer gave it the "Goldwyn touch"—"12,153" authentic Russian props, the studio blurbs boasted, a $260,000-village set that was levelled to the ground with "2000 sticks of dynamite, 500 gallons of gasoline," and enough "flying debris and embers" to injure "more than 100 persons . . . none seriously."

For "class," Goldwyn, unable to secure Prokofieff or Shostakovitch, commissioned American composer Aaron Copland to do the score, then invited Ira Gershwin to set words to some of the melodies. "I did quite a lot of work on *The North Star*," Ira said, but added, "I felt very little would be used as songs tend to hold up the action in a more or less documentary melodrama."[10] Finding himself called upon to do "a folk song or two," he put simple words to "No Village Like Mine" and "Loading Time At Last Is Over." Both are sung in the early part of the movie by the children of the village as part of their peaceful daily routine. Then, as the children are singing "The Younger Generation," a Russian soldier hears the onset of a German air raid and shouts, "Stop the singing!" And stop it does—for the entire rest of the film. After the air raid, the children lament, "We are not young anymore," and as the German army takes over the village, and bleeds the Russian children to supply plasma for their soldiers, there are no more songs. Such a film certainly met Ira's insistence upon an unconventional setting for his lyrics, but where song is the powerful link between the child and adult in *Lady in the Dark*, in *The North Star* both song and childhood are abruptly relegated to the past.

His next film assignment was a much more conventional "backstager" musical called *Cover Girl*, but it did give Ira the opportunity to work with Jerome Kern. Kern had been casting about for a new collaborator ever since Oscar Hammerstein had turned his back on Hollywood and returned to the Broadway stage. Known as a difficult collaborator, one who staunchly refused to change even one note of his sonorous melodies to accommodate his lyricists, Kern proved to be Ira's most irascible musical partner. From the very start they could not even agree on a place to work. Although they lived only a few blocks away from one another in Beverly Hills, neither would budge to accommodate the other's work habits. Ira liked to write lyrics in his house in Roxbury Drive, where he was surrounded with his library of poetry anthologies and reference works. He finally gave in to Kern's insistence that they begin work at the composer's residence; once the melody was completed, however, Ira would set a dummy lyric to it and then escape back to his study to wrestle with the real words.

Nowhere was the rift more apparent—as well as Ira's antipathy to romantic ballads—than in Kern's soaring "big" melody for *Cover Girl*. Not only would he have to say "I love you" yet once more, Ira would have to do so with an unusual musical pattern. The melodic line, sweeping even for Kern, was repeated, at a slightly higher or lower interval, in each section of the refrain—with no "release" whatsoever. Even the producer of the film, Arthur Schwartz, a composer himself, was puzzled by the music when Kern first played it; only when Schwartz asked Kern to play it again, without his usual harmonic flourishes, could the producer discern the strange melodic contour.

No melody ever gave Ira more difficulty. From the very first he was stumped over what to do with the long opening phrase of seven notes. As always, the title was the hardest part of the lyric, but with this melody he could not even tell whether the title should be a one-syllable word on the first long note, or the first three notes, or the entire seven-note strand. In one version, Ira settled on a four-syllable title phrase, "Midnight Music," which the composer liked but which launched Ira into the kind of melodramatic exclamation Oscar Hammerstein so often used in setting Kern's sonorous melodies:

> And oh, there never was such music!
> Darkened streets began to shine
> the moment midnight music made you mine.

Although Kern liked the alliteration of that last line, Ira told himself "Keep it simple, keep it simple," and started all over again from scratch. An impatient Kern sarcastically suggested Ira try working from the dummy title the composer had used on the sheet-music—"Watching Little Alice" (to which someone had waggishly added a capital "P").

Finally, Arthur Schwartz called Ira one day to tell him the ballad had to be completed immediately so that it could be filmed. Ira tried stalling, saying he was still at work on a new version, the fourth, but Schwartz insisted he read whatever words he had over the phone. "I heaved an enormous sigh of relief at not having to go down to the studio to face anyone with this lyric," Ira said. To the "mentally pooped" lyricist, the version he read over the phone, "Long Ago and Far Away," seemed "just a collection of words adding up to very little."[11] Only later did Ira realize that he had indeed "come through, as requested, with a good simple lyric," one that brought out the melody with unobtrusive, but perfectly singable, words. The first line modulates between long and short open vowels:

> Long *ago* a*nd* far a*way*

Then Ira shifts to closed *i* and *e* vowels:

> *I* dreamed a dr*ea*m one day—
> and now that dr*ea*m is here b*esi*de m*e*.

Deft as the vowel placement is, however, Kern's soaring lines pull Ira into uncharacteristic platitudes that go all the way back to his earliest pollyanna weather formulas:

> Long the skies were overcast,
> but now the clouds have passed:
> you're here—at last!

Only at the conclusion does he manage any verbal invention at all, as he plays on the different meanings of "long" as a verb and an adjective:

> That all I longed for long ago was you.

Given the song's nostalgic appeal to soldiers in World War II, "Long Ago and Far Away" became enormously popular—Ira Gershwin's biggest hit in terms of annual sales of recordings and sheet-music. Although he was pleased to see it climb to the top of radio's "Hit Parade," Ira once more voiced his misgivings that such "Top Ten" institutions tended to promote songs less on the basis of quality than popularity. As for the quality of "Long Ago and Far Away," Ira dismissed this "Miss Simplicity" ballad with the same rigorous criticism he levelled at "Love Walked In"—"Neither says anything new."[12]

By contrast, he felt, his other lyrics for *Cover Girl* "were so much richer in rhyme and reference."[13] That richness, as always in Ira Gershwin's lyrics, stemmed from complexities in the music he had to set. In the title song, for example, Kern suddenly shifts from a simple strand of repeated notes to an abrupt melodic figure that traverses ten intervals. Ira adroitly stitched the musical rift together with a sequence of embedded rhymes on "Mona *Lisa*/she's *a*" and "*vision*/*El*ysian." For another song, Ira gave Kern "Put Me to the Test," an unused song he and George had written for *A Damsel in Distress*, in the hopes that his new collaborator would take inspiration from it. Kern performed an unusual feat of musical alchemy: he substituted new notes—but in exactly the same rhythmic pattern—for the ones George had written. "I gave him the lyric," Ira observed, "I didn't think he'd take the tune too."[14] Even though his old lyric now had a new melody, Ira still revised the catalogue to make it suitable for film audiences, changing the allusions to Noel Coward and Gandhi that would titillate Broadway audiences to such Hollywood items as Flash Gordon and Red Ryder.

The most complex melody in the film was one that Ira himself had to elicit from his collaborator. Years before, Kern had played a tune for Ira that ever since had haunted the lyricist. When he asked Kern about it, however, the composer had no record of the melody and could not even remember it. Ira then enlisted the help of Kern's daughter Betty, who also recalled the elusive melody, and together she and Ira hummed enough of it to jog Kern's memory. One can see why Kern had difficulty reconstructing the melody—and why the tune had so haunted Ira; with its key shifts, abrupt repeated notes, and unusual structures it was precisely the kind of musical setting that would challenge his artistry in the way George Gershwin's had.

Given his role in reviving the song, Ira had the temerity to do what no other lyricist would dream of doing with Jerome Kern—ask the imperious composer to change the music to fit the words. As he had done with George during their last year of collaboration, Ira beseeched Kern to alter his melody to accommodate the lyric; in this case, by splitting the opening note into two notes to accommodate a two-word title—"Sure Thing." With uncharacteristic cooperativeness, Kern not only complied but even complimented his collaborator by saying "in fact, the two notes make a better announcement."[15] Ira's inspiration for the title reflects his love of the racetrack, where he regularly placed bets according to intricate word associations with horses' names. While his gambling skills were notorious for their lack of success, his lyrical touch was on the nose. In the verse he sets up what seems to be a straightforward song about horse-racing:

> The favorite doesn't always win,
> no matter what the odds.
> Since nobody knows how they'll come in—
> I leave it to the gods.

In the chorus (which Kern called, with characteristic aplomb, the "burthen"), Ira weaves racetrack argot such as "picked you out of the blue" and "win or lose, what comes up, you're thumbs up with me" into a Runyonesque paean that foreshadows the slangy love songs of *Guys and Dolls*:

> If love can fig*ure*
> out a *sure*
> thing, that *sure*
> thing is you.

All of this vernacular grit was lost in the film, however, when "Sure Thing" was presented not as a contemporary love song but a period-piece. In a flashback scene, the song is performed by Rita Hayworth playing her own grandmother—a turn-of-the-century vaudeville star. Her dazzling legs hidden by layers of Gibson-girl frills, Hayworth does not even dance, merely strolls across the stage with a parasol to a slow waltz rhythm that robs "Sure Thing" of all of its intricate energy. What, in the hands (and feet) of Fred Astaire and Ginger Rogers, could have been a racy jazz duet, comes across as a genteel, Gay '90s canter.

Still, *Cover Girl* was hailed as a musical that evoked the sophistication of Fred Astaire and Ginger Rogers films. Despite its period flashbacks and a "conventional" storyline, all other aspects of the film were the "work of a production company which knows, cares about, and enjoys what it is doing."[16] In casting Gene Kelly the studios hit upon a young dancer who not only could fill Astaire's shoes but could sing and act as well. Although Rita Hayworth was a dynamic dancer, she could not sing, and so her voice had to be dubbed—a practice that became increasingly common in Hollywood. In the early days of film musicals all singing was dubbed, but it was dubbed by the singers themselves, so that on screen they could concentrate on dancing and movement. But when Astaire or Rogers filmed their pre-recorded songs, they performed them with all the movements and expressions of the professional singer; when a non-singing actress, like Hayworth, tried to put over a song dubbed by someone else, she invariably seemed stilted ("she looks," one reviewer quipped, "as if she were daring you to stick your head in her mouth").[17] Given that awkwardness, intimate duets, particularly ones combined with dances, had to be avoided and without such numbers the Astaire-Rogers magic would never be fully recaptured.

Increasingly, Hollywood studios, with the exception of MGM, were turning from the creation of original musicals to making film versions of successful Broadway shows. Wartime shortages made it difficult for studios to maintain the huge production staffs needed to create scripts and songs for musicals from scratch; it was far easier—and safer—to take a successful Broadway show and put it on film. Now that the Broadway musical had undergone an extraordinary revival with the onset of integrated musicals after *Oklahoma!*, Hollywood, it seemed, could count on a series of "sure things." Producers need only put their creative stamp on their product by substituting a screen star for a Broadway one (Gordon MacRae for Alfred Drake in *Oklahoma!*, Betty Hutton for Ethel Merman in *Annie Get Your Gun*, Mitzi Gaynor for Mary Martin in *South Pacific*, etc.).

The dearth of original Hollywood musicals, coupled with the resurgence of stage musicals, enticed composers and lyricists back to Broadway. Jerome Kern, recognizing the significance of what Richard Rodgers and Oscar Hammerstein, his own long-time lyricist, had accomplished with *Oklahoma!*, rushed back to New York to make his own contribution to the integrated musical. In 1945, while planning an "Americana" musical about Annie Oakley, Kern collapsed on the streets of New York and died a few days later. Rodgers and Hammerstein, who were the producers of the musical, then turned to Irving Berlin, the old warhorse who, at nearly sixty years of age, topped everyone by writing a string of songs that were not only perfectly integrated into the plot and characters of *Annie Get Your Gun* but also went on to become independent hits as well.

Berlin demonstrated that, at a time when the world of music was changing profoundly, a lyricist was most secure when he was his own composer. In a span of a few years, all the great songwriting teams of the era had dissolved—the Gershwins, Kern and Hammerstein, Rodgers and Hart, Howard Dietz and Arthur Schwartz, as well as such Hollywood collaborators as Leo Robin and Ralph Rainger and Al Dubin and Harry Warren. Even Yip Harburg and Harold Arlen separated, despite their film triumph in 1939 with *The Wizard of Oz* and the success of *Bloomer Girl* in 1944, their own contribution to the "Americana" musical drama inaugurated by *Oklahoma!* Arlen's primary lyricist in Hollywood had now become Johnny Mercer, while Harburg, blacklisted by the film industry for his long-standing political views, remained on Broadway where, with composer Burton Lane, he continued the development of the integrated musical with *Finian's Rainbow*. As composers and lyricists successfully played out a collaborative game of musical chairs throughout the 1940s, a game that spanned Broadway and Hollywood, Ira Gershwin was left standing without a long-term collaborator.

At first the void created by Kern's departure was filled by Kurt Weill's return to Hollywood near the end of 1943. Weill first was assigned the task of writing a score for a film version of *Lady in the Dark*. The results, however, appalled him—and Ira. The studio cut out songs and revamped Weill's careful orchestrations. Most dumbfounding was the treatment of "My Ship"; while the haunting melody is heard throughout the movie, the all-important lyric is never sung. Weill then wanted to do an original film musical, and Twentieth Century-Fox, bucking the trend toward Broadway remakes, invited him and Ira Gershwin to do a film that promised to be as revolutionary a Hollywood musical as *Oklahoma!* had been for Broadway. *Where Do We Go from Here?* offered Weill what he regarded as "frankly an experiment in opera form, in which the music and lyrics are integrated with the story, advancing it rather than retarding it as is the case with most musical films."[18] Ira Gershwin greeted the project with equal relish, as "the first movie musical I know that has some of the flavor of *Of Thee I Sing* in the writing and the music." What intrigued both lyricist and composer about *Where Do We Go from Here?* was an extended fantasy sequence that called for an unbroken stretch of plot-carrying lyrics rather than the traditional film presentation of songs as performances. The basic story concerns an American patriot named Bill, who is classified 4-F but still labors for the war effort by collecting scrap metal and doing dishes at a USO. As he longs for the battlefield, he comes across a magical lamp that produces a bumbling genie; when Bill makes a wish to go to war, the genie mistakenly whirls him back in history. First he lands at Valley Forge in 1776, then finds himself sailing with Columbus in 1492, and from there he travels to Dutch New Amsterdam. Since the whole sequence was a fantasy, characters could burst into song and dance for no reason, and the historical settings gave the songwriters the kind of freedom they had envisioned in their plans for a costume musical set in the Restoration.

When Bill is assigned by General Washington to spy on Hessian troops in a Trenton tavern, for example, he listens to them sing "A Song of the Rhineland," where Ira Gershwin plays with lyrical imagery that is as anachronistic as Weill's thumping waltz rhythms:

> Life is milk and honey-er
> where the sun is sunnier,
> and the rain is rainier
> and the brain is brainier;
> where the heart is mellower
> and the hair is yellower,
> and the girls is juicier
> and the goose-step goosier.

The intrusion of the hero's World War II perspective on Germanic *Gemütlichkeit*, gives a satiric edge to Ira's playful suffixes:

> where the stork is storkier
> and the pig is porkier
> and the beer is beerier
> and the soup superior;
> where the wine is winier
> and the Rhine is Rhinier
> and the Heine's Heinier
> and what's yours is minier.

Even more innovative was the Columbus sequence, in which Weill and Gershwin created what has been termed a miniature *opéra bouffe*.[19]

When the bumbling genie plunks Bill down on the *Santa Maria*, he finds himself in the midst of a mutiny. The sailors chant their anger at Columbus for "sailing westward ho" since the "world is flat—like that" and thus there is "no land to land on where we go." Columbus appeals to their patriotism, warning that Queen Isabella has hocked her jewels to fund the mission; thus, if they fail, Isabella, too, "will be flat—like that!" The sailors are unmoved, however, and the cook warns Columbus that no appeal will quell their anger:

> Yes, Commodore, their stomachs are in an ugly mood
> on top of getting nowhere they are fed up with the food.

The very mention of food invokes an aria of nostalgic lament:

> Every night we are in tears
> when we think of macaroni
> and it seems like forty years
> since we tasted minestrone.
> Long to drink again the vino
> with the wife and the bambino.

Bill, however, steps in to save the day, unveiling a picture of the future America with the clairvoyance of a 1945 American man-in-the-street. Instead of grandiose patriotic visions, he paints the kind of vista likely to appeal to sailors of any era:

> The girls are delightful,
> their sweaters are quite full . . .
> what pictures you'll pin up
> if you keep your chin up.

Between the prospects of a "flat" Isabella and such a full-bodied future, the sailors are swayed, but when Bill lets slip that the New World will be named America, Columbus, outraged that his discovery will be named after that "two-bit explorer Amerigo Vespucci," orders the ship to turn back to Spain. Before the order can be carried out, however, a sailor cries "Land Ho!" and the crew exultantly presses onward.

The twelve-minute sequence still stands as the longest continuous stretch of sung dialogue in film history. Weill wrote to a friend back in New York, "I have turned out a job here which I can be proud of," while Ira, more cautiously, observed, "A lot of effort and imagination has gone into this film and I hope the results warrant it."[20] While *Where Do We Go from Here?* won acclaim from critics for the musical fantasy sequence, the rest of the movie, with its emphasis on rationing, scrap-metal drives, and servicemen's canteens, had little appeal for war-weary audiences. *Where Do We Go from Here?* went, as they say, nowhere.

Before the film's release, Ira and Kurt Weill, still enthusiastic over their achievement in film operetta, returned to the stage musical they had shelved back in 1942. Together with playwright Edward Justus Mayer, they scrapped plans for the Restoration musical about Nell Gwynne and decided to adapt Mayer's own play *The Firebrand* into a musical. Not only had *The Firebrand*, based on Benvenuto Cellini's *Autobiography*, been a success back in 1924, it had included a song, "The Voice of Love," for which a young lyricist named Ira Gershwin had provided the words.

"We have set ourselves quite an ambitious task," Ira observed, "especially as this is the first time I am doing a costume piece." The Renaissance, bursting with poetry, gave him the opportunity to "do a lot of things in fun that I'd hesitate to experiment with if the show were placed in modern times."[21] The linguistic exuberance of the period licensed all sorts of verbal play, and rhyme itself, as Ira observed, was then in glorious flower:

> the Italians had been making use of this verbal or syllabic harmoniza-
> tion for some centuries. (Petrarch declared the Italians learned the de-
> vice from the Sicilians; the Sicilians stated they acquired it from the
> Provençals; the Provençals felt they'd inherited the chiming effect from
> their erstwhile masters, the Arabians, while the Germans maintained
> they had adopted it from the Scandinavians. And so on.)[22]

Given such a poetic setting, Ira unleashed all of his light-verse wit. What resulted, however, were lyrics that were too verbally clever, calling attention to themselves rather than the music and dramatic context.

The most pyrotechnic lyrics were the ones Ira wrote for Cellini's patron, the lecherous Duke, "Alessandro the Wise":

> My art collection features Botticelli and Da Vinci,
> but also I collect young women who are plump and pinchy.

With an obvious delight in his own rhyming—as well as sexual prowess—the Duke flaunts his literate lechery:

> I educate the female mind,
> the which I do in private.
> No matter what erotica
> their shelves are lacking—I've it.

When the Duke attempts to seduce Cellini's model Angela, he is more caught up in his own rhyming powers than with the object of his desire:

> It's always been a pleasure
> to dedicate a measure
> to the lady who intrigues me at the time.
> Diana and Roxana
> and Lana and Susannah
> were names I sang in rhythm and in rhyme.
> Cornelia and Aurelia,
> Cecilia and Ophelia
> inspired lovely lyrics from my pen—
> but Angela is something else again!

In "A Rhyme for Angela," as we have seen, Ira's failure to come up with a match for her name portends the Duke's failed suit.

In the climactic, albeit abortive, seduction scene, Ira has the Duke succumb to utter linguistic impotence. As early as 1924, Ira had wanted to write a song lyric "based on spoonerisms"—the "accidental transposition" of syllables that turns a simple phrase such as "our dear old queen" into "our queer old dean."[23] Finally, given the dramatic context of *The Firebrand of Florence*, Ira found a lodgment for his light-verse wit. As the Duke woos Angela, he is so fearful of the danger of Cellini lurking nearby that he mumbles,

> I know where there's a nosy cook,

which Angela then corrects to

> My lord, you mean a cozy nook?

Then he proceeds to suggest that "there we two can kill and boo," which she again corrects to "bill and coo," only to have him launch into her praises with,

> I love you for your sturgeon vile,

which she then straightens out:

> My lord, you mean my virgin style?

Soon, Angela herself falls into spoonerisms:

> How masterf'ly you stress your puit!
> I mean the way that you press your suit.

At the conclusion the Duke finally manages to untwist his syllables,

> And so I offer wedless bliss,

while Angela can only wish he had remained tongue-tied:

> I'd rather it were bedless wiss.

It is the spoonerisms, however, rather than the dramatic situation that come to the fore, leaving Ira open to the criticism that the lyrics were self-indulgent.

The one song that manages to balance wit and passion is, fittingly, a diatribe against poetry. In "Sing Me Not a Ballad" the earthy Duchess, in contrast to her Duke's linguistic efflorescence, dismisses the flowery words and other accoutrements of chivalry:

> Gallantry I find archaic,
> poetry I find prosaic.
> Give me the man who's strong and silent:
> inarticulate—but vi'lent.

She then launches into an all-out assault on romantic effusions in words perfectly suited to what Ira termed Weill's wonderfully "astringent music":

> Sing me not a ballad,
> send me not a sonnet.
> I require no ballad:
> rhyme and time are wasted on it.
> Save your books and flowers;
> they're not necessaries;
> Oh, the precious hours
> lost in grim
> prelim-
> inaries!

She concludes with one of Ira's characteristic turnarounds of a stock phrase:

> Spare me your advances—
> just, oh just make love!

Had Ira taken some of the Duchess's advice, he might have better contained his own witty flights within the musical and dramatic framework of *The Firebrand of Florence*.

His own poetic excesses, unfortunately, were part of an over-all conceptual problem with the musical, which alternated between swashbuckling, romantic operetta and tongue-in-cheek self-deprecation, as if it were a patchwork collaboration between Sigmund Romberg and Gilbert and Sullivan. At first, however, Ira had the highest hopes for *The Firebrand of Florence*. Weill's score, he felt, was "the best job he's ever done—it's a more rounded score than *Lady in the Dark*." When Ira arrived in New York in December of 1944 to begin rehearsals, he exulted that "it's going to have the best singing I've been connected with since the original *Porgy and Bess* company." Soon his confidence grew stronger: "On the whole, I'd say things look pretty good with this opus." Although he reminded himself that "naturally lots of things can go wrong before the opening and lots more after," he could not contain his enthusiasm: "We're all pretty optimistic and know we're connected with something worth while doing artistically—and (this we hope) financially."[24]

By the time *The Firebrand of Florence* opened, casting problems had widened the fundamental fissures between book and lyrics. While their voices were superb, newcomers Earl Wrightson as Cellini and Beverly Tyler as his model Angela lacked the "authority and presence"[25] to sustain the lead roles in a Broadway show. They could not maneuver the difficult transition from witty, light-verse ballads, such as "You're Far Too Near Me," to the soaring bombast that pitted Cellini's longings for artistic immortality ("Work is my destiny, my relentless destiny") against her romantic demands ("Love is my destiny; work is my enemy, urging you onward, ever onward . . . "). Even more damaging was the casting of Duke Alessandro. Originally, Walter Slezak was to have played the lecherous Duke, but he soon withdrew, and the role was given to British comedian Melville Cooper, who lacked the kind of boisterous ribaldry Slezak would have brought to the role. The loss of Slezak took its toll as well on the performance of Lotte Lenya, Weill's wife, who was cast, or, as some said, miscast, in the role of the Duchess. What the role called for was an aging, yet still brassy siren, but Lenya's performance fell far short of such erotic demands. *The Firebrand of Florence* closed after forty-three performances.

Ira took the failure with unusual bitterness: "It looks as if nine months of hard work have been shot to hell."[26] Most of the songs are unknown today, but they do survive in an unusually apt form: with wartime restrictions, Weill and Gershwin made a recording, on a home tape machine, of much of the score for *The Firebrand of Florence* and sent it to New York to give the show's director their sense of how each number should be performed. With Weill at the piano, occasionally interjecting bits of choral numbers in his thick German accent, Ira Gershwin sings virtually the entire score in a voice that resembles that of Groucho Marx. The tape was transformed, with all of its made at home sound problems, into a collector's recording, where it constitutes a kind of "closet" musical performed solely by composer and lyricist.

Even with a stronger score, book, and cast, it is doubtful whether *The Firebrand of Florence* would have been a success. As a costume operetta set in Renaissance Italy it ran against the grain of audience tastes which, in the wake of not only *Oklahoma!* and *Bloomer Girl* but a European war, had come to delight in musicals that radiated Americana. Even after World War II, such native settings and themes continued to appeal to audiences with *Annie Get Your Gun* and *Finian's Rainbow*. It was to such American material that Kurt Weill turned, collaborating with Langston Hughes on *Street Scene* and, just before he died, contemplating a musical based on *Huckleberry Finn*. It is tempting to imagine what might have resulted had Kurt Weill and Ira Gershwin transformed *Huckleberry Finn*, a novel so rooted in American music and vernacular speech, into a musical drama. But Kurt Weill returned to the Broadway stage, and Ira Gershwin, in Hollywood, sought out another, albeit ghostly, collaborator—his brother George.

11

CHANGING MY TUNE
1946–1951

You know, I always avoided George when I could because he would ask me what I was doing, tell me to get busy, and all that . . . I always felt that if George hadn't been my brother and pushed me into lyric writing, I'd have been contented to be a bookkeeper . . It sounds like a pompous word but George inspired me. He was always full of new ideas, and he was so good a musician, that I could do things with lyrics that I couldn't do with just a songwriter. I'm not just interested in writing songs. I like to do things with a twist, things that you might even call artistic.

—Ira Gershwin

A T his death, George Gershwin left a legacy of dozens of completed songs, for which words could still be set, and stacks of tunebooks with many more songs sketched in fragmentary form. On top of this "new" material were many songs that had been cut from shows and films, such as "Ain't It Romantic?" which was discarded from *Oh, Kay!* in 1926 and went into the trunk as "Melody No. 44."[1] With revised lyrics, Ira knew, such gems might shine in new productions. Still other songs, such as "Love Is Here To Stay" and "They Can't Take That Away from Me," had been wasted in their original contexts; showcased in better productions these might finally garner the recognition they merited. Such a treasure of musical material, all of it sitting in Ira's home, was a constant temptation to continue his collaboration with George at the same time that he was working with other composers. Although Ira Gershwin always wore the mask of Rip Van Winkle, nothing should dispel the myth of his indolence more than the fact that in the years that followed his brother's death he pursued not one career but two.

Ira's first efforts at working with George posthumously came when he received an invitation from the planners of the 1939 New York World's Fair to provide a new "Gershwin" theme song for the event. For musical assistance, Ira turned to Kay Swift. The classically trained composer had once had nothing but disdain for popular songs until her brother played her a recording of several songs by George Gershwin, including "Stairway to Paradise." In 1924 she had met George at a party she gave with her husband at the time, financier James Warburg, and by 1926 she and George were romantically involved. They spent a great deal of time together at the piano, and soon Kay Swift was serving informally as George's musical secretary, even as she established herself as a popular composer with successes such as "Fine and Dandy." George would play ideas for her, and together they would work songs out on two pianos, including one piece that Ira dubbed "Her Waltz, His Waltz, Their Waltz."

Although their romance cooled when George left for Hollywood, they continued to write to one another on a regular basis until George's death. To Ira, Kay Swift seemed the most likely collaborator to help him with the musical archaeology:

> She knew almost everything George had ever written, had frequently taken down sketches as he composed in his New York apartment, and had total musical recall. (At one time she could play from memory the entire *Porgy and Bess* vocal score of 559 pages.)[2]

Ira found that she even worked much as George did, rummaging around in the tunebooks, pulling out strands from several different melodic fragments, then piecing them together. For the New York World's Fair anthem, she wove several melodies, including a 1930s song called "Come, Come, Come to Jesus," into "Dawn of a New Day." Ira, in turn, took the formula of pollyanna weather songs and gave it a solemn twist that envisions a glorious future beyond the Depression: "See the sun through the gray—it's the dawn of a new day."

Their successful collaboration prompted Ira, in the lull after *Lady in the Dark*, to consider plans for using George's unpublished music in a full-scale musical, *Birds of a Feather*. While the script, by Bella and Samuel Spewack (who later adapted *The Taming of the Shrew* into the book for Cole Porter's *Kiss Me, Kate*), was good, Ira felt that it lacked enough love interest for songs. Perhaps recalling the problems with *Let 'Em Eat Cake*, Ira decided against the undertaking, noting that when a show "is done with the posthumous music it ought to have a more romantic background than the one *Birds* presents."[3]

Clearly, though, he was determined to resuscitate the unpublished songs in one form or another, and in 1946 he felt he had finally found the perfect vehicle for them. Twentieth Century-Fox, mindful of the Broadway success of Americana musicals like *Oklahoma!* and *Bloomer Girl*, planned just such a period piece around its biggest female star, Betty Grable. In *The Shocking Miss Pilgrim*, Grable would play a New York secretary who comes to Boston in the 1870s as that city's first female typewriter. The fact that such a story would prohibit Grable from displaying her legs did not deter the studio bosses. Nor did the fact she could not sing, now that dubbing was the fashion, though the studios made sure that her co-star, Dick Haymes, could sing (though he could do little else).

Still, Ira was intrigued by the challenge of writing a score, with the flavor of a historical period, from George's legacy of music. Initial plans called for him to work with either Harry Warren or Harold Arlen, but when neither composer was available, Ira approached producer William Perlberg with the possibility of creating an entire score out of George's unused musical material. Once Perlberg, as Ira put it, "sold the studio on the idea," Kay Swift was called in once more:

> We spent ten weeks going carefully through all my brother's notebooks and manuscripts; from them she played and then copied for me well over a hundred possibilities—forty or fifty complete tunes (several of which . . . I had started setting lyrics to in George's lifetime), plus verses, plus themes for arias, openings, &c.[4]

By Ira's own account, he had a staggering amount of musical material to work with—100 songs, fifty of them complete. Equally amazing was the fact that the musical trove could yield enough songs with the period flavor needed for *The Shocking Miss Pilgrim*. "I can't use some of the rhythmic and modern stuff and have to go in more for charm,"[5] but clearly there was plenty of material that could be used for the film—as well as future musicals.

The best "charm song" of the film, "Aren't You Kind of Glad We Did?" was a revision of a duet the Gershwins had written in the 1930s. In the original song Ira gave a twist to the romantic euphoria formula by writing what he termed an "Epithalamium of the Depression," a duet for two lovers who decide to marry despite their penury. While the Gershwins had "no particular show in mind" at that time, Ira hoped one day one might come along calling for this particular lodgment.

"Since no libretto ever called for the situation," he lamented, "this nuptial notion gathered dust for a dozen years."[6] Working on *The Shocking Miss Pilgrim*, he realized that the song could be revised into a "Mid-Victorian Colloquy" for the scene where Betty Grable, recently arrived in Boston, is given a carriage tour of the city by her employer, Dick Haymes. After the tour he takes her to dinner at a fashionable restaurant, but as he is seeing her home, they suddenly realize they have violated Boston propriety by failing to have a chaperon.

Ira found that his original lyric for the first two sections of the refrain suited the film's satire of Boston gentility just as well as it had the Depression couple:

> Honestly, I thought you wouldn't;
> naturally, you thought you couldn't;
> and probably we shouldn't—
> but aren't you kind of glad we did?
> Actually, it all was blameless;
> nevertheless, they'll call it shameless,
> so the lady shall be nameless—
> but aren't you kind of glad we did?

The original release and the final section of the chorus, however, had a slangy directness that anchored it too firmly in the 1930s:

> Socially, I'm rather hazy;
> financially, I've not a dime.
> Realistically, we're both ka-ra-zy—
> but we'll have one hell of a time.
> Though creditors may try to floor us,
> though relatives will carp and bore us—
> for us no anvil chorus!
> Whatever we did we're glad we did.

In rewriting these sections to fit the situation of *The Shocking Miss Pilgrim*, Ira needed more lyrical room than George's original music allowed, so Kay Swift added some "grace notes" to the melody, lengthening various lines of the chorus to give Ira extra syllables. With her extra notes, Ira could have Dick Haymes manfully shoulder responsibility for the social crime:

> I'm a rounder, a bounder, a cad, a Boston blighter.

Then, by lengthening Grable's line by one note, Kay Swift enabled Ira to provide her witty concurrence:

> You shouldn't be seen alone with your typewriter.

Kay Swift did not have to add a note to the film's other comic number, "The Back Bay Polka," only transform the tempo of "Heigh-Ho the Merrio," a British "folk song" the Gershwins had written for *Damsel in Distress*, into the rousing rhythms of a most un-Bostonly dance:

> Don't speak the naked truth—
> what's naked is uncouth;
> It may go in Duluth—
> but not in Boston!
> . . . somewhere the fairer sex
> has curves that are convex,
> and girls don't all wear specs—
> but not in Boston!

In the film, "The Back Bay Polka" is sung by a quartet of rooming-house tenants who call themselves "The Outcasts," and their unconventional characters—painter, poet, lexicographer, and composer—inspired Ira to work some particularity into his light-verse catalogue of Boston taboos:

> Books that are out of key
> we quickly bury;
> you will find liberty—
> in Mr. Webster's dictionary . . .
> Painters who paint the nude
> we keep repressing;
> we take the attitude
> even a salad must have dressing . . .
> No song except a hymn—
> and keep your language prim:
> you call a leg a "limb"
> or they boot you out of Boston!

For the romantic ballads of *The Shocking Miss Pilgrim*, Kay Swift had to perform more extensive musical excavations and reconstructions, and Ira had to rework, yet once more, the formulas of romantic longing and euphoria. Out of a melodic fragment in George's tune-books, Swift wove a lovely song, and Ira took inspiration from that achievement and came up with the title "Changing My Tune":

> No more the feeling
> that my world is reeling,
> no fearing I'll fall in a swoon;
> problems are all picayune.

In another stratum of the tunebooks, "Gershwin Melody No. 51," Kay
Swift struck what she called a "goldmine," and Ira faced what he termed
the task of performing "variation #4,708,903 1/2, Series E, on the Three-
Little-Words theme." As arduous as that task had become he still came
up with an artfully simple lyric, singable in its long open and closed
vowels, memorable in its subtle repetitions of rhyme, from the opening title phrase,

> For you—
> for me—
> for evermore,

through the release,

> we found, by finding each other,
> the love we waited *for*,

to its final reprise:

> what a lovely *wor*ld this *wor*ld will be
> with a *wor*ld of love in st*or*e
> *for* you, *for* me, *for* everm*or*e.

Given such artfulness, one can sympathize with Ira Gershwin's irritation at a singer who recorded the song but sang these closing
lines as:

> what a lovely world this world would be
> with a *love that can endure*
> for you, for me, for evermore.

With the pompous sentimentality of "love that can endure" the singer
lost the vernacular ease of "love in store" as well as a true rhyme
(end*ure*/m*ore*). Ira ranted, "On the album jacket, the vocalist is quoted:
'No, I don't read music . . . and all my own training was by ear.'" "Good
girl," he quips, "—but how about reading the words."[7]

   The Shocking Miss Pilgrim earned what Ira dismissed as the usual
studio acclaim— "'Best we ever had,' 'Out of this world,' etc., etc." In
his own characteristically understated terms, he gave it the highest
praise possible: "I will say it's a very good Gershwin score."[8] At the time
he could not foresee that the film would be sabotaged by production
problems—strikes, miscasting, multiple changes of directors—and that
Grable fans would not like seeing their darling's gams swathed in
petticoats and her hair done up in braids (in a historically accurate
depiction of how nineteenth-century office women protected them-

selves from the new machines). Still, Ira could bask in his and Kay Swift's achievement, though, as was his wont, he gave George most of the credit: "The music, outside of a few grace notes . . . was all my brother's. So, thanks to Perlberg's trust in the notebooks, manuscripts, and me, a score materialized—the first posthumous one, I believe, for a film musical."9

Pleased with the results of posthumous collaboration, and with the dozens of completed songs and over a hundred melodic fragments, including lots of "rhythmic and modern stuff," still in the Gershwin "trunk," Ira could look forward to more new "Gershwin" musicals. It was at that point that he heard from George S. Kaufman. To Kaufman and co-playwright Nunnally Johnson, it seemed that the spate of home-spun Americana period-pieces launched by *Oklahoma!* had run its course and that Broadway audiences by 1946 were ripe for a return to "smart" musicals. What more urbane theme could titillate audiences, they thought, than divorce? Not one divorce, no, but couple after couple after couple uncoupling with a string of ex's so long no one could keep them straight, not even the beleaguered lawyer at the plot's center. Such sophisticated social confusion, Kaufman was certain, would be the butt of many a gag and spark witty curves on the tiredest of lyrical formulas.

It seems that Ira's willingness to write the lyrics for this ill-conceived and ill-timed venture was based on his assumption that it would give him an opportunity to collaborate on another score with George. After he had agreed to do *Park Avenue*, however, he received another letter from Kaufman, explaining that, through some confusion, Ira's desire to use George's music had not been communicated to him in time. He and Johnson, therefore, had already invited composer Arthur Schwartz to provide the music. While Ira must have been disappointed, the choice of Schwartz made sense. He had collaborated with lyricist Howard Dietz some dozen years earlier on *The Band Wagon*, *The Little Show*, and other smart revues, producing such urbane melodies as "I Guess I'll Have To Change My Plan" and "By Myself." Kaufman's reassurance that "Arthur's grasp of the book delights me" may have been a subtly pointed reminder to Ira of the major liability of having a posthumous collaborator.

Working with Kaufman, as always, had its own liabilities. Bent upon gags, his script outline gave Ira little inspiration in the way of characters or situations. For an opening number, the playwright suggested "fast dancing goings-on" with "some-such title" based on what was to become the show's one and only joke: "When I Was Married to

Your Mother (I Remember Her Well)." Ira tried other titles but they only reflected the script's permutations on its single theme: "What Do You Do Between Marriages" and "I Don't Know Where My Next Husband Is Coming From." Kaufman also suggested other lame variations for the first-act finale, such as "You Can't Tell the Husbands and Wives Without a Scorecard." When it came to suggesting a theme for a "straight love song," however, the anti-romantic Kaufman was at a loss: "a wedding, the nature of their lives together—God knows what. Anyhow—NUMBER."

With such uninspiring suggestions, it is remarkable that Ira came up with even serviceable lyrics; that he produced some cleverly comic ones resulted from his equation of linguistic confusion with marital confusion. By wrenching language, he could reflect the disarray of the couples who divide and reunite through the course of the story. One inspiration for such entangled syntax and spouses came from his recollection of an old Alley songwriter:

> I met Dave Clark in the early Twenties at the billiard-and-pool parlor on 52nd Street—a hangout frequented nightly by songwriters. Clark was always neatly dressed, clean-shaven, and soft-spoken, even though over the years the poor chap's brains had become disordered . . . Despite his mental handicap, every once in a great while Dave would turn out a new song—with words somewhat Gertrude Steinish . . . A publisher Dave didn't take to was a "faint little man"; of another annoyer he said: "I never liked him and I always will" . . . Even before I knew Dave I'd heard of his liking a Broadway show and recommending it to many with: "Don't miss it if you can."[10]

Such linguistic convolutions inspired Ira to write "Don't Be a Woman If You Can," which catalogues the daily choices women face over clothing, nail polish, hairdos, and perfume:

> Shall it be Chanel or Flattery,
> Sexy or Assault-and-Battery,
> Innuendo, Radiant, or Dash-of-Bed . . .
> wondering which will make love burgeon:
> Courtesan or Vestal Virgin,
> Jezebel or Farmer's Daughter—
> which one leads them to the slaughter?
> See-Me-Later or Narcissus,
> Midnight Passion, Morning Kisses?
> Worried which one will beguile 'um,
> till you're fit for the asylum.

Ira's syntactical skewing spills over into other lyrics, such as "There's Nothing Like Marriage for People" and "There's No Holding Me (When I'm Holding You)." A similar clash between words and music occurs in "Sweet Nevada," in which Ira Gershwin and Arthur Schwartz salute the divorce capital of America—in a waltz:

> Young woman, go West,
> unfeather your nest!
> . . . one rushes to arrive there;
> your girlish glands revive there.
> Oh, how one feels alive there . . .
> they glorify the credo
> be true to your libido.

Even the big romantic ballad got a twist as the leading boy and girl, seeing the meaninglessness of marriage for the multiply divorced adults who surround them, agree to call off their wedding; still thinking in illogical terms, Ira has them toast farewell, not to the past, but to the future with "Good-bye to All That."

For all of Ira's witty play with language, *Park Avenue* could not make light of its premise, as Arthur Schwartz realized during the Boston try-out when a recently divorced friend told him she had wept through most of the performance. Far from bucking the trend toward Americana musicals, what Ira termed this "so-called 'smart' show" closed after only nine weeks. Musing upon the back-to-back debacles of *The Firebrand of Florence* and *Park Avenue*, he stoically quipped, "Heigh ho—guess I can't afford to do any more flops—two in a row is about six too many."[11] Despite such insouciance, Ira Gershwin never again wrote for the stage, even though the Broadway musical had at last achieved the kind of integration between song and story that the Gershwin brothers had always sought. With the release of *The Shocking Miss Pilgrim* early in 1947, to disappointing reviews, Ira Gershwin withdrew from Hollywood musicals as well. He dug no further into his brother's tunebooks and, with his Van Winkle mask firmly in place, announced that, at age fifty, he was "determined to rest."[12] His days were spent at the racetrack, in poker games, on the golf course, reading, answering correspondence—even opening his home as a meeting place for friends who were organizing resistance to the House Un-American Activities Committee.

Clearly it would take a tremendous opportunity to lure him out of semi-retirement—and, in 1949, one came: another chance to write for

Fred Astaire. Little did Ira realize it would also mean the chance to
write for Ginger Rogers as well, for the pair's final movie and one of
their best, *The Barkleys of Broadway*. The reunion of Astaire and Rogers
came about through a Hollywood version of musical chairs. The film
Easter Parade had originally paired Gene Kelly with Judy Garland, but
when an accident sidelined Gene Kelly, Fred Astaire was brought in
to replace him. Since Garland did not radiate the sensuous elegance
of Rogers, Irving Berlin took advantage of her slapstick talents in numbers such as "A Couple of Swells," for which she and Astaire blackened
their teeth, smudged their faces, and donned ragged tuxedos in a burlesque parody of the classic Astaire-Rogers routines. As a follow-up to
Easter Parade, MGM cast Astaire and Garland as a bickering vaudeville
couple in *You Made Me Love You*. For songs, they paired Ira Gershwin
with one of Hollywood's most experienced composers, Harry Warren.
Warren's jazzy, riffish music for *42nd Street* had revolutionized film
musicals, and he had continued writing such rhythmic hits in Hollywood as "Lullaby of Broadway," "Chattanooga Choo Choo," and "On the
Atchison, Topeka and the Santa Fe." With a strong script by newcomers
Betty Comden and Adolph Green, and Arthur Freed, already renowned
for his talented production unit at MGM, as producer, the movie
seemed a surefire success.

Ira Gershwin and Harry Warren wrote several songs, including
some comic numbers tailor-made for Judy Garland—"Natchez on the
Mississip,'" a parody of songs about the South ("Natchez" being the
only "spot that's not been done by Tin Pan Alley"), and a hillbilly parody,
"The Courtin' of Elmer and Ella." Once into rehearsals, however, Garland's emotional problems, exacerbated by her addiction to the drugs
prescribed by studio doctors, forced Freed to replace her. When Ginger
Rogers agreed to step in, the film took on a different dimension. While
some of the more farcical numbers, like the hillbilly parody, had to be
cut, Rogers demonstrated her own flair for comic songs. One of the
wittiest of these emerged after the title of the picture was changed
from *You Made Me Love You* (a Garland signature song) to *The Barkleys
of Broadway*. Astaire suggested that he and Rogers, as "the Barkleys,"
do a "Scottish" song. Ira and Harry Warren went to the cottage the
studio provided for songwriters and stayed only the short time it took
for Warren to come up with a suitable tune.

Ira then retreated to his study and, thinking in terms of the combative married couple in the script, took the notion of a "Scottish fling"
and wedded it to the kind of romantic "fling" a dour Scottish husband
and wife might imagine. In "My One and Only Highland Fling" (with

"highland" pronounced "hee-land") he created one of the wittiest variations of what he called the "Euphoria Revisited" formula. Admittedly
ignorant "about Scottish dialect,"[13] he browsed through his verse anthologies and steeped himself in the poetry of Robert Burns. Burns
was an apt choice since his dialect poems were truly song lyrics—new
words he put to traditional airs. Ira recognized that music could give
a lilt to the long vowels in such simple expressions as "Where early
fa's the dew" and "Gie'd me her promise true." Similarly, as he pondered
such alliterative phrases as "red, red rose" and "gang aft a-gley." Ira
knew such bristling consonants would nimbly trip off the tongue of
Fred Astaire:

> When I went romancin'
> I gie'd no thought to any weddin' ring;
> every bonny lassie was my highland fling.
> No chance was I chancin';
> I'm not the mon you dangle on a string.
> I was canny, waitin' for the real, real thing.

In Rogers's refrain, she matches him, consonant for consonant, "burr-
ing" her *r*'s just as crisply:

> When I went a-dancin',
> no special lad I was encouragin';
> every likely laddie was my highland fling.
> No glance was I glancin';
> well—nothin' really worth the mentionin'—
> hopin', watchin', waitin' for the real, real thing.

While their consonants roll, however, Fred and Ginger, dressed in
kilts and tams, deliver the song in rigid and expressionless fashion.
Frowning through his fricatives, Fred recalls "that fatal day in the fling
I was flung with you" and concludes with a cascade of hissed *h*'s and
rolling *r*'s:

> Oh, now my hea-r-rt is pr-r-rancin,'
> dr-r-runk as a lo-r-rrd and happy as a king.
> The yea-r-r-rs I'll weather-r-r-r-r
> in the hame or on the heather-r-r-r
> with my one and only highland fling.

Not only did Ira study the poetry of Robert Burns, he combed the "Mc"
and "Mac" entries in *Who's Who* and the Los Angeles phone book.
In a Scottish version of his light-verse litany of Russian names in

"Tchaikowsky," he has the married pair recall one another's former flings:

> I thought you were fallin' for Andy McPherson
> —Nae, nae, he became an impossible person.
> But what about you and that Connie MacKenzie?—
> She talked when I putted and drove me to frenzy.
> But what of the lad known as Bobbie MacDougal?
> —It pays to be thrifty, but he was too frugal.
> And weren't you daft about Maggie McDermott?—
> I tasted her cookin'—'twould make me a hermit.
> How jealous I was of MacDonald McCutcheon!
> —His neck had a head on, but there wasn't much in.

While Ira's comic lyric fitted perfectly into Warren's Scottish melody for "My One and Only Highland Fling," he found Warren's rhythmic, driving phrasing difficult to set in other songs. In the big solo dance for Astaire, Warren's phrases ended in two strong beats, posing the problem that, as P. G. Wodehouse once warned Ira, was "the greatest challenge (and greatest worry)" in lyric writing—"to come across a section of a tune requiring three double rhymes."[14] The fact that it was a straight "performance" dance number only added to Ira's woes; he had always felt most constrained by the formula he called "Turns with Terpsichore"—lyrics *about* dancing that allowed few witty curves. He had once enlivened the hackneyed idea of "Dancing Shoes" with the clever "Fidgety Feet," but now he was at a loss.

Retreating to his study, Ira leafed through his reference works, where, in Bulfinch's *Mythology*, he noticed a picture of the god Mercury in winged cap and shoes. Reaching from classical mythology into his vernacular bag, he came up with a clever title phrase—"Shoes with Wings On"—that ended, as Warren's rhythm required, in two strong accents. It took ten days of "leaden rather than mercurial" work, however, before Ira could deck out the other words "to fit Warren's tricky tune." Finally, feeling like "a suddenly unburdened Atlas,"[15] he arrived at a snappy sequence of colloquial phrases:

> I've got shoes with wings on—
> and living has no strings on—
> I put those magic things on—.

Then, as Warren's melody suddenly shifts from abrupt phrases to an extended flight, Ira's syntax soars with it:

> and I go flyin' with 'em
> and the town is full of rhythm
> and the world's in rhyme.

This close fit of rhythm and rhyme, in turn, inspired one of Fred Astaire's most ingenious solos. In a stage skit he plays a cobbler who tries on a pair of shoes left by a mysterious customer (perhaps the trickster god Mercury himself). The shoes set Fred dancing against his will, and as he vainly struggles *not* to dance the shoes seemingly whirl and propel him around the set in a physical manifestation of the way Ira's lyric is pulled by Warren's driving, insistent rhythm.

His lyric for the other dance number, "Swing Trot," was far less effective. Cast in the even more constricting formula of the "newest craze dance" formula, the song was put in the picture at Astaire's commercial (rather than artistic) insistence; at age fifty he was on the verge of retirement, and he needed a song to help plug his new chain of dance studios. Warren's melody was appropriately bumptious, but Ira mustered only a modicum of wit for the assignment:

> It's bill and coo-y, tea for two-y,
> just watch your partner's eyes grow dewy;
> *entre nous-y*, you're slightly screwy.

Harry Warren was disappointed that "Swing Trot" was wasted as background music during the rolling of the titles.

The composer was even more disappointed to find that only four of the fourteen songs he wrote for the film made the final cut. Along with "Swing Trot," "Shoes with Wings On," and "My One and Only Highland Fling," there was only one other of his melodies, "You'd Be Hard To Replace," that survived. This last should have been the film's big romantic ballad, but Warren's lovely melody ran up against Ira Gershwin's longstanding antipathy to saying "I love you" in thirty-two bars. For the lyric Ira dug into his trunk and found a song, "Hard To Replace," which he'd written with Jerome Kern in the years after George's death. Even after reworking the lyric for Warren's melody, Ira still relied on padding—"where else in all this world such loveliness and such grace"—a string of clichéd images—from "laughter in those eyes" to "moon and stars and skies," and his peccadillo—inverted word order: "without you by my side no future can I face." Once slated to be a classic Astaire-Rogers dance duet, "You'd Be Hard To Replace" is almost tossed away in the film as Astaire casually sings it to Rogers after they've had a marital spat. Since they're both in bathrobes, no dance follows.

On top of all of these disappointments Warren encountered a composer's greatest nightmare—an interpolation. The ballad that was given the most spectacular treatment in the film was not "You'd Be Hard To Replace" but George and Ira Gershwin's "They Can't Take That Away from Me," which Fred, in black tuxedo, and Ginger, in white gown, dance as a throwback to their 1930s musicals. The song that George felt had been thrown away in *Shall We Dance?* was thus finally redeemed in *The Barkleys of Broadway*, but at a price—the bitterness of Harry Warren. "I didn't take kindly to this," Warren said years later. "Not that I didn't like the song, but there isn't a composer alive who likes having a song by someone else interpolated into his score."[16] The interpolation, according to Ira, was the idea of Freed; others have said it was inspired by associate producer Roger Edens. "I would never have suggested it," Ira insisted, adding hopefully, "but I guess it was all right with Harry." Clearly, it was not. For all of his success, Harry Warren always felt that writing for films gave him far less freedom and fame than writing for Broadway. "Out here in Hollywood," he frequently said, "a songwriter is the lowest form of life." Although he had nearly as many hits during his lifetime as Cole Porter, his name was nowhere near as familiar. Certainly, his experience with *The Barkleys of Broadway* did little to alleviate his sense of professional inferiority. Whatever the reason, Harry Warren, who wrote successfully into the 1960s, never again collaborated with Ira Gershwin, although the two men remained good friends.

If George's ghost had been appeased by the resurrection of "They Can't Take That Away from Me," it must have rejoiced over Ira's next revival of their work—*An American in Paris*. Gene Kelly had suggested to Arthur Freed, the reigning genius of MGM musicals, that they do a picture about an ex-GI who remains in Paris to paint after the war. That was, as Freed himself put it, an instance of how "pictures start in strange ways":

> Ira Gershwin is one of my closest friends, and I grew up with George Gershwin in New York when I was first writing songs. I used to spend a lot of time over at the Gershwins'. I still spend every Saturday night with Ira at his house, and we either play poker or pool. So one night I was with Ira Gershwin playing pool and afterwards, it was about two in the morning, we sat talking about pictures and I said, "Ira, I've always wanted to make a picture about Paris. How about selling me the title *An American in Paris*?" He said, "Yes, if you use all Gershwin music."[17]

Ira had wanted to reach into George's tunebooks to create more new songs, but Freed wanted him simply to reverse his usual procedure; instead of tailoring his lyrics to fit into dramatic context and character, he could select numbers from his repertoire with George and the film would be built around them. At most, Ira found, he was asked to rewrite "a line here and there in the old songs,"[18] to integrate them more fully into the new film.

Any dissatisfaction Ira may have felt, however, disappeared when Freed brought in young Alan Jay Lerner to write the screenplay. Lerner, a brilliant lyricist himself, fresh from the triumphs of *Brigadoon* and *Paint Your Wagon*, was the most perfect librettist, short of himself, Ira could ever want. As a lyricist, he built the story around the Gershwin songs—but with integration and particularity in mind:

> All I knew at this time was that I was going to write the story as if the Gershwin music had been written for it. I didn't want it to be just a cavalcade of songs. I wanted to write a story so the songs would appear because of the emotional and dramatic situation. I wanted them to seem like the original emotional expressions written for those particular moments in the film.[19]

The result, as film critic Gerald Mast observed, is that "the musical numbers, not the plot" carry the film, which is "less a story than a tone poem," and "number for number no filmusical can rival *An American in Paris* for musical integrity."[20]

Others in Arthur Freed's stable of talent, such as musical director Johnny Green, shared Lerner's insistence that song and story be wed:

> We were all "theater *Menschen*": we were all people from the theater, all of us, and, whether it's a tri-dimensional stage or a bi-dimensional screen, it's theater. So the *dramatic* values of the songs were most important to us. How do they apply to the story line? What can we make of it? Something that has both entertainment and good drama.[21]

Then there was Gene Kelly's singing—as well as dancing—contribution:

> the one advantage that nonsingers like myself have over good singers is that we can almost talk what we have to say. We want the audience to hear the words. We're very particular about our lyrics.

All of that talent, under Vincente Minnelli's direction, would be showcased in sets inspired by Impressionist paintings. Who, indeed, could ask for anything more?

Drawing upon both famous and obscure Gershwin songs, *An American in Paris* showcases them more spectacularly than any other film. The heroine, Leslie Caron, is introduced dancing to "Embraceable You" while costumes, sets, and orchestrations shift, like George's music, between jazzy American and European classical traditions. That same cultural shift introduces Gene Kelly, whose first number, "By Strauss," recycles the Gershwins' European waltz parody, while his next, "I Got Rhythm," presents him as the thoroughly American ex-GI dancing with kids on the streets of Paris. To reinforce the contrast, Ira added additional lyrics to "I Got Rhythm" that allude to American movie stars, from Charlie Chaplin to Hopalong Cassidy. Conversely, Ira added a new chorus to "'S Wonderful" to provide a Franco-American duet between Kelly and Georges Guetary. The Frenchman exults "'S *magnifique!*" and 'S *élégant!*" while Kelly shoots back with "'S what I seek" and "'S what I want." Finally they unite in bilingual camaraderie:

> You've made my life so ting-a-lish;
> I'll even overlook your Eng-a-lish!
> 'S *exceptionnel!* 'S no bagatelle—
> That you should care for me!

Ira's witty wordplay here extended across languages, for, as Gerald Mast astutely observed, "the ''S' stands in as easily for the French 'c'est' as the English 'it's,' which are both contractions in the first place."[22]

Ira's greatest resuscitation, however, came with "Love Is Here To Stay," thrown away as a background number in *The Goldwyn Follies.* Its dynamic and moving rendition by Gene Kelly had a large part in making it the enduring classic it has become—a fitting restoration for the last song the brothers wrote together. Ira's work on *An American in Paris* stretched over two years and included working on the ticklish arrangements for copyright permissions to use his and George's songs in the new film. The Gershwins, like most songwriters—Irving Berlin being the major exception—did not hold the copyrights for their songs, and Ira found that the various music publishers who did could be quite recalcitrant about granting permissions:

> The publishers have put up all sorts of arguments about the restrictions Metro wants. It's all very complicated and negotiations have been going on for nine (count 'em) nine months.[23]

Once filming was completed in 1951, however, Ira found the effort all worthwhile:

Everyone connected with the piece has outdone himself. A lot of integrity and ingenuity has gone into the making and I'll be very surprised if this isn't recognized by the critics and public . . . Some of the songs like "By Strauss," "Love Is Here To Stay," "Tra-La-La," and a couple of others aren't well known but will be easy to take. All in all, quite a picture . . . I think the studio is going to have everything it hoped for when the project started. It's really one of the best ever.[24]

For once, the public, the critics, and even the Motion Picture Academy of Arts and Sciences agreed: *An American in Paris* won seven Oscars, including Best Picture—the first musical so honored since 1936. More than any other work, *An American in Paris* represents the culmination of Ira Gershwin's mission to ensure his brother's legacy, enshrining some of their greatest songs in a perfectly integrated dramatic setting.

12

Lonelier and Tougher
1951–1954

In his lyric-writing, Ira is a plodder—and I don't mean that disrespectfully, I mean it in the best sense. He digs and digs and digs. He edits. He goes over and over his work to change maybe only a line or just a word . . . Ira hates writing ballads. If I want to get him, all I have to say is, "Ira, we have a film to do and there are six ballads in it."

—Harold Arlen

WHEN Burton Lane learned that he would be working with Ira Gershwin on songs for MGM's 1953 film *Give a Girl a Break*, the young composer reacted with trepidation. Even though he had collaborated with Yip Harburg on *Finian's Rainbow* and Alan Jay Lerner on *Royal Wedding*, Lane still regarded Ira Gershwin with awe. When he met his legendary collaborator at the studio, Lane confessed that he was so nervous that he had taken two aspirin. "Me too," Ira responded, in what Lane took as a gesture of kindly reassurance, but which may have reflected Ira's own anxiety, given the fact that he had not collaborated since 1949. His work on *An American in Paris* had consumed most of his time since then, but the enormous success of the film made him receptive to a new proposal from MGM, which had established itself as the premiere studio for film musicals. Although *Give a Girl a Break* would not be mounted by Arthur Freed, Vincente Minnelli, and their "Royal Family" of choreographers, designers, and technical staff, it would be directed by Stanley Donen, who had done *On the Town*, and star a host of young talent, including Marge and Gower Champion, Debbie Reynolds, and Bob Fosse. *Give a Girl a Break* thus promised to be another MGM success in the tradition that began with *The Wizard of Oz* and included such gems as *For Me and My Gal*, *Meet Me in St. Louis*, and *Singin' in the Rain*.

Knowing only that the film would be a typical "backstager," with three young starlets vying for the lead in a Broadway musical, Ira suggested a title, "Applause, Applause," and Lane took it home and worked up a rhythmic tune. The next day he played the melody for Ira. As he played music whose abrupt phrasing would give most lyricists fits, Lane "felt an arm on his shoulder; he looked up, and there was Ira in a rare demonstrative moment, beaming down with appreciation and approval."[1]

Part of Ira's delight may reflect the fact that Lane's music for "Applause, Applause!" was reminiscent of those George Gershwin melodies which, as he once put it, gave a lyricist so little room to "turn around." Taking its rhythmic spurts, Ira crafted a literate "clapping lyric":

> Applause, applause!
> Vociferous applause—
> from orchestra to gallery
> could mean a raise in salary ...
> We live, we thrive—
> you keep us all alive
> with "Bravo!" and "Bravissimo!"
> (We're dead if it's *pianissimo*.)

Had *Give a Girl a Break* been more successful, "Applause, Applause!" might have taken its place alongside such other Broadway anthems as Porter's "Another Op'nin', Another Show" and Berlin's "There's No Business Like Show Business."

For Lane, working with "The Jeweller" revealed some of the fine points of the lyricist's mosaic art. "In Our United State" is an extended simile, in the manner of the metaphysical "conceits" of Donne and Marvell, where two lovers envision their marital future in political terms. They pledge to "avoid foreign entanglements," declare a "Declaration of Dependence," and plan a future "House with cute Representatives." In setting such words to Lane's melody, Ira resorted to a strategy he sometimes had to adopt with George Gershwin's music—avoidance of rhyme. Ira realized that these polysyllabic political terms would "jingle" if they rhymed with one another, so he matched the endings of Lane's short lines with unrhymed words. When words like "treasury" and "unconstitutional" are paired, he explained, they "give an unexpected tickle to the ear; they may dangle but do not jangle."[2] As always, the music came first in songwriting, and Ira stressed that while a simple phrase might take a certain accentual pattern when read aloud,

> I *won't* investigate
> in *our* united state,

the musical downbeat dictated a different pattern of verbal stress:

> *I* won't investigate
> *in* our united state

While Ira lamented that "where *song* is involved, music frequently makes for prosodic perversion,"[3] in other songs he displayed his uncanny knack for finding colloquial shards that perfectly matched the musical phrase. In the title song, "Give a Girl a Break," for example, he filled four different refrains with vernacular phrases that let the three starlets strut their stuff:

> Hey, gorgeous!
> Yes, sir! You're jus'
> what I ordered from the start . . .
> Hey, single!
> If we mingle—
> things will be jake . . .
> Why back up?
> Don't I stack up?
> Do I have to draw a chart?

While Burton Lane was impressed by such craftsmanship, he, like Harry Warren, found that Ira Gershwin had wearied of the thirty-two-bar ballad. "It Happens Every Time," which should have been the film's big romantic hit, saddles a lovely Lane melody with such clichéd phrases as "Each time I fold you in my arms—lo and behold, a million charms."

Despite the weak ballads, the quality of the rhythmic songs might have ensured the success of *Give a Girl a Break*. The film's story, however, was threadbare. Not only had Hollywood worn out the dramatic conventions of the "backstager," the studios seemed to have exhausted their inventiveness in presenting songs as "performances." When the Gershwins and Lanes saw the screening, Lane quipped that the film should be retitled *Give a Song a Break* and even tried to have his and Ira's name removed from the credits. Leonore Gershwin asked her husband if he owned any stock in MGM; when Ira admitted he did, she snapped, "Sell it!" (which he dutifully did—at a substantial loss). Even the studio seemed embarrassed by the film, premiering it at a theater in Brooklyn instead of the usual Manhattan outlets.

Anger at MGM's treatment of his songs in *Give a Girl a Break* may have made Ira more receptive to Warner Brothers invitation to write songs with Harold Arlen for *A Star Is Born*, a film that was to be Judy Garland's great comeback vehicle after years of breakdowns and addiction. While Arlen's music, rooted in jazz and blues, was even closer than Burton Lane's to that of George Gershwin, he had also composed the opulent melody for "Over the Rainbow," so Warner Brothers regarded him as the natural choice to write music for Garland. After years on the blacklist, Yip Harburg was out of the question, so the studio turned to Ira Gershwin for the lyrics. Not only would Ira be working with Harold Arlen, another old friend, Moss Hart, was to write the screenplay. Ira knew from his experience with Hart on *Lady in the Dark* that *A Star Is Born* might be a backstager about Hollywood musicals but the songs would be tightly integrated into the story and characters.

Hart set to work on the script fully aware of the difficulties he faced. *A Star Is Born* was to be a musical remake of a successful dramatic film of 1937 (which was, in turn, based on the still earlier film *What Price Hollywood?*), about an alcoholic film star who commits suicide after nurturing a young starlet to fame. Since no script for either of the previous versions of the film existed, Hart had to study the 1937 movie—a risky undertaking since, as an excellent film in its own right, it could have stymied his efforts to update the story and incorporate songs:

> It was a difficult story to do because the original was so famous and when you tamper with the original, you're inviting all sorts of unfavorable criticism. It had to be changed because I had to say new things about Hollywood—which is quite a feat in itself as the subject had been worn pretty thin . . . Add to that the necessity of making this a musical drama, and you'll understand the immediate problems.[4]

From the outset, Hart decided to conform to Hollywood's conventional presentation of songs as performances but to make them integral to the developing relationship between the young, insecure singer and her adoring but self-destructive mentor.

Garland alone would sing in the picture, and, since she would be playing the part of a singer, she would always have an "excuse" for bursting into song, either on stage or in a private performance. The role made new demands on her acting talents, however, as well as those of her co-star. Several major actors had been considered for the role of the alcoholic and suicidal Norman Maine, most notably Cary Grant, but, as James Mason put it, "in the end it came to me and I grabbed it smartly before it slipped away." What probably put off Grant and other stars, according to film historian Ronald Haver, was the prospect of having to be "subordinate to Judy Garland" in the song sequences, merely reacting with smiles and gestures as she sang. Few actors of Mason's caliber, Haver notes, could have played "second fiddle to Judy Garland."[5] Not only did Mason's reactions to her singing deepen the presentation of each song, his own poise as an actor elicited a powerful dramatic performance from Garland.

In his initial script outline, Hart introduced Garland and Mason in a "performance" number that not only establishes their "singer—sung to" relationship but also their mutual dependency. Garland, playing an unknown singer named Esther Blodgett, is performing with a band at a huge Hollywood benefit when Mason, as film star Norman Maine, drunkenly staggers on stage. She manages to save him from embarrassment by incorporating his antics into her act, then deftly escorts him offstage. He, in turn, musters the poise to bring her back for a bow that makes the whole affair seem a carefully rehearsed duet. Later that night Mason seeks her out to thank her for saving him and finds her singing in an after-hours jam session at a local dive. Recognizing her extraordinary talent, the one thing he still respects after all his years in Hollywood, he determines to transform Esther Blodgett into the star, "Vicki Lester."

At that point in his work, Hart presented his collaborators with what Ira Gershwin always longed for but seldom received in Hollywood—a clear outline of where his lyrical lodgments would be placed in the film. Hart initially envisioned seven songs for *A Star Is Born*, each designed to "chart the emotional development of the characters as surely as the speeches and the action advance the surface manifestations of the story":

1. Benefit show—Esther and orchestra
2. "Dive" song—Esther and small group
3. Movie rehearsal song (happy type), partly reprised complete at preview.
4. Song on recording stage (marriage proposal with interruptions)
5. Honeymoon song in motel; to be reprised later

6. Malibu beach house song (funny song; she tries to cheer Norman up)
7. Reprise of 5, probably sung over suicide or at end.[6]

From working with Ira and Kurt Weill on *Lady in the Dark*, Moss Hart knew how a song could express depths of character more articulately than any dialogue. After a long meeting with Moss Hart at Ira Gershwin's home, the songwriters went to work.

Well aware of his lyricist's antipathy to ballads, Arlen suggested they begin with the first two numbers—the rhythmic song for the Hollywood benefit and the bluesy torch song Garland would sing in the dive. Since breaking into songwriting back in the late 1920s, Arlen had steeped himself in blues and jazz, resisting the musical confines of the thirty-two-bar chorus. George Gershwin himself had admired the way Arlen's melody for "Stormy Weather" not only stretched beyond the standard format but avoided the use of repeated phrases that were such a commonplace in Tin Pan Alley melodies. Equally innovative were Arlen's rhythm songs, such as "(You've Got Me In) Between the Devil and the Deep Blue Sea" and "Ac-cent-tchu-ate the Positive," which challenged lyricists with their abrupt, percussive phrases.

"Composer Arlen," Ira exulted, "is no thirty-two bar man,"[7] and for the benefit number Arlen regaled his lyricist with no less than a forty-eight-bar chorus. Ira, in turn, responded to his new-found freedom with a sequence of crisply alliterative colloquial phrases:

> You wanna have bells that'll ring?
> You wanna have songs that'll sing?
> You want your sky a baby blue?
> You gotta have me go with you!

Moss Hart had suggested that Ira write the "kind of song you can never hear the lyrics to,"[8] since the scene of Garland steering the drunken Mason through a dance routine would distract the audience from the song itself. Amused at the playwright's suggestion, Ira wrote an utterly simple "throwaway" lyric, but nevertheless made it subtly integral to the dramatic context so that the audience subconsciously grasps the relationship between the characters. "Gotta Have Me Go with You" not only underscores Garland's efforts to get Mason offstage, it foreshadows Mason's insistence that she trust him enough to abandon her job with the band and let him transform her into a movie star.

While "Gotta Have Me Go with You" would be subordinated to the action on screen, the next song, the "dive" number, would be the

central focus of the scene. What was called for was a "great" song
that would reveal "Esther Blodgett's" enormous talent to Mason, so
Arlen unwound what he called one of his "tapeworms"—an unusually long and intricately patterned blues composition he had written
years earlier during his period of collaboration with Johnny Mercer.
The song had no verse, but was sixty measures long, and instead of
the usual AABA pattern of the thirty-two-bar chorus it progressed in
a complex ABABCAD structure. At first, however, he played Ira only
the first two A-sections. "I know how Ira's ear works," Arlen explained,
"and was sure he would like the theme, one that I'd had for some
time—an eight-bar phrase." Once he heard that melody, Ira, a lyricist
who usually found the title the hardest part of his job, leaned over
the piano and whispered, "the man that got away." Arlen replied, "I
like."

What is doubly remarkable about Ira's sudden inspiration, is that,
as Lawrence Stewart points out,[9] the eight-bar melody Arlen played
for him was not the title-phrase, which comes later in the melody.
Perhaps Arlen's bluesy vamp stirred memories of the music of George
Gershwin, Ira's own long-lost collaborator. Whatever its source, the
title is one of Ira's wittiest transformations of a vernacular catch-phrase
(the angler's lament for "the one that got away"). Though grammarians,
much to Ira's amusement, kept trying to correct it to "The Man Who
Got Away," the poetry, as in "They Can't Take That Away from Me,"
was all in the "that." Just as the singer's "that" harshly reduces the lost
man to a mere thing, she mocks the fact that she nevertheless longs
for his return by coldly addressing herself as a forlorn "you" ("for you've
been through the mill") rather than speaking in the first person as a
hopefully expressive "I."

When Ira set to work on putting syllables to the eight-bar opening,
however, inspiration came much more slowly. Lawrence Stewart, his
secretary, saw to it that all of Ira's manuscripts were carefully pre-
served. Thus it is possible to follow the full evolution of some of his
lyrics. From the nine sheets of lyrical revisions, most covered in typescript and scrawled with pencilled changes and notations, we can see
how sentimentally the song started out:

> There's just no sleeping.
> Your eyes are red with weeping.
> Though you know better,
> you're waiting for that letter.

Gradually, Ira moves closer to his characteristic vernacular style:

> You can't erase him
> and you're too proud to chase him . . .
> there'll be no sun-up
> and misery is one up. . . .

Discarding those versions, Ira tried a witty sequence of imagery that reflects the world of Hollywood:

> The song is played out,
> the moon is in a fade-out.
> The stars won't glimmer,
> the autumn wind is grimmer—.

Focusing on "The stars won't glimmer," Ira reworked it with harsher consonants, replacing "glimmer" with "glitter," which not only kept the tinselly Hollywood feel of "played out" and "fade out" but inspired a biting feminine rhyme:

> The night is bitter,
> the stars have lost their glitter.

Then he took "the autumn wind is grimmer" and made it starker still by changing the single, specific "wind" to the more vaguely oppressive and unceasing "winds":

> The winds grow colder.

The next line begins with "and," but instead of continuing the sequence of natural imagery the simple connective suddenly shifts the focus of the lyric:

> and suddenly you're older.

Like Hemingway, another master of the simple word deftly placed, Ira Gershwin uses "and" to link logically discontinuous—but emotionally wedded—phrases.

Such subtle shifts kept the lyric moving with Arlen's snaky melody, and, as those musical phrases unwind, Ira intensifies them with driving internal rhymes, though in his early efforts the rhymes were too prominent and the wit too redolent of light verse:

> Yessiree that's how it is
> he had me in a tiz,
> I guess I got the biz.

As Lawrence Stewart observes, Ira Gershwin had to struggle against his "tendency to write wittily" as he caught himself

> drifting continually into smart expressions which he had to excise from the song itself; these worked their way into the margins of his manuscripts, as though he was compelled to be ingeniously inventive, even when the material would not permit it. So there are humorous rhymes: "groovy, movie, and hotter than Vesuvi." There are couplet asides: "I rate a razzing, Perhaps he's Alcatrazing." (As Gershwin points out, this would have been fine in "Boy, What Love Has Done to Me," in *Girl Crazy*, but is far too smart here.)[10]

Having staved off his penchant for Gilbert's dazzle, Ira crafted the "simpler" but more toughly poignant rhymes of his final version:

> the writings on the w*all,*
> the dreams you dreamed have *all*
> gone astray . . .
> The man that *won* you
> has *run* off
> and *undon*e you . . .
> No more that all-time thr*ill*
> for *you*'ve
> been thr*ough*
> the m*ill,*
> and never a n*ew*
> love w*ill*
> be the same.

Just as skillful as Ira's use of rhyme is his juxtaposition of unrhymed and rhymed phrases to reflect the singer's sudden shifts between stoic resolve and desperate longing:

> Good riddance, good-bye!
> Ev'ry trick of his you're on to.
> But fools will be fools—
> and where's he gone to?

Stewart, who sat in on the session when Ira and Harold Arlen worked together, recalled how

> the collaboration was so close that each made suggestions on the music and words: one ceased being merely a lyricist and the other a composer. Their separate functions blended together . . . they had slowed down in their schedule and were spending whole days on the pursuit of *le mot juste.*[11]

One can see this coalescence of verbal and musical pattern as Arlen's melody twists through its intricate structure, and Ira adroitly skews his syntax and suffixes:

> The road gets rougher,
> it's lonelier and tougher.

The awkward "lonelier" (instead of the more accepted "more lonely") was one of Ira's last revisionary touches to the lyric, penciled in on the final draft. Placed where it is, "lonelier" is forced into alignment with "rougher" and "tougher," intensifying its emotional resonance. Later, when Arlen breaks out of this musical segment, Ira drops rhyme altogether for a prosaic wail whose poetic power comes from the alliteration in two ordinary colloquial compounds:

> there's just no let-up
> the live-long
> night and day.

Having brought his lyric to this climax, Ira Gershwin struggled for a denouement that would bring the song back down to earth. His first version, like his initial opening, was too sentimental:

> Oh tell me if you can
> what song is sadder than. . . .

Then he over-corrected by again becoming too slangily "smart":

> you always will be his.
> Oh what a sucker is. . . .

After more false starts, he found the vernacular road back to his inspired title, a road rough with consonants but paved with "memorable" rhymes:

> Ever since this world beg*an*
> there is nothing sadder th*an*
> the one-m*an* wom*an*
> looking for the m*an*
> that got away.

"The Man That Got Away" was Ira Gershwin's last great standard, coming exactly thirty years after "The Man I Love," their themes of innocent longing and bitter loss neatly bracketing a career devoted to variations on simple romantic formulas.

While "The Man I Love" was shunted in and out of three different musicals, "The Man That Got Away" was filmed as brilliantly as any song could be. While done as a "performance," it is still perfectly integrated into *A Star Is Born*, foreshadowing Mason's sudden alcoholic disappearance after he persuades Garland to leave the band, as well as his ultimate escape into suicide (he later drowns himself in the ocean). The superb interplay between Arlen's shifting melody and Ira's equally intricate lyrical movement inspired the director George Cukor in his filming of "The Man That Got Away":

> When you look at something, you're used to seeing the whole of a thing—then suddenly you see a section, arbitrarily, not composed. Just a section of something cut off. In the David painting "Sacre de Napoleon," when the detail is reproduced in an art book, you see a head to one side, bits of other heads cut off here and there. And I thought, "Why not do that in a movie?" So I decided that we could do that when she sang "The Man That Got Away." I wanted the camera to follow her, always in front . . . sometimes she would go to the side and almost disappear out of the frame . . . all in one long take, for the whole musical number.[12]

Cukor's conception posed extraordinary difficulties for the cameraman, who recalled it as "the toughest lighting problem I ever had": with Garland "moving in and out of pools of light" it "was tough because here she is in a place where she was definitely lit right, then she'd move over here and she'd get into this light here, that would hit her on this side, and the light didn't make her look good."[13]

If Cukor's conception was difficult for the cameraman, it was doubly so for the performer. "It isn't easy for an actor or actress to carry a long take," Cukor observed, "you have to be strong. I wanted to do it with Judy because I knew she could sustain it." Cukor's confidence in Garland's talent and endurance were fulfilled by "The Man That Got Away." "In making a movie," Garland reflected, "there's no audience to play to, only a large crowd of technicians." Her solution was to transform those technicians into her "stage" audience:

> I would try to make the electricians and the cameramen and the others react to the song . . . If it was the blues, I would try to make them feel in the spirit of the song. Only when they had shown the emotion the particular song was supposed to evoke did I feel that I had reached them.[14]

With all the problems in lighting, staging, and sound, "The Man That Got Away" took twenty-seven takes, over three days of filming, every one of which, the cameraman recalled, Garland performed with the same power and poise.

Having undergone as much revision in its filming as it had in its creation, "The Man That Got Away" combined the artistry of a great lyricist and composer, writer and director, performers and technicians. One of the small but crucial elements in the scene is James Mason's reaction to Garland's performance. Moss Hart's script called for a "slow look of amazement and pleasure" to spread over his face as she sings, realizing as he does that she possesses the talent that he cherishes. "As the number finishes," Hart specified, "the effect on him is electric—he starts to applaud—then drops his hands and keeps staring at the bandstand."[15] Mason does not applaud because he realizes the song is not done as a performance but for the aesthetic pleasure of the musicians themselves. The bartender expresses his astonishment that musicians, who play for hire all evening, would then gather after midnight to "jam" for themselves. Mason's face, however, with a look that was probably similar to the expression Burton Lane once saw on Ira Gershwin's face, reveals his shared joy in the practice of art for its own sake.

While such artistry went into A Star Is Born, commercial demands would leave much of it, including some of Gershwin and Arlen's best songs, on the cutting-room floor. Unaware of what lay ahead for this star-crossed film, the songwriters, at Arlen's urging, went to work on the film's ballads. While Ira did not relish the assignment, he could take inspiration from the integral relation the ballads would bear to the characters of Garland and Mason, as well as comfort from the fact that the dramatic context of the film would undercut the romantic sentiments of his lyrics. "Here's What I'm Here For," for example, with Ira's turnaround of the title phrase—"I'm here for you"—gains ironic poignancy as an expression of Garland's utter reliance upon Mason's Pygmalion-like conception of her.

Similarly, with "Someone At Last," the seemingly clichéd conclusion—"With that someone I'll be someone at last"—deepens as an expression of Garland's inability to imagine an identity for herself apart from Mason's conception. As Hart conceived the number, "the humor came from overproduction,"[16] so what was needed was a lyric so simple it would lend itself to a parody of Hollywood production numbers. He wanted Garland to sing "Someone At Last" as a "private performance" to cheer up her despondent husband at their Malibu home. With his career languishing as hers is on the rise, Mason finds himself out of work and turning into the mere "husband" of his famous creation. Trying to accept the role—and keep from drinking—he fixes dinner for her and, like a dutiful wife asks her, "What went on at the studio today?" Hart's script has Garland force a laugh and cheerily report,

"We started shooting the big production number today—and it's the production number to end all production numbers! It's an American in Paris, Brazil, the Alps, and the Burma Road! It's got sex, schmaltz, patriotism . . ." She launches into the production number, taking all the parts herself—the ballet, the chorus boys, the show girls, the director, the leading man, a burlesque of herself, singing the main song, using anything she can lay her hands on in the room for props. She leaps on and off sofas, turns over chairs—it is a tour de force designed solely to make Norman forget himself and laugh.[17]

In the film Garland sings the simple phrases of the lyric over and over in a series of silly roles and accents—a French torch singer, Chinese sing-song girl, Brazilian samba dancer. The whole scene, at once inane and touching, was "carefully rehearsed," director George Cukor noted, "very carefully rehearsed to give the effect of improvisation, of spontaneity."[18] So, too, was Ira Gershwin's lyric, based on an unused song in the 1927 musical *Funny Face*, carefully revised to seem like the tossed-off fare of Hollywood wordsmiths.

In the course of working on the script, Hart added another production number that gave Ira the opportunity to parody Hollywood's pollyanna weather songs, from "Singin' in the Rain" to "April Showers." In "Lose That Long Face" he took up that hackneyed formula and exaggerated the already strained clichés:

> Does the day look painful?
> The future glum?
> Does the sky look rainful
> . . . are you in a va-cu-um?

In Hart's scene Garland rehearses "Lose That Long Face" in an equally strained version of production numbers—as a ragamuffin child selling newspapers in the slums who, unaccountably, bursts with infectious good spirits. During a break in rehearsal, she goes to her dressing room and breaks down in tears. When the director comes for her, she confesses that her marrying Mason has not kept him from destroying himself with alcohol. "I hate to go home at night—and listen to his lies," she sobs, "but my heart goes out to him, because he *does* try . . . but I hate him for failing!" In utter hopelessness, she asks, "No matter how much you love some one—how do you live out the days?" At that point she must go back on the sound stage and muster her spirits for another dose of Hollywood cheer.

For what the songwriters hoped would be the major hit of the picture, "It's a New World," Harold Arlen crafted one of his opulent, soaring melodies, and Ira, as Yip Harburg had done with "Over the Rainbow," pushed wit aside and pulled out all the lyrical stops:

> The tears have rolled off my cheek
> and fears fade away ev'ry time you speak;
> a new world though we're in a tiny room,
> what a vision of joy and blossom and bloom!

Within the film, however, these soaring, optimistic strains were sharply undercut. Hart's outline called for song "5" to be sung by Garland to Mason on their honeymoon, but then reprised near the end of the film as Mason commits suicide. While Garland's tremulous voice emanates from off camera, warbling the clichés of Tin Pan Alley optimism, he calmly walks out of their Malibu home and into the ocean, entering a "new world" indeed, and plunging Garland into one where she must seek an identity apart from him.

Even as Gershwin and Arlen were working on their songs, production on *A Star Is Born* was paralyzed by a technological development second only to the advent of "talkies"—the wide-screen process called "CinemaScope." CinemaScope transformed the screen into something more like a stage. Instead of the numerous camera shots that were built into a sequence of images, actors and sets had to be carefully arranged for a single "master shot." One of the appeals CinemaScope had for the studio heads was that it was cheaper to take such a single mastershot rather than the numerous "medium shots, close shots, and dolly shots" that were required in traditional camera work. The effect, however, particularly on such intimate films as *A Star Is Born*, was to forgo subtle camera movements and blow everything up into gigantic, but static, proportions. George Cukor, who had originally come to Hollywood as a "dialogue" director to help actors cope with the advent of sound, now found himself the victim of the new wide screen:

> We couldn't move the camera up or down, because of distortion, and we couldn't move back and away from the camera. Everything had to be played out on a level plane—if someone were too much upstage, they would be out of focus. And you weren't really to come in really close on faces. It was rather like what happened when sound came in—you were supposed to forget everything you'd learned.[19]

CinemaScope had been developed by Twentieth Century-Fox and as production began on *The Robe*, the first "epic" film to use the new process, other studios slowed or shut down filming to await the results. As with the advent of "talkies," studios feared that if the CinemaScope revolution was successful, their films would be immediately outdated. Despite the success of *The Robe*, Jack Warner refused to follow other studios in leasing CinemaScope from Twentieth Century-Fox. Instead he was determined to fight back with a wide-screen process of his own, and announced that the first film in "WarnerSuperScope" would be *A Star Is Born*. Both George Cukor and Moss Hart adamantly opposed filming such an intimate story on a wide screen, but Warner would not relent, and production was delayed for months. The first results of WarnerSuperScope, especially the scene where Garland sings "The Man That Got Away" in the dive, strengthened Cukor's opposition; not only did the Warner process distort the images, it was particularly poor in filming night scenes. Since so many scenes took place at night, Jack Warner reluctantly gave in, and in late September announced that *A Star Is Born* would be filmed for a traditional screen.

No sooner had filming begun, however (including retakes of "The Man That Got Away"), than the two other Warners, Albert and Harry, noting the industry-wide movement to CinemaScope, informed their recalcitrant brother that CinemaScope, not WarnerSuperScope, would be the order of the day at Warner Brothers. Since *A Star Is Born* was the biggest picture under production on the Warner lot, they also ordered that it, despite its intimate story, be the first candidate for CinemaScope. Problems with the new process, along with Cukor's characteristic slow pace of filming and Judy Garland's equally characteristic unreliability, dragged filming out for months. One thing that was quickly becoming apparent was that the running time of the film grew longer and longer and consequently production costs were soaring. Hart's script had lengthened the original story by adding depth and complexity to the characters; then the musical numbers further drew out the time. Both Hart and Cukor, moreover, kept imagining additional small shots and scenes that enriched the film but made it longer still. Despite the mounting length and costs, the quality of the emerging film excited everyone, so much so that Hart and Cukor insisted upon rewriting and refilming more than a dozen scenes to bring them up to the level of the rest of the picture. One retake, at Hart's suggestion, was of "The Man That Got Away." With Garland in a different costume and make-up, and the brown tones of the previous set replaced by reds and blues, the final, stunning version of "The Man That Got Away" was filmed.

While the retakes added nearly a quarter of a million dollars to a film that already, at over four million dollars, was the most expensive film Warner Brothers had ever made, the artistry of *A Star Is Born* seemed to justify its extravagance. It was at this point, however, that less artistic figures and forces projected themselves into the frame. The producer of the film, Sidney Luft, was married to Judy Garland, and he wanted to be sure that she had a sure-fire "big number" to cement the success of her comeback. Luft also was concerned about the length of the film, which he thought would necessitate an intermission. Garland's big number could thus be used to climax the first half of the film, marking her full emergence as a Hollywood star, while the second half would trace the downfall of Norman Maine. Nearly a year after "completing" their songs for *A Star Is Born*, Ira Gershwin and Harold Arlen were summoned back to the studio. Although they had already provided two different songs for Garland's "stardom" number, "Green Light Ahead" and "Dancing Partner," they were now told to come up with something more "socky," a song that would inspire the choreographer with an idea for a blockbuster production number to showcase Garland's talent.

Arlen had been in New York working on his new musical, *House of Flowers*, but he managed to get back to Hollywood, where he and Ira wrote yet a third song, "I'm Off the Downbeat." Ira, inured to the ways of Hollywood, began to fear the worst—an interpolation:

> Everything about the picture looks great. There's only one problem: what to do about a production number that's to wind up the first half (the showing is to have an intermission—the picture runs about three hours so far). The situation in the film is the sneak previewing of Vicki Lester's first movie—a showing which makes her a star overnight. All that's necessary is to put Vicki in a good number for four or five minutes, then show the audience's enthusiastic acceptance of a new star, as they fill out the preview cards in the lobby. Arlen and I wrote three songs for this spot: "Green Light Ahead," "I'm Off the Downbeat," and "Dancing Partner," all good by anyone's standards, but it seems that the choreographer couldn't get any production ideas. Could be that they may even interpolate an outside number which would be a shame.[20]

Despite Ira's feeling that all three of their songs were good "by anyone's standards," Sidney Luft thought they were all "bad songs." Jack Warner concurred; his knee-jerk Hollywood instincts told him what was called for is a "big musical number . . . we gotta show what makes her a big star."

When Harold Arlen suddenly became ill, Ira saw the writing on the wall:

> Know no more about possible interpolation in *Star*. With Arlen in hospital (he's on the mend but it'll be weeks before he'll be able to leave) and with an over four million investment in the film, naturally producer and

management are nervous . . . I certainly won't like it if an outside number
is interpolated but I'm not going to lose any sleep over it; there's too little
sleep left as it is.[21]

What Luft and Warner wanted, as it turned out, was something no
songwriter could supply—a barrage of songs that were *already* proven
hits. The highlight of a Judy Garland concert, Luft reflected, came
when she sat at the edge of the stage and sang a medley of standards.
That, he realized, was what was needed for *A Star Is Born*—an anthology of "Garland's Greatest Hits."

To provide a framework number for such a medley, Luft sought
out Roger Edens. While not a great songwriter, Edens had a knack for
presenting a number. After all, he had written the number that had
made Garland a star in *Broadway Melody of 1938*; taking a song from
1913, "You Made Me Love You," Edens wrote a new verse for it, "Dear
Mr. Gable," which little Judy sang to a photograph of her favorite star.
To make the lyric suitable for a young girl, Edens bowdlerized such
lines in Joseph McCarthy's original lyric as "Gimme, gimme, gimme
what I cry for—you know you got the brand of kisses that I die for,"
replacing them with more genteel longings: "I must tell you what I'm
feeling—the very mention of your name sets my heart reeling." Edens
went to his trunk and pulled out a "concert" piece called "Born in a
Trunk," a sentimental monologue recounting a singer's interminably
slow rise to stardom, from the day she was "born in a trunk in the
Princess Theater in Pocatello, Idaho." The song dragged out every
showbiz cliché—from "stopped the show" through the "show must go
on"—and wrenched some terrible rhymes, such as being born on a
"Friday" with "they used a make-up towel for my didy." The tedious
narrative was drawn out even further as Garland stopped to perform
all of the songs she had sung along the long, long way to fame—"I'll
Get By," "You Took Advantage of Me," "Melancholy Baby," and others.
There was even a Gershwin song, but, ironically, with a lyric not by
Ira but Irving Caesar—"Swanee."

"Born in a Trunk" took nearly two weeks to film, added another
quarter of a million dollars to production costs, and, worst of all, tacked
fifteen more minutes onto the film. George Cukor, who had no role in
the filming of the "Born in a Trunk" sequence, objected to it on grounds
of length and the fact that it added nothing to the dramatic development
of character or plot. Ira Gershwin, who, as a mere songwriter had far
less to say about the film, grasped the essential problem of the number
when he saw the screening: while it was "excellent for its original

purpose" as a concert piece for Judy to deliver from the stage directly to a live audience, on the CinemaScope screen it was a "Big Mistake." Whereas on Broadway his insight would have been sought out and taken seriously, in Hollywood he could only throw up his hands and say "all none of my business."[22] He consoled himself by saying, "Anyway La Garland does right by 'The Man That Got Away.' "

With the addition of "Born in a Trunk," *A Star Is Born* ran over three hours—more than twice as long as an ordinary film. Complaints from theater owners ruled out an intermission, since it would limit "turnover"—the number of showings (and hence box-office receipts) per day. Even without an intermission, it could only be shown five times a day, with the first feature beginning at eight in the morning. That limited turnover cut into the profits of a film whose productions costs had finally run to more than five million dollars, making it one of the most expensive films ever made. Shortly after opening in late September of 1954, the losses from limited turnover became apparent; in order to have any hope of making the ten million dollars necessary to offset the five million spent on the picture, nearly half an hour had to be carved out of *A Star Is Born.*

Who decided on what was cut remains a mystery, but whoever made the cuts made them not in tiny segments but wholesale swatches of film. When George Cukor, who had been out of the country at the time, saw the results he was outraged at "the way they just hacked into it":

> If they thought it was too long there were other ways of shortening it besides chopping and hacking out vital bits. Had we been allowed, Moss Hart and I could have sweated out twenty minutes which would have been imperceptible to the audience. That's something which I can't understand. Producers spend millions of dollars to do pictures and then suddenly, right out of the blue, they say, "Let's chop this out, then that . . ." It's one of the great sorrows of my career, the way the picture was cut by the studio. Judy Garland and I felt like the English queen who had "Calais" engraved on her heart. Bloody Mary, wasn't it? Neither of us could ever bear to see the final version.[23]

That final version, unfortunately, was the only one to survive. To this day, no complete copy of the original, uncut version has ever been found (although a recent discovery of some of the lost footage led to the making of a partial restoration).[24]

Among the severest losses were two songs by Harold Arlen and Ira Gershwin, "Lose That Long Face" and "Here's What I'm Here For," their finest ballad. Not only were these excellent musical numbers, they "had been designed to complement and enhance the dramatic structure of the story; cutting them not only lessened the impact of certain scenes but also seriously damaged Moss Hart's carefully structured continuity, which, in the original, maintained a careful balance between the musical and the dramatic." "Born in a Trunk," however, remained virtually intact, though even as great a Garland lover as Noel Coward squirmed at having to endure "montage after montage and repetition after repetition" and found himself "wishing that dear enchanting Judy was at the bottom of the sea."[25]

Even the smaller cuts damaged the over-all quality of the film. Lost were many of Hart and Cukor's subtlest touches—bits of dialogue, camera close-ups, background shots—designed to deepen the characters of Mason and Garland. Without those nuances, as Elia Kazan candidly told Moss Hart, the cut version of *A Star Is Born* puts "too much self-pity into the feelings of the two leads"—and, one could add, blunts the satiric edge of some of the lyrics. The intimacy of their relationship was already strained by the wide screen, and Kazan was especially alert to the dangers of CinemaScope. At the time he was fending off Warner Brothers pressure to film *East of Eden* in Cinema-Scope, and he dreaded what the wide screen had done to the "proportions" of *A Star Is Born*—especially to the songs: "Everything had been blown up or glamorized. Numbers which were supposed to be the essence of informality were informal on such a huge scale!"[26]

The cuts took their toll on *A Star Is Born* at the Academy Awards ceremony, which, ironically, figures so prominently within the film itself. George Cukor was not even nominated for Best Director, and, in the six categories the film was nominated for, it won nothing. James Mason lost out to Marlon Brando, and the Best Actress award went to Grace Kelly. *A Star Is Born*, the film that was to have launched Garland's great comeback, effectively ended her career in movie musicals. Harold Arlen and Ira Gershwin were also among the losers. The veteran songwriters saw "The Man That Got Away" passed over for the work of a newer team—Sammy Cahn and Jule Styne's "Three Coins in the Fountain." For Ira, it was his third nomination and third loss. Arlen scornfully tacked the Oscar nomination citation on his bathroom wall and devoted most of the rest of his career to the Broadway musical theater. Ira Gershwin consoled himself more philosophically. Reflecting that his two previous Oscar nominations, "They Can't Take That Away from Me" and "Long Ago and Far Away," had also lost and had also used "away" in their title, he wryly advised himself to do "away with 'away.' "[27]

13

THE LONG, LONG NIGHT
1954–1983

I guess I've always considered perfection, or as close as I can
come to it, my armor. And I know that even if the lyric failed,
I had done my very best . . . a career of lyric-writing isn't one
that anyone can muscle in on; that if the lyricist who lasts
isn't a W. S. Gilbert he is at least literate and conscientious;
that even when his words at times sound like something off
the cuff, lots of hard work and experience have made them so.
                                              —Ira Gershwin

D URING the many months of delay in the filming
of *A Star Is Born*, Harold Arlen and Ira Gershwin were commissioned by Paramount to write
songs for another film, *The Country Girl*. Ira was intrigued by the script,
an adaptation of Clifford Odets's "strong psychological study," with
Bing Crosby playing an alcoholic singer trying for a comeback, Grace
Kelly, his long-suffering wife, and William Holden, a tough-nosed
Broadway director putting on a "revolutionary" new musical. Although
The Country Girl was another "back-stager," Ira realized immediately
"the result won't be a musical."[1] *The Country Girl*, like *A Star Is Born*,
has tragic rather than comic overtones, but it moves even farther from
the formulas of the film musical in putting songs into an ironic relation
to their dramatic context.

What Ira Gershwin and Harold Arlen had to write, therefore, were
generic popular songs that could then be done, in traditional Hollywood
style, as sprightly performances set against the grim background of
the story and its characters. "It's Mine, It's Yours," for example, is a
standard pollyanna weather song that promises "if you want blue skies
about" just "try a cheerful song and a valentine." Crosby delivers the

number, however, in a desperate audition for the lead role in the new
musical, a role that might help his recovery from alcoholism and alleviate the guilt he feels over the death of his son (guilt which, he later
admits, was only a crutch he used to excuse the failure of his career).

The film's only ballad occurs in a flashback to Crosby, at the height
of his career in the 1930s, cutting a hit record. What was called for,
as Ira saw it, was "an imagined hit song of that period."[2] Therefore he
could write a straightforward lyric of romantic euphoria, "The Search
Is Through," dressing it up with a flourish of the allusive wit common
to songs of the 1930s:

> In my *Who's Who*
> you've got what it takes:
> the Who, the Where, the When, the Why.

Gershwin and Arlen found, however, that "The Search Is Through"
was "no hit in the period in which it was written—the middle Fifties,"[3]
when the romantic ballads of Tin Pan Alley were being supplanted by
the new sound of rhythm and blues.

The best song in *The Country Girl* was a rhythmic number done
not as part of the Broadway show but, like "The Man That Got Away,"
as an impromptu performance in a night club. Crosby is sitting at the
bar, dolefully nursing a drink, but when the night-club singer launches
into a torch song, he joins her for a jazzy duet. For this scene, Harold
Arlen, more in his element, concocted a "slow rock" melody, and Ira
Gershwin, also more comfortable in a rhythmic number than a ballad,
reached down into the vernacular for his patented, turnaround phrases:

> Love and learn,
> learn a lot,
> It's the be-and-end-all—
> then it's not;
> it's a dream, it's a plot;
> it's something out of Seventh Heaven—
> then something misbegot!

They had originally planned to entitle the song "Love and Learn," but
when Ira found that there were already three songs with that title, he
penned the more scholarly "Dissertation on the State of Bliss." That
combination of literate wit and brassy colloquial language makes one
wonder what would have been the impact on popular music had Harold
Arlen and Ira Gershwin continued to collaborate. Certainly Arlen, of
all the traditional composers, was the one most versed in the anteced-

ents of the new "rhythm and blues," and in Ira Gershwin he would have had a lyricist capable of handling even the earthiest slang. Had they continued to write songs together, the rift between the old and the new popular music perhaps might not have become so absolute.

The one song in *The Country Girl* that called for a measure of integration and particularity was written for the "revolutionary" musical Holden is directing. Set in a new western territory at the turn of the century, the show is clearly modeled on *Oklahoma!* In their effort to emulate Rodgers and Hammerstein, Arlen and Gershwin produced "The Land Around Us," a song that comes off as "an uninspired excerpt from *Oklahoma!*" Bing Crosby, in a cowboy hat, leads his fellow "settlers" in a celebration of the town they will build, envisioning the "post-office" here and the "high-school" there. For Arlen and Gershwin, two of the most urbane songwriters of their time, such small-town sentiments did not come easy. As Arlen himself admitted, "We didn't give it our best."[4] Even "The Land Around Us," however, is effective dramatically, as it extols the virtues of small-town life in a film that is itself set against the grittiest New York City background.

Although Arlen continued composing after *The Country Girl*, Ira Gershwin effectively "quit as a songwriter in 1954."[5] On the one hand it seems strange that a lyricist, still in his fifties and at the height of his career, would withdraw from songwriting. By that time, however, the winds were indeed changing, growing colder for lyricists like Ira Gershwin. The year 1954 saw the full emergence of a new style in popular music when a song called "Rock Around the Clock" topped the record sales charts, and then, a year later, was showcased in a film called *Blackboard Jungle*. The year also saw one of the last of the great, full-scale, original film musicals, *Seven Brides for Seven Brothers*. After that, when Hollywood made a musical, it was usually either a remake of a successful Broadway show or a low-budget rock musical aimed at a teenage audience.

The career of Johnny Mercer, the lyricist for *Seven Brides for Seven Brothers*, shows how limited opportunities were for such craftsmen after 1954. Mercer, like Ira Gershwin, was a pure lyricist, not adept at adapting his own libretti as were such newer "book and lyric" writers as Alan Jay Lerner and Frank Loesser. Though he doggedly tried for success on Broadway, Mercer's lyrics went down with a series of shows, from *Texas Li'l Darlin'* (1950) to *Saratoga* (1959). All that Hollywood could offer Mercer in this era was piecework—setting words to movie theme songs, such as "Moon River" and "Days of Wine and Roses." While some of these were well-crafted songs that became popular, such

"theme" songs were a far cry from the kind of dramatic context Ira
Gershwin wanted for his lyrics.

With the demise of films that called for a full score of original
songs, Ira Gershwin, lyricist, became what George had always called
him—"Ira, the scholar." Shortly after George's death, Ira had established the Gershwin Archive at the Library of Congress, where he
deposited George's unpublished music. In 1953 he started "to get all
the scrap books about George in some sort of order. Big job. What
with the letters, photographs, records, etc., looks like a year's work,
on and off."[6] With the assistance of Lawrence Stewart, Ira began going
through manuscripts, correspondence, and other documents, catalogu-
ing and annotating them for deposit at what he impishly abbreviated
as the "L.o.C."

What promised to be a year-long project stretched out for decades.
Ira, believing as always "that George Gershwin was the immortal Gershwin,"[7] was surprised to learn that an archive had been established in
his name as well, so he dutifully added what he had saved of his own
manuscripts, correspondence, and other papers. Along with building
the Gershwin archive, Ira tried to salvage Gershwin songs that had
been slighted or cut in their original productions. Such resuscitative
work drew him deep into his own creative past, all the way back to
his first lyric, "The Real American Folk Song," which had been dumped
by Nora Bayes when George had refused to change its ending to suit
her taste. Now, more than forty years later, Ira, with what must have
been wry reminiscences, had it published in sheet-music. Finally published, too, was his first "comic" lyric, "Harlem River Chanty," which
had been cut, as had so much of his exquisite work, through "show
doctoring": when the producers of *Tip-Toes* decided to change the
setting from New York to Florida, "Harlem River Chanty" simply
proved too integral to the original setting to survive the change. Perhaps
his wittiest lyric, "Just Another Rhumba," whose only fault was that
its word-play had failed to amuse Hollywood mogul Sam Goldwyn,
now, too, could be finally resurrected and published.

Along with preserving the past, Ira updated it. When a revival of
Of Thee I Sing was mounted in 1952, he rewrote some of the lyrics for
audiences who could not be expected to recognize that "Posterity Is
Just Around the Corner" alluded to Herbert Hoover's pledge of 1932
about prosperity. In the process of updating, however, the lyrics lost
some of their topical bite, as when

> Who cares what banks fail in Yonkers,
> long as you've got a kiss that conquers?

became

> Who cares how history rates me,
> long as your kiss intoxicates me?

He also updated "Love Is Sweeping the Country" so it could serve as a campaign song for Adlai Stevenson. Stevenson's "fearless attitudes with no platitudes" appealed to Ira Gershwin, who gave the candidate a professional compliment for his way with words—words that, like words a good lyricist provides a singer—one can "lean" on:

> Adlai's sweeping the country!
> He will be the next Prez.
> We'll be leaning
> on words with meaning,
> for he means every word he says.

The revival was as disappointing as Stevenson's run for the presidency, however; as was an off-Broadway production of *Of Thee I Sing* in 1969. The critics, such as Clive Barnes, focused on what had frequently been the problem in a Gershwin musical:

> The book by Kaufman and Ryskind should have been slammed shut in Philadelphia 38 years ago. It is not just weak, it is tottering. It is not just bad, it is terrible. The story, the jokes, the dialogue—the entire caboodle—would today give even the dimmest Broadway producers (well, perhaps not the dimmest) apoplexy.[8]

Amid the debacle, however, one thing stood out: "George and Ira Gershwin remain as fresh as ever":

> The Gershwins may still be out on their own ahead of the field in the American musical theater. Also this is an extraordinarily advanced kind of musical comedy. The Gershwins were here actually straining toward proper, or more likely, improper, operetta and had the courage to use arias, ensembles, even, as unlikely as it sounds, recitatives, and the musical aspect of the show. . . is as fresh as tomorrow.

If the response to these revivals of *Of Thee I Sing* was prophetic, it would mean that weak books would continue to plague the songs of the Gershwins. In their life-long efforts to wed words and music to a dramatic context, the Gershwins had relegated many of their finest songs to the status of period-pieces. Their most enduring legacy, it seemed, would be one of songs, not shows. Of those songs, moreover, it would be the least integral ones that became the greatest standards—the rhythmic numbers and, above all, the great romantic ballads that Ira had so long before wearied of writing. In one of the greatest of those ballads, he made a tiny but significant revision; for years, he had wanted to change the title of "Love Is Here To Stay" to his original idea for the song: "*Our* Love Is Here To Stay," but he felt he could not alter a song that had become a standard. Finally, with the publication of *The George and Ira Gershwin Songbook* in 1960, he added what Lawrence Stewart aptly calls that "warming pronoun."[9]

Almost immediately after his effective retirement from songwriting, Ira Gershwin initiated another scholarly project that took him back to his youthful poetic aspirations. The inspiration for this endeavor may have gone back as far as 1930, when a reviewer praised his lyrics for *Strike Up the Band*:

> If they were printed in a book, I should buy it and find something more than the accident of alphabetical arrangement in the fact that it would be placed on my shelves next to the works of W. S. Gilbert.[10]

Ira now began thinking of reversing Gilbert's procedure: where Gilbert had published his poems first, then had Sullivan set them to music, Ira considered taking words that had been fused with music and publishing them separately as a collection of lyrics. Only one other lyricist of his generation, Oscar Hammerstein, had published a similar collection, but since many of Hammerstein's lyrics had been written before Richard Rodgers set them to music, there seemed more justification in presenting them as poetry. According to Lawrence Stewart, Ira had always accepted Franklin Pierce Adams's judgment that Hammerstein alone was the "poet" among his peers, yet he always thought "his own talent" was "for light verse," and he "clearly had the poet's desire for his works to be collected together in one volume, where they could escape the impermanence of flimsy sheet-music."[11]

As Ira himself put it, more whimsically, he was thinking "of having a go at a book about lyrics."[12] The project that began so casually resulted, nearly five years later, as *Lyrics on Several Occasions*, a collection, with commentaries, of well over one hundred of his own lyrics (though still only a fraction of the more than 700 songs he wrote during his career). In compiling the book, Ira Gershwin reflected upon the paradoxical art of songwriting as he had come to regard it after a lifetime of practice, an art related to, yet distinct from poetry.

The first lyric for which he wrote a commentary, "The Babbitt and the Bromide," underscored the poetic aspect of his craft, since it had been anthologized in the *Anthology of Light Verse* edited by Louis Kronenberger. In making his other selections, Ira relied heavily upon his "comic" lyrics, perhaps because they stood up better on the page as poems. Taking his title from Matthew Prior's *Poems on Several Occasions*, he established continuity with his beloved eighteenth century and also stressed the "occasional" nature of his lyrics by noting the dramatic context of the film or stage musical into which he had tried to integrate his lodgment. In his rambling, eighteenth-century style subtitle, he expanded upon that dramatic dimension of his art:

> A selection of stage & screen lyrics written for sundry situations; and now arranged in arbitrary categories to which have been added many informative annotations & disquisitions on their why & wherefore, their whom-for, and their how; and matters associative.
> by Ira Gershwin, *Gent.*[13]

While *Lyrics on Several Occasions* allies the art of the lyric with that of poetry, Ira emphasized the primacy of music in the creation of song by posting a warning as intimidating as Mark Twain's "Notice" to readers seeking a motive, moral, or plot in *Huckleberry Finn*:

> Since most of the lyrics in this lodgment were arrived at by fitting words mosaically to music already composed, any resemblance to actual poetry, living or dead, is highly improbable.[14]

In many of the commentaries, Ira takes pains to point out the problems posed by having to fit music and words together and details the way the artistry of a simple song lay in how skillfully lyric and melody coalesce. The fact that he chose to open *Lyrics on Several Occasions* with "The Man I Love," where his artistry consists in how perfectly the words are fitted to George's music, counterbalances the implication that lyrics are "poetic" creations. The choice of "The Man I Love" also runs counter to Ira's presentation of his lyrics as lodgments written to fit a specific dramatic occasion. Cut from three different musicals, "The Man I Love" survived and has endured as a pure "pop" song—a romantic ballad that simply, wittily, and movingly performs the task Ira Gershwin had increasingly sought to avoid—saying "I love you" in thirty-two bars.

Performance of that task with a light-verse curve became the organizing principle of *Lyrics on Several Occasions*. Instead of clustering lyrics together by chronology or by the musical show for which they were written, Ira grouped them according to the lyrical formulas upon which they were based. He even gave many of those formulas a witty twist, entitling the category of torch songs "Ladies in Lament" and that of dance numbers "Turns with Terpsichore." Such an arrangement enables the reader to see how each lyric works its own subtle transformation of the basic formula. Under the category he dubbed "The Importunate Female," for example, we find such diverse songs as "I Can't Get Started," "Someone To Watch Over Me," and "Sing Me Not a Ballad"—three songs completely different, in tone, character, and dramatic context, yet all built upon the same formulaic romantic plea. Ira Gershwin found the scholarly task of compiling and annotating *Lyrics on Several Occasions* "just as difficult, bemusing, and time-consuming" as, originally, the lyrics had been. Like Huck Finn, who, after completing his own opus, expresses relief that "there ain't nothing more to write about, and I am rotten glad of it, because if I'd knowed what a trouble it was to make a book I wouldn't a tackled it and ain't agoing to no more," Ira Gershwin sighed, "this book is unique in that its author isn't looking forward to doing another."[15]

Amid the chorus of critical acclaim for the published volume came a brief but sweeping personal tribute from the lyricist who had first shown Ira and his contemporaries that light verse could be wed to music: "The lyrics," P. G. Wodehouse wrote, "are wonderful. I've always considered you the best of the whole bunch."[16]

Ira Gershwin continued his scholarly activities—editing, compiling, annotating his brother's, and his own, works—for nearly thirty years. Although he occasionally tinkered with putting lyrics to one of George's unused melodies, his imagination, as always, required a full-scale dramatic and musical "property" for his lyrics. Ever since he had begun posthumous collaboration with his brother, Ira insisted that the show that contained new Gershwin songs must have "intellectual excitement."[17] Only once during this extensive period did Ira find a project exciting enough to induce him to re-enter the gritty, pressured, uncertain world of writing songs for a show.

At a party in 1964, director Billy Wilder asked Leonore Gershwin what it would take to get Ira back into work. "To be asked by someone he admires,"[18] she replied. On that, Wilder, known for his darkly comic satires, asked Ira to provide lyrics for a film that would portray the popular music business in all of its crassness and venality. The film, whose title, *Kiss Me, Stupid*, was a parody of Tin Pan Alley ballads at their most ludicrous, would star Dean Martin, playing a caricature of himself as a boozy singing star, who stops for gas in a small desert town between Las Vegas and Hollywood. The garage owner, played by Cliff Osmond, is an aspiring lyricist who, when he recognizes Martin, disconnects his fuel pump to detain the great "Dino" long enough to persuade him to sing some of Osmond's songs on his television show.

The story turns ugly when Osmond rushes to the house of his composer, played by Ray Walston, and pleads with him to use his beautiful wife as "bait" to keep the lecherous Dino in town for the night so they can "plug" their songs. When Walston, already insanely possessive of his wife, refuses, they hire a prostitute, played by Kim Novak, to impersonate Walston's wife and sleep with Martin.

While Ira may have relished the chance to skewer an industry whose commercialism had frequently slighted his finest work, he must also have been intrigued by the unique challenge the film posed. The songs the two amateurs demonstrate for Martin could not really be good songs, yet they could not simply be bad either; they would have to be, as Ira put it, "just somewhat obvious."[19] The prospect of re-creating, after a lifetime of lyrical mastery, the work of talented but amateur songwriters, pulled Ira's imagination back to his own apprenticeship years. Wilder, who expected Ira to suggest such Hollywood stalwarts as Henry Mancini or André Previn as a collaborator, was pleasantly surprised when Ira proposed working with George Gershwin. With the help of Roger Edens, who had confected the "Born in a Trunk" medley for Judy Garland, Ira hoped that once more the Gershwin trunk would give birth to the needed numbers.

Wilder told them he needed only three songs—a couple of novelty songs (Wilder cited the example of "Doggie in the Window" as the kind of inane nonsense that appealed to public taste) and an "Italian ballad" designed for Dean Martin. Turning first to the "Italian" song, Ira thought that the two amateurs might typically dream of writing a follow-up to a big hit like "That's Amore," much the way he himself, back in 1917, imagined writing a "second 'Poor Butterfly,'" with George Gershwin and co-lyricist Lou Paley. As "Arthur Francis," in fact, Ira had written just such a song back in 1920, with Vincent Youmans, entitled "Bambino":

> See, I buy-a this new mandolino
> jus' to sing-a my love to you.
> Oh please-a don't treat-a me mean-o,
> Maraschino, I'll be true.

Even then, he had to rein in his light-verse wit to meet Tin Pan Alley's standards of simplicity. In his original lyric he had the ardent Italian lover aver:

> I'll climb to your window
> like in da romance,
> I no give a rap if I rip-a da pants.

But that cleverness—and its crackling consonants—had to be toned
down to the more singable and straightforward

> The love moon is bright
> so let's make-a da hay.
> Come make-a with me monkey business till day.

What he now needed to do, with some of George's music, was to create
the illusion of apprentice work with the artful artlessness of a master.

Looking over "Wake Up Brother and Dance," an unused song from
the film *Shall We Dance*, Ira remembered that he had once told George
that "it reminded me a lot of an Italian song we used to hear on the
East Side when I was a kid."[20] With its tempo changed to a waltz, Ira
wrote a lyric in an Alley genre he usually avoided—the "girl's name"
song. Selecting the name of the most popular Italian film star of the
day, he wrenches his rhymes excruciatingly:

> Listen to me, Sophia,
> have you any idea
> how much you mean to me-a?

Imagining how his fledgling lyricist would struggle to find Italian termi-
nology, Ira has him scan sheet-music for inspiration:

> I'm all *agitato*,
> ev'ry heart string *vibrato*,
> ev'ry look *passionato* . . .
> it's love *crescendo*,
> never ever *diminuendo*.

As he toyed with bilingual phrases, he struck upon a clever pairing of
American slang and arch Italian:

> All the others were so-so,
> not a one *amoroso*—.

He then followed with an even cleverer match of American slang,
Italian, and classical allusion:

> Be my *inamorata*—
> hot-like,
> not like
> a Lysistrata.

Too clever for his amateurs, Ira must have decided, for he cut those
lines and pushed the lyric over the top by switching to culinary Italian:

> you're sweeter than spumoni,
> sweeter even than zabaglione.

In the film Wilder had composer Ray Walston demonstrate the number to a bored Dean Martin and an enraptured Kim Novak. In order to get rid of Walston—and get at Novak—"Dino" agrees to take "Sophia," sardonically praising it as the next "That's Amore" and "Arrivederci Roma."

For the "nutty" number Wilder suggested Ira simply use "Blah, Blah, Blah," which had been written for *Delicious* in 1931, but Ira wanted a new creation, so he dug deeper into the Gershwin trunk. In "You Know How It Is," a song that was cut from the 1928 production of *Rosalie*, Ira had confected an image of romantic incompleteness that had always tickled him:

> Ev'ry poached egg needs a piece of toast;
> you know how it is.
> Philadelphia needs the *Sat. Eve. Post*;
> you know how it is.

In the 1930s, the heyday of list songs, Ira had reused the image and lengthened the catalogue:

> I'm a poached egg without a piece of toast;
> Philadelphia without the *Sat. Eve. Post*;
> George Jean Nathan without a play to roast
> when I'm without you.

At that point, however, no full song emerged, and Cole Porter's 1935 song, "A Picture of Me Without You," used the same idea of a catalogue of romantic incompleteness ("Picture Ogden Nash without a rhyme . . . Mr. Bulova without the time . . ."). Still, Ira had a fondness for his fragment, and recycled it into the trial scene of *Lady in the Dark*—but it was cut during tryouts. When he and Kay Swift were organizing George Gershwin's manuscripts in 1945, Ira recalled the music and sang it to her, and she wrote it down as an eight-bar theme and put it among the unpublished manuscripts.

When Ira sang the fragment and suggested the items could be changed and updated for the 1960s, Wilder liked the idea. Sitting down at the piano with Roger Edens, Ira suggested that the eight-bar musical fragment could be completed by adding a bridge based on another early Gershwin song, "Are You Dancing?," and with some tempo changes the musical metamorphosis was accomplished. He then

recast the entire lyric as he imagined two amateur songwriters might
attempt to create a contemporary catalogue song in the tradition of
Cole Porter. Probably no lyric ever gave Ira Gershwin more delight.
He filled seventeen pages of manuscript with items for his catalogue
of incompleteness until he achieved precisely the kind of images he
thought amateurs would think "topping":

> I'm a bullfight—
> without a matador;
> Casanova—
> the night he didn't score . . .
> I am Groucho
> without a single brother;
> I'm a Whistler
> who never had a mother.

Stressing the contemporary nature of catalogue allusions, he included
images from the 1950s and '60s:

> I'm a missile
> that can't get into space,
> Monte Carlo
> without a Princess Grace
> Perry Mason
> the time he lost a case.

For only the second time in his career, Ira confessed to Lawrence
Stewart, he relied upon a rhyming dictionary: "In looking up rhymes
for 'toast' he found 'hitching-post,' "[21] and promptly tied the lyric to it.
When Ella Fitzgerald asked him for a female version, he came up with
a dozen more items, including a variation on his original image:

> I'm a girlfriend
> without a thing to boast—
> any egghead
> would have me diagnosed
> as a poached egg
> without a piece of toast—
> each time I'm without you.

While Ira's prolonged work on this lyric may have resulted from years
of lyrical inactivity, its theme of incompleteness, coupled with George's
music, may have felt like sustained collaboration with his brother.
Perhaps sensing that longing beneath the witty allusions, Wilder sug-

gested the song be retitled "When I'm Without You," but Ira held firm for his beloved image of incompleteness.

Wilder staged "I'm a Poached Egg" in a way that highlighted the crudity of song salesmanship even more than he had with "Sophia." When Dean Martin steps into the men's room of the gas station, Osmond pushes Walston in after him and tells his composer to serenade the singer with "I'm a Poached Egg." As the lyricist listens to his collaborator's voice through the bathroom window, he is clearly enthralled at his own wit. However, when Walston sings:

> I'm Vienna
> without the Viennese,
> I'm Da Vinci,
> without the Mona Lis'—

Martin groans, and, as he comes out of the men's room, he shakes his head at the lyricist and mutters incredulously, "Mona Lis'?"

In the course of filming, Wilder decided that the other number for the film need not be quite such a "nutty" song. What he wanted instead was a genuine romantic ballad, "something strong like 'Love Walked In.' "[22] Instead of bristling at the request for yet another ballad, Ira relished the opportunity "to write another Gershwin ballad that might become a standard." As his imagination drifted back to his earliest efforts to say "I love you" in thirty-two bars, Ira recalled a song he had written back in 1921. He and George, together with co-lyricist Lou Paley, had visited a summer camp in the Adirondacks. "It was cold as hell," Ira recalled, "I slept in bed with my clothes on,"[23] but the three novices were determined to crank out a "hit." George came up with a suitable melody, but Ira and Lou Paley gave it a lyric as "Phoebe," which was so simple it bordered on the banal:

> Phoebe—Oh, Phoebe!
> Let me be your boy;
> for your smile so true
> makes me feel I must have you.[24]

Although it was never published, George had saved his manuscript for "Phoebe," and Ira and Kay Swift had filed it as Melody Number 89 when they went over the musical notebooks in the 1940s. Taking the music from the verse of "Phoebe," Ira used it for the verse of the ballad for *Kiss Me, Stupid*. For the refrain, which was written first, he took another of George's melodies from the 1920s, a sensuous, bluesy number that had gone into the files as Melody Number 57.

With the music for this posthumous collaboration set, Ira did more archival searching and came up with another of his own apprentice efforts, an unpublished lyric he had written in 1922 to a song by composer Richard Meyers called "Mary-Louise." There he found a promising phrase, "I never knew that I could care as I do, all day and all the night through," which he reworked into one of his finest title-phrases, rich in long vowels and liquid consonants, at once casually colloquial and yet understatedly moving:

> all the livelong day
> and the long, long night.

Knowing that "All the Livelong Day (and the Long, Long Night)" would be sung in the climactic scene where Martin demands his payoff tumble with Novak, Ira considered changing it to "All the Live-long Day and Love-long Night," but feared so "integral" a lyric would be thought too risqué.

With its beautiful melody and the simple, but artful, title-phrase, "All the Livelong Day" might well have become another great Gershwin standard. Once again, however, Ira subordinated his lyric to the demands of its dramatic "occasion"—in this case altering music and lyric just enough to mark them as amateurish while not utterly ruining the song. Back in the 1940s, Kay Swift had made a note on the "Phoebe" manuscript that a musical "figure" needed to be added to the refrain. Now, Ira asked Roger Edens if he could add the necessary notes. Edens, who had concocted the lilting vamp that introduces Gene Kelly's slogging rendition of "Singin' in the Rain," found a similar "whoo-whoo calling phrase" in the verse to "Phoebe." Edens then unified both parts of the song by using that vamp in the refrain, and Ira seized upon it to give his lyric the necessary amateurish touch—dragging out syllables to fit the added notes:

> what do I do-oo-oo?
> dream about you-oo-oo?

Except for that single, intentional blemish, the rest of Ira's lyric rides the thin line between simplicity and banality as it touches upon one romantic cliché after another, from

> felt this way the first time you came in sight,

to the pollyanna weather imagery of

> suddenly my gloomy old sky turned magic'ly bright

He then pushes clichés further still with:

> summer, spring and fall-time
> you're my one and all time.

Then, just as the lyric threatens to descend hopelessly into banality, Ira returns to his exquisite title via another simple colloquial phrase:

> All I live for now is to hold you tight
> all the livelong day and the long, long night.

By using "All" first as a pronoun then an adjective, Ira managed yet one more subtle play with language.

Asked by Wilder to suggest a dramatic context for the song, Ira came up with a clever idea. Thinking in "scholarly" terms, Ira believed he could educate the public about how lyricists work from a "dummy" lyric, temporary, often nonsensical phrases to help them remember the melody while they worked on the real version. Lyricists seldom worked from a full-fledged dummy lyric (covering all the music of a tune), but Ira, after he had completed the real lyric for "All the Livelong Day," concocted one for his amateur songwriters:

> When it's wintertime, many flowers droop.
> There's a saying old,
> "Summer is not so cold."
> Some like turtle better than onion soup.
> Ala kazam
> "How's your wife, Sam?"
> I'm what I am.

It would be funny, Ira told Wilder, if the amateur composer, while nervously demonstrating the song to Dean Martin, mistakenly sang this dummy lyric instead of the real one. Thus Ira, as always, was willing to sacrifice his lyric to its dramatic context—in this case substituting a dummy lyric for the real ballad in order to enhance the comic moment.

Billy Wilder, however, perhaps sensing the superb quality of this ballad, presented "All the Livelong Day" as the one genuinely moving moment in an otherwise bleakly satirical film. So harsh was that overall cynical tone that when *Kiss Me, Stupid* was released it was derided as "tasteless," and even Dean Martin refused to record any of the songs. Thus Ira's, and George's, efforts, once more suffered unjustly because of their dramatic vehicle. Even though the film now is celebrated as a classic satire, with prostitution and adultery used as metaphors for the crass operations of the popular music industry, the songs have not survived. Ironically, the scene Wilder created to encase "All the Livelong Day" was the only suggestion that there could also be artistry in that industry. As Walston demonstrates the song to Dean Martin and Novak, we see a kind of morality-play triptych. Walston, the songwriter, is flanked on the one side by Martin, an emblem of the industry at its most crudely commercial; on his other side is Novak, the image of a public that uncritically embraces whatever sentimental or mawkish wares the industry grinds out. As he plays and sings, however, Walston withdraws from both of them, performing "All the Livelong Day," finally, for himself.

When Martin, at the end of his lecherous rope, interrupts and shouts, "I'll buy this one, too!" just to get Walston out of the house, the composer turns to him and quietly says, "This one is not for sale." Then, oblivious to them, he again sings the lovely conclusion:

> All I live for now is to hold you tight,
> all the livelong day and the long, long night.

As the camera closes in, the composer's face wears a look of sheer delight in the song for its own sake, not for its commercial or popular success. It is a look similar to that of James Mason as he listens to Garland sing "The Man That Got Away," to the look Burton Lane saw on Ira Gershwin's face, as must have George Gershwin, Kurt Weill, Harold Arlen, and all of Ira's other collaborators. Thus in this last song, Ira Gershwin, who had long sought to integrate his lyrics into their dramatic context, was finally given an occasion that captured the artistry he had, for a lifetime, brought to the creation of song—that "joint art of words and music," he was always fond of saying, "two arts under emotional pressure coalescing into a third."

Although Ira Gershwin after *Kiss Me, Stupid* never again ventured into the commercial world of songwriting, he continued in his role of scholar—editing, compiling, annotating his brother's and his own works. In 1966, he became "Ira, the scholar" officially when the University of Maryland awarded him an honorary Doctor of Fine Arts degree. (Ira, who had worked in shipping at B. Altman's department store before trying his hand at lyrics, wryly pointed out that the D.F.A. did not stand for "Division Freight Agent.") After the awards ceremony, Leonore observed that the honorary degree "meant more to her than his Pulitzer had," and Ira concurred:

> I know what she means ... When you're young and get an award, it doesn't mean much. But when you're seventy and get one—then it really means something.[25]

During the same trip east, he was honored at a luncheon at the Library of Congress. While he always regarded the honors accorded to George—the naming of streets and schools, prizes, commemorative medals—as his brother's proper due, Ira was genuinely taken aback when such recognition came to him. "Did you ever think you'd see the day," he confided to a friend, "that Ira Gershwin would be a guest of honor at the Library of Congress?"[26]

The greatest and most fitting tribute he received came in 1967 at the Museum of the City of New York. The museum had vied with the Library of Congress for the acquisition of Gershwin material. Ira responded to the curator's plea for certain memorabilia that belonged in the city that had nurtured the brothers Gershwin and whose rhythms and idioms they, in turn, had transformed into song. He assembled a collection of documents, art works, and other "Gershwiniana" particularly appropriate for a museum devoted to the city of theatrical flair, such as George's red silk cummerbund and a tile-table given to Ira by actor Louis Calhern (each inlaid ivory tile had a picture that alluded to one of his lyrics—a clock without hands for "Bidin' My Time," a broom for "Love is Sweeping the Country," etc.). One of those items, the engraved cigarette lighter George had given Ira on the opening night of *Girl Crazy*, inspired the title of an exhibition that celebrated the opening of the archive: "GERSHWIN: George the Music/Ira the Words." At last, it seemed, both brothers were accorded equal recognition. Extending the festivities city-wide, Mayor John Lindsay also honored both George and Ira by proclaiming "Gershwin Week in New York."

To grace the exhibition, a special collector's edition of "Hi Ho!," the first song the Gershwins wrote for Astaire in Hollywood, was published. Thirty years before, the song was peremptorily dropped from *Shall We Dance* even before filming began; now it was reincarnated in an elegant black and white cover, imprinted with the signatures of composer and lyricist and sporting a bright red ribbon. "Hi Ho!," along with all of the brothers' songs, did indeed seem here to stay. One of the most popular items in the exhibition was a panel that displayed Ira's extensive worksheets for "I'm a Poached Egg." Glancing at the display, he remarked, "This Gershwin sure uses up a lot of paper."[27]

In his last years, Ira Gershwin still clung to the hope that some of George's unused music could be salvaged. Gene Kelly worked with some of the melodies, and Ira himself envisioned a "suite inspired by locations in New York City."[28] Nothing came of these projects, however. With the assistance of Michael Feinstein, Ira took a few of the melodic fragments he had earlier set lyrics to and edited them for a final time. One of these last compositions, "Saying My Say," might serve as a last word for a master of words:

> There's no stopping me
> I've come here to say my say,
> Don't try topping me,
> I've just got to say my say.

Having said his say in a lifetime of song, Ira Gershwin died as quietly as he had lived, on August 17, 1983.

23. Goldberg, *Tin Pan Alley*, 230.

24. Ira Gershwin, *Lyrics on Several Occasions*, 42.

25. Harburg, "From the Lower East Side to 'Over the Rainbow,' " 140–41.

26. Rick Altman, *The American Film Musical* (Bloomington: Indiana Univ. Press, 1987), 134–35.

27. James Ellis, "Introduction," *The Bab Ballads By W. S. Gilbert* (Cambridge: Harvard Univ. Press, 1970), 21–22.

28. Ian Bradley, *The Annotated Gilbert and Sullivan* (Middlesex: Penguin, 1982), 104–5.

29. Oscar Hammerstein, *Lyrics* (New York: Simon and Schuster, 1949), 19–20.

30. *New York Tribune* (clipping, annotated "Spring, 1925") in Ira and Leonore Gershwin Trusts Archive, Los Angeles, California.

31. P. G. Wodehouse, *Author! Author!* (New York: Simon and Schuster, 1962), 15.

32. Meyerson and Harburg, *Who Put the Rainbow in "The Wizard of Oz"?*, 18.

2. Boy Wanted: 1918–1924

1. Edward Jablonski, "Brother Act: The Gershwins," *George and Ira Gershwin's "Girl Crazy"* (New York: Roxbury Recordings, Inc., 1990), 29.

2. Harold Meyerson and Ernie Harburg, *Who Put the Rainbow in "The Wizard of Oz"?* (Ann Arbor: Univ. of Michigan Press, 1993), 19.

3. Deena Rosenberg, *Fascinating Rhythm: The Collaboration of George and Ira Gershwin* (New York: Dutton, 1991), 20.

4. Robert Kimball and Alfred Simon, *The Gershwins* (New York: Atheneum, 1973), 42–43.

5. David Ewen, *George Gershwin: His Journey to Greatness* (New York: Ungar, 1970), 38–39.

6. S. N. Behrman, *People in a Diary* (Boston: Little, Brown, 1972), 242.

7. "Lyricist of 'Saga of Jenny' Et Al.," unattributed news clipping, Jablonski-Stewart Archive, Harry Ransom Humanities Research Center, University of Texas, Austin.

8. Robert Kimball, *The Complete Lyrics of Ira Gershwin* (New York: Alfred A. Knopf, 1993), 4.

9. *Ibid.*

10. Rosenberg, *Fascinating Rhythm*, 32–33.

11. Kimball and Simon, *The Gershwins*, xxii.

12. "News of the Drama: In Which Ira Gershwin Is Considered," *New York Times* (Jan. 19, 1930).

13. Kimball, *The Complete Lyrics of Ira Gershwin*, 6.

14. *Ibid.*, 6–7.

15. Ewen, *George Gershwin*, 52.

16. Edward Jablonski, *Gershwin* (New York: Doubleday, 1987), 46.

17. Ira Gershwin, *Lyrics on Several Occasions* (New York: Alfred A. Knopf, 1959), 323.

18. Lawrence Stewart, who served as Ira Gershwin's secretary for many years, has pointed out in a letter to me that such inversions reflect Ira's fondness

NOTES

1. Bidin' My Time: 1896–1917

1. S. N. Behrman, *People in a Diary* (Boston: Little, Brown, 1972), 249

2. Edward Jablonski, *Gershwin* (New York: Doubleday, 1987), 238.

3. George Gershwin, "Introduction," *The George Gershwin Songbook* (Ne York: Simon and Schuster, 1932).

4. Alec Wilder, *American Popular Song: The Great Innovators, 1900–19.* (New York: Oxford Univ. Press, 1972), 150.

5. Ira Gershwin, *Lyrics on Several Occasions* (New York: Alfred A. Knoɲ 1959), 362.

6. Robert Kimball, *The Complete Lyrics of Ira Gershwin* (New York: Alfrɛ A. Knopf, 1993), xvi.

7. Anthony Burgess, *This Man and Music* (London: Hutchinson, 1982 105–6.

8. Behrman, *People in a Diary*, 242–43.

9. Quoted in Deena Rosenberg, "Notes," *Ella Fitzgerald: The George an Ira Gershwin Songbook* (Verve Record VE-2-2525).

10. Joan Peyser, *The Memory of All That: The Life of George Gershwi* (New York: Simon & Schuster, 1993), 28.

11. Ira Gershwin, ". . . But I Wouldn't Want To Live There," *The Saturdɑ Review* (Oct. 18, 1958), 27.

12. Robert Kimball and Alfred Simon, *The Gershwins* (New York: Athɛ neum, 1973), xxii.

13. Ira Gershwin, " . . . But I Wouldn't Want To Live There," 48.

14. Harold Meyerson and Ernie Harburg, *Who Put the Rainbow in "Tʰ Wizard of Oz"?* (Ann Arbor: Univ. of Michigan Press, 1993), 18.

15. Ira Gershwin, *Lyrics on Several Occasions*, 215.

16. Ira Gershwin, "Words and Music," *New York Times* (Nov. 9, 1930).

17. *The Collected Poetry of Dorothy Parker* (New York: Modern Librarʸ 1959), 43.

18. E. Y. Harburg, "From the Lower East Side to 'Over the Rainbow,' *Creators and Disturbers: Reminiscences by Jewish Intellectuals of New Yorᵏ (New York: Columbia Univ. Press, 1982), 141–42.

19. Carolyn Wells, *A Vers de Société Anthology* (New York: Charles Scrib ner's Sons, 1907), xxv.

20. Meyerson and Harburg, *Who Put the Rainbow in "The Wizard o Oz"?*, 19.

21. Max Wilk, *They're Playing Our Song* (New York: Atheneum, 1973), 222

22. Ira Gershwin, *Lyrics on Several Occasions*, ix.

for periodic sentences (where the word order suspends the meaning of the sentence until the last word has been reached—"a wonderful dramatic device"). Stewart adds, "Ira was a great student of the 18th century, when that rhetorical structure was so frequently employed." Stewart's points are illuminating, but I would still maintain that inversion runs counter to Ira Gershwin's own stated aim of making lyrics sound like "rhymed conversation."

19. *Primrose* included lyrics by a young British songwriter, Desmond Carter, and it may be that Carter was involved in the revisions of "Boy Wanted," although Gershwin biographer Edward Jablonski asserts that Carter's primary contribution to *Primrose* was a series of comic patter songs such as the "Gilbert and Sullivanish 'Isn't It Terrible What They Did to Mary, Queen of Scots?'" (Jablonski, *Gershwin*, 79–80).

20. One of the few songs the brothers wrote together during these years turned out to be one of their most successful, "Stairway to Paradise." Ira had written a lyric called "A New Step Every Day" in 1919, and three years later Buddy DeSylva suggested they rewrite it for a production number in the 1922 *Scandals*. After revising Ira's line, "I'll build a staircase to paradise," the two lyricists recast the song into a jazzy dance number that went on to become an independent hit.

21. Unattributed news story, Jablonski-Stewart Archive, Harry Ransom Research Center, University of Texas, Austin.

22. Ira Gershwin, *Lyrics on Several Occasions*, 119.

23. *Ibid.*, 335.

24. *Ibid.*, 119.

25. Alec Wilder, *American Popular Song* (New York: Oxford Univ. Press, 1972), 293.

26. Ewen, *George Gershwin*, 95.

27. Jablonski, *Gershwin*, 47.

28. Ira Gershwin, "Questionnaire for Lyric Song Writers," *New York Sun* (April 19, 1923).

29. Kimball, *The Complete Lyrics of Ira Gershwin*, 38.

30. Wilder, *American Popular Song*, 122.

31. Wilfrid Mellers, *Music in a New Found Land* (New York: Alfred A. Knopf, 1965), 389.

32. Ira Gershwin, *Lyrics on Several Occasions*, 4.

33. *Ibid.*

34. I want to thank my colleague Michael Hancher for pointing out this witty skewing of verb tenses.

35. Meyerson and Harburg, *Who Put the Rainbow in "The Wizard of Oz"?*, 181.

36. Wilder, *American Popular Song*, 129.

37. Mellers, *Music in a New Found Land*, 388.

3. That Certain Feeling: 1924–1927

1. William R. Taylor, "Broadway: The Place That Words Built," *Inventing Times Square: Commerce and Culture at the Crossroads of the World*, ed. William R. Taylor (New York: Russell Sage Foundation, 1991), 212–18.

2. John B. Kennedy, "Words and Music," *Collier's* (Sept. 28, 1928), 52.

3. Lehman Engel, *The American Musical Theater* (New York: Macmillan, 1967), 30.

4. Fred Astaire, *Steps in Time* (New York: Harper & Bros., 1959), 126–28.

5. Robert Kimball and Alfred Simon, *The Gershwins* (New York: Atheneum, 1973), 39.

6. In 1982, a treasure trove of scores and manuscripts from shows by the Gershwins, Kern, and other songwriters was discovered at the Warner Brothers warehouse in Seacaucus, N. J.

7. Ira Gershwin, *Lyrics on Several Occasions* (New York: Alfred A. Knopf, 1959), 173.

8. Gerald Mast, *Can't Help Singin': The American Musical on Stage and Screen* (Woodstock, N.Y.: Overlook Press, 1987), 72. I also am indebted to singer Brian Kent for the analysis of "Fascinating Rhythm."

9. "Trying To Interview Gershwin Brothers," *Boston Globe* (Dec. 13, 1931).

10. Ira Gershwin, *Lyrics on Several Occasions*, 173.

11. Kimball, *The Complete Lyrics of Ira Gershwin*, 48.

12. Deena Rosenberg, *Fascinating Rhythm* (New York: Dutton, 1991), 91.

13. *American Popular Song: Six Decades of Songwriters and Singers*, eds. James R. Morris, J. R. Taylor, and Dwight Blocker Bowers (Washington: Smithsonian Institution Press, 1984), 38–39.

14. Astaire, *Steps in Time*, 55.

15. F. Scott Fitzgerald, *Tales of the Jazz Age* (New York: Charles Scribner's Sons, 1922), 85–86.

16. S. N. Behrman, *People in a Diary* (Boston: Little, Brown, 1972), 256.

17. *New York Herald Tribune* (Dec. 2, 1924).

18. *New York Sun* (Dec. 2, 1924).

19. Ira Gershwin, *Lyrics on Several Occasions*, 119.

20. *Ibid.*, 120.

21. Rosenberg, *Fascinating Rhythm*, 130.

22. Wilder, *American Popular Song* (New York: Oxford Univ. Pres, 1972), 132–33.

23. Ira Gershwin, *Lyrics on Several Occasions*, 41.

24. *New York Herald Tribune* (Dec. 29, 1925).

25. *New York Evening Post* (Dec. 29, 1925).

26. *New York World*, (Dec. 29, 1925).

27. *Thou Swell, Thou Witty: The Life and Lyrics of Lorenz Hart*, ed. Dorothy Hart (New York: Harper and Row, 1976), 53.

28. *New York Herald Tribune* (May 31, 1925).

29. *New York Herald Tribune* (May 31, 1925).

30. *Variety* (Dec. 30, 1925).

31. *Minneapolis Star Tribune* (Dec. 7, 1991).

32. P. G. Wodehouse and Guy Bolton, *Bring on the Girls!* (New York: Simon and Schuster, 1953), 223.

33. Edward Jablonski, *Gershwin* (New York: Doubleday, 1987), 133.

34. Ira Gershwin, *Lyrics on Several Occasions*, 262.

35. David Ewen, *George Gershwin* (New York: Ungar, 1970), 45.

36. Ira Gershwin, *Lyrics on Several Occasions*, 111.

37. Howard Dietz, *Dancing in the Dark* (New York: Quadrangle, 1974), 20–21.

38. Ira Gershwin, "Marginalia," *The George and Ira Gershwin Songbook* (New York: Simon and Schuster, 1960), xi-xii.

39. Wodehouse and Bolton, *Bring on the Girls!*, 191.

40. Wayne Shirley, "Introduction," *Oh, Kay!* (Smithsonian Collection Recording, LP R 008), 5.

41. Jablonski, *Gershwin*, 131.

42. Shirley, "Introduction," 6.

4. 'S Wonderful: 1927–1930

1. Fred Astaire, *Steps in Time* (New York: Harper & Bros., 1959), 151.

2. *Ibid.*, 152.

3. *Ibid.*, 153.

4. Ira Gershwin, *Lyrics on Several Occasions* (New York: Alfred A. Knopf, 1959), 24.

5. *Ibid.*, 280.

6. Fred Thompson and Paul Gerard Smith, *Funny Face* (typescript, 1928), Act I, Scene 3, 6–7.

7. Astaire, *Steps in Time*, 154–55.

8. Robert Kimball and Alfred Simon, *The Gershwins* (New York: Atheneum, 1973), 80.

9. *New York World* (Jan. 11, 1928).

10. Edward Jablonski, *Gershwin* (New York: Doubleday, 1987), 173.

11. Ira Gershwin, *Lyrics on Several Occasions*, 94–95.

12. *Ibid.*, 37.

13. Jablonski, *Gershwin*, 189.

14. Ira Gershwin, *Lyrics on Several Occasions*, 152.

15. *Ibid.*, 271.

16. Ethel Merman, *Merman: An Autobiography* (New York: Simon and Schuster, 1978), 38.

17. *Ibid.*, 39.

18. Ira Gershwin, *Lyrics on Several Occasions*, 204.

19. *Ibid.*, 342.

5. Sweeping the Country: 1930–1933

1. Tommy Krasker, "What Price Cheese?" *Strike Up the Band* (Electra Nonesuch 79273), 17.

2. Edward Jablonski, "The Gershwins Go to War," *ibid.*, 24.

3. Laurence Bergreen, *As Thousands Cheer: The Life of Irving Berlin* (New York: Viking, 1990), 250.

4. John Mueller, "Preaching to the Masses: "Strike Up the Band" and War," *Strike Up the Band*, 34.

5. Ira Gershwin, *Lyrics on Several Occasions* (New York: Alfred A. Knopf, 1959), 224.

6. Laurence Maslon, "George S. Kaufman: The Gloomy Dean of American Comedy," *Strike Up the Band*, 30.

7. *New York Evening Post* (Jan. 15, 1930).

8. *New York World* (Jan. 15, 1930).

9. Jablonski, "The Gershwins Go to War," 26.

10. Maslon, "George S. Kaufman: The Gloomy Dean of American Comedy," 31.

11. Percy N. Stone, "Ira Gershwin's Light Is Shining Without George's Reflected Glory," *New York Herald Tribune*, (Dec. 27, 1931).

12. Ira Gershwin, *Lyrics on Several Occasions*, 304–5.

13. Stone, "Ira Gershwin's Light Is Shining". . . .

14. Ira Gershwin, *Lyrics on Several Occasions*, 332.

15. *Ibid.*, 55.

16. Stone, "Ira Gershwin's Light. . . ."

17. Edward Jablonski, *Gershwin* (New York: Doubleday, 1987), 239.

18. *Ibid.*, 228.

19. *Ibid.*, 241.

20. Robert Kimball, *The Complete Lyrics of Ira Gershwin* (New York: Alfred A. Knopf, 1993), 194.

21. Jablonski, *Gershwin*, 239.

22. Ira Gershwin, *Lyrics on Several Occasions*, 162.

23. Jablonski, *Gershwin*, 245–46.

24. Deena Rosenberg, *Fascinating Rhythm* (New York: Dutton, 1991), 260.

25. Jablonski, *Gershwin*, 242.

26. Ira Gershwin, *Lyrics on Several Occasions*, 57.

27. *New York Times* (Oct. 23, 1933).

6. Necessarily So: 1933–1935

1. Deena Rosenberg, *Fascinating Rhythm* (New York: Dutton, 1991), 265.

2. *Ibid.*, 272.

3. Edward Jablonski, *Gershwin* (New York: Doubleday, 1987), 263.

4. Frank Durham, *DuBose Heyward: The Man Who Wrote "Porgy"* (Columbia: Univ. of South Carolina Press, 1954), 124.

5. *Ibid.*

6. Rosenberg, *Fascinating Rhythm*, 273.

7. Hollis Alpert, *The Life and Times of "Porgy and Bess": The Making of an American Classic* (New York: Alfred Knopf, 1990), 91.

8. Ira Gershwin, *Lyrics on Several Occasions* (New York: Alfred A. Knopf, 1959), 360–361.

9. *DuBose Heyward: The Man Who Wrote "Porgy,"* 125.

10. *Ibid.*

11. According to Frank Durham, Dorothy Heyward claimed Ira Gershwin wrote the lyric to "A Woman Is a Sometime Thing" (*DuBose Heyward: The Man Who Wrote "Porgy,"* 125).

12. *Ibid.*, 126.

13. Rosenberg, *Fascinating Rhythm*, 274.

14. Ira Gershwin, *Lyrics on Several Occasions*, 360.

15. *Ibid.*, 359–60.

16. *Ibid.*

17. *DuBose Heyward: The Man Who Wrote "Porgy,"* 125.

18. Ira Gershwin, *Lyrics on Several Occasions*, 149.

19. Alpert, *The Life and Times of "Porgy and Bess,"* 91.

20. Ira Gershwin, *Lyrics on Several Occasions*, 83.

21. Alpert, *The Life and Times of "Porgy and Bess,"* 121.

22. Hall Johnson, "*Porgy and Bess*—A Folk Opera," *Opportunity* 14 (Jan. 1936), 26.

23. William J. Mahar, "Black English in Early Blackface Minstrelsy: A New Interpretation of the Sources of Minstrel Show Dialect," *American Quarterly* 37 (Summer 1985), 261–66. I also am indebted to my colleague Genevieve Escure for my discussion about dialect.

24. James Weldon Johnson, "Preface," *God's Trombones: Seven Negro Sermons in Verse* (New York: Penguin, 1927), 8.

25. James Weldon Johnson, "Dialect Poems," *St. Peter Relates an Incident: Selected Poems* (New York: Viking Press, 1935), 69–70.

26. Jablonski, *Gershwin*, 289.

27. *New York Herald Tribune* (Oct. 11, 1935).

28. Jablonski, *Gershwin*, 289.

29. *New York World-Telegram* (Oct. 11, 1935).

30. Jablonski, *Gershwin*, 289.

7. Fun To Be Fooled: 1934–1936

1. Ira Gershwin, "Marginalia," *The George and Ira Gershwin Songbook* (New York: Simon and Schuster, 1960), xiv.

2. David Ewen, *All the Years of American Popular Music: A Comprehensive History* (Englewood Cliffs, N. J.: Prentice-Hall, 1978), 400.

3. Harold Meyerson and Ernie Harburg, *Who Put the Rainbow in "The Wizard of Oz"?* (Ann Arbor Univ. of Michigan Press, 1993), 76.

4. *Ibid.*, 78.

5. *Ibid.*, 77.

6. *Ibid.*, 79.

7. *Ibid.*, 83.

8. *Ibid.*, 81.

9. *Ibid.*, 77.

10. Max Wilk, *They're Playing Our Song* (New York: Atheneum, 1973), 223.

11. Ira Gershwin, *Lyrics on Several Occasions* (New York: Alfred A. Knopf, 1959), 54.

12. Robert Kimball, *The Complete Lyrics of Ira Gershwin* (New York: Alfred A. Knopf, 1993), 244–45.

13. Ira Gershwin, *Lyrics on Several Occasions*, 100.

14. *Ibid.*

15. *Ibid.*

16. *Ibid.*, 246.

17. *Ibid.*, 195.

18. *Ibid.*, 194–95.

19. For some of those songs, of course, Ira had a co-lyricist, such as Gus Kahn, for *Show Girl*, and P. G. Wodehouse, for *Rosalie*.

20. Deena Rosenberg, *Fascinating Rhythm* (New York: Dutton, 1991), 323.

8. HERE TO STAY: 1936–1938

1. Early exceptions to this rule of thumb were black musicals, such as *Hallelujah!*, which relied upon the racial convention that the "spontaneity" of blacks enabled them to break into song and dance without needing an "excuse."

2. Edward Jablonski, *Gershwin* (New York: Doubleday, 1987), 207.

3. Ira Gershwin, *Lyrics on Several Occasions* (New York: Alfred A. Knopf, 1959), 151.

4. "Trying To Interview Gershwin Brothers," *Boston Globe* (Dec. 13, 1931).

5. Deena Rosenberg, *Fascinating Rhythm* (New York: Dutton, 1991), 325.

6. *Ibid.*, 325.

7. Harold Meyerson and Ernie Harburg, *Who Put the Rainbow in "The Wizard of Oz"?* (Ann Arbor: Univ. of Michigan Press, 1993), 93.

8. Rosenberg, *Fascinating Rhythm*, 325.

9. *Ibid.*, 321.

10. *Ibid.*, 352.

11. Jablonski, *Gershwin*, 300.

12. Rosenberg, *Fascinating Rhythm*, 321.

13. Alec Wilder, *American Popular Song* (New York: Oxford Univ. Press, 1972), 122.

14. Rosenberg, *Fascinating Rhythm*, 326.

15. Ira Gershwin, *Lyrics on Several Occasions*, 170.

16. Rosenberg, *Fascinating Rhythm*, 272.

17. *Ibid.*, 322.

18. Ira Gershwin, *Lyrics on Several Occasions*, 48.

19. Rosenberg, *Fascinating Rhythm*, 352.

20. Ira Gershwin, *Lyrics on Several Occasions*, 287.

21. Rosenberg, *Fascinating Rhythm*, 351.

22. Fred Astaire, *Steps in Time* (New York: Harper and Bros., 1959), 212–22.

23. Rosenberg, *Fascinating Rhythm*, 351.

24. Astaire, *Steps in Time*, 229.

25. Ira Gershwin, *Lyrics on Several Occasions*, 345.

26. Astaire, *Steps in Time*, 229.

27. Ira Gershwin, *Lyrics on Several Occasions*, 345.

28. *Ibid.*, 66.

29. *Ibid.*, 97.

30. Jablonski, *Gershwin*, 314.

31. Ira Gershwin, *Lyrics on Several Occasions*, 141.

32. *Ibid.*, 284.

33. Robert Kimball and Alfred Simon, *The Gershwins* (New York: Atheneum, 1973), 235.

34. Jablonski, *Gershwin*, 327.

35. Kimball and Simon, *The Gershwins*, 235.
36. Edward Jablonski and Lawrence A. Stewart, *The Gershwin Years* (Garden City, N.Y.: Doubleday, 1958; rev. ed. 1973), 306–7.

9. This Is New: 1939–1941

1. Robert Rice, "Rice and Old Shoes," *P. M.* (Feb. 3, 1941).
2. Deena Rosenberg, *Fascinating Rhythm* (New York: Dutton, 1991), 372.
3. *Ibid.*, 373.
4. Moss Hart, *Lady in the Dark* (New York: Random House, 1941), 9.
5. *Ibid.*, 12.
6. Ira Gershwin, *Lyrics on Several Occasions* (New York: Alfred A. Knopf, 1959), 50.
7. Hart, *Lady in the Dark*, 13.
8. Edward Jablonski, *Gershwin* (New York: Doubleday, 1987), 331–32.
9. Rosenberg, *Fascinating Rhythm*, 376–77.
10. *Ibid.*, 376–80.
11. Ira Gershwin, *Lyrics on Several Occasions*, 202.
12. *Ibid.*, 144.
13. *Ibid*, 209.
14. *Ibid.*
15. Hart, *Lady in the Dark*, 60–65.
16. Ira Gershwin, *Lyrics on Several Occasions*, 50.
17. Hart, *Lady in the Dark*, 79.
18. *Ibid.*, 83.
19. Rice, "Rice and Old Shoes."
20. Lehman Engel, *The American Musical Theatre*, (New York: Macmillan, 1967), 55–56.

10. Sing Me Not a Ballad: 1941–1945

1. Deena Rosenberg, *Fascinating Rhythm* (New York: Dutton, 1991), 384.
2. Edward Jablonski and Lawrence Stewart, *The Gershwin Years* (Garden City, N.Y.: Doubleday, 1958; rev. ed. 1973), 322.
3. *Jewish Ledger* (Dec. 10, 1937).
4. *Music Business* (Oct. 1946).
5. Ira Gershwin, *Lyrics on Several Occasions* (New York: Alfred A. Knopf, 1959), 42.
6. *Ibid.*
7. ". . . But I Wouldn't Want To Live There," *The Saturday Review.* (Oct. 18, 1958), 48.
8. Edward Jablonski, *Gershwin* (New York: Doubleday, 1987), 334.
9. *Ibid.*, 335.
10. *Ibid.*, 336.
11. Ira Gershwin, *Lyrics on Several Occasions*, 275.
12. Jablonski and Stewart, *The Gershwin Years*, 304.
13. Ira Gershwin, *Lyrics on Several Occasions*, 276.
14. Jablonski, *Gershwin*, 338.

15. Ira Gershwin, *Lyrics on Several Occasions*, 15.

16. *The Nation* (April 8, 1944), 428.

17. *Ibid.*

18. Jablonski, *Gershwin*, 342.

19. Jablonski and Stewart, *The Gershwin Years*, 301.

20. Jablonski, *Gershwin*, 342.

21. *Ibid.*, 343.

22. Ira Gershwin, *Lyrics on Several Occasions*, 321.

23. *Ibid.*, 131.

24. Jablonski, *Gershwin*, 343–44.

25. *Ibid.*

26. *Ibid.*

11. Changing My Tune: 1946–1951

1. Edward Jablonski, *Gershwin*, (New York: Doubleday, 1987), 130.

2. Ira Gershwin, *Lyrics on Several Occasions* (New York: Alfred A. Knopf, 1959), 70.

3. Jablonski, *Gershwin*, 347.

4. Ira Gershwin, *Lyrics on Several Occasions*, 70.

5. Jablonski, *Gershwin*, 348.

6. Ira Gershwin, *Lyrics on Several Occasions*, 21.

7. *Ibid.*, 281–82.

8. Jablonski, *Gershwin*, 348.

9. Ira Gershwin, *Lyrics on Several Occasions*, 70.

10. *Ibid.*, 124.

11. Jablonski, *Gershwin*, 346.

12. *Ibid.*, 350.

13. Ira Gershwin, *Lyrics on Several Occasions*, 61.

14. *Ibid.*, 290.

15. *Ibid.*

16. Jablonski, *Gershwin*, 352.

17. Donald Knox, *The Magic Factory: How MGM Made "An American in Paris"* (New York: Praeger, 1973), 37.

18. Jablonski, *Gershwin*, 355.

19. Knox, *The Magic Factory*, 40.

20. Mast, *Can't Help Singin'* (Woodstock, N.Y.: Overlook Press, 1987), 254.

21. Knox, *The Magic Factory*, 53.

22. Mast, *Can't Help Singin'*, 75.

23. Jablonski, *Gershwin*, 354.

24. *Ibid.*, 355–57.

12. Lonelier and Tougher: 1951–1954

1. Edward Jablonski, *Gershwin* (New York: Doubleday, 1987), 359.

2. Ira Gershwin, *Lyrics on Several Occasions* (New York: Alfred A. Knopf, 1959), 301.

3. *Ibid.*

4. Ronald Haver, *A Star Is Born: The Making of the 1954 Movie and Its 1983 Restoration* (New York: Alfred A. Knopf, 1988), 45.

5. *Ibid.*, 71.

6. *Ibid.*, 57.

7. Ira Gershwin, *Lyrics on Several Occasions*, 109.

8. Haver, *A Star Is Born*, 52.

9. Deena Rosenberg, *Fascinating Rhythm* (New York: Dutton, 1991), 393.

10. *Ibid.*

11. *Ibid.*, 391.

12. Haver, *A Star Is Born*, 125.

13. *Ibid.*, 129.

14. *Ibid.*, 195.

15. *Ibid.*, 125.

16. Edward Jablonski and Lawrence Stewart, *The Gershwin Years* (Garden City, N.Y.: Doubleday, 1958; rev. ed. 1973), 321.

17. Haver, *A Star Is Born*, 178.

18. *Ibid.*, 180.

19. *Ibid.*, 126–133.

20. *Ibid.*, 189.

21. Jablonski, *Gershwin*, 362.

22. Haver, *A Star Is Born*, 190.

23. *Ibid.*, 215.

24. For the story of that discovery and restoration, see Haver, *A Star Is Born*, 212–16.

25. *Ibid.*

26. *Ibid.*, 193.

27. Ira Gershwin, *Lyrics on Several Occasions*, 248.

13. The Long, Long Night: 1954–1983

1. Edward Jablonski, *Gershwin* (New York: Doubleday, 1987), 363.

2. Ira Gershwin, *Lyrics on Several Occasions* (New York: Alfred A. Knopf, 1959), 142.

3. *Ibid.*

4. Jablonski, *Gershwin*, 364.

5. *Ibid.*

6. *Ibid.*, 366.

7. *Ibid.*, 367.

8. *New York Times* (March 3, 1969).

9. Edward Jablonski and Lawrence Stewart, *The Gershwin Years* (Garden City, N.Y.: Doubleday, 1958, rev. ed. 1973), 335.

10. *Ibid.*, 328.

11. *Ibid.*, 328.

12. Jablonski, *Gershwin*, 367.

13. Ira Gershwin, *Lyrics on Several Occasions*, i.

14. *Ibid.*, ix.

15. *Ibid.*, vii.

16. Deena Rosenberg, *Fascinating Rhythm* (New York: Dutton, 1991), 397.

17. "Gershwin Songs To Be Released," *New York Times* (Feb. 1964).

18. Jablonski and Stewart, *The Gershwin Years*, 319.

19. *Ibid.*, 321.

20. *Ibid.*, 322.

21. *Ibid.*, 323.

22. *Ibid.*, 321.

23. *Ibid.*, 324.

24. In *The Gershwin Years* (p. 325), Lawrence Stewart gives the "original Twenties lyric" as:

> I sit in Childs and order
> breakfast for one.
> I feel just like a boarder—
> 'magine my condition
> when my one ambition
> has, for oh, so long! been to hold you tight—
> all the livelong day and the long, long night.

25. Jablonski and Stewart, *The Gershwin Years*, 312.

26. Jablonski, *Gershwin*, 369.

27. Jablonski and Stewart, *The Gershwin Years*, 314.

28. Kimball, *The Complete Lyrics of Ira Gershwin*, 388.

Credits

BIDIN' MY TIME (Music and Lyrics by George Gershwin and Ira Gershwin)
© 1930 (Renewed) WB Music Corp. for the United States; Chappell & Co. and New World Music Company (Ltd.) administered by WB Music Corp. for all British Reversionary Territories; New World Music Company (Ltd.), administered by WB Music Corp. for all other countries.

BITTERSWEET (Music by William Daly or Lewis E. Gensler, Lyrics by Ira Gershwin)
Lyric © 1993 Ira Gershwin Music administered by WB Music Corp. for the United States and all other countries.

BLAH, BLAH, BLAH (Music and Lyrics by George Gershwin and Ira Gershwin)
© 1931 (Renewed) WB Music Corp. for the United States; Chappell & Co. and New World Music Company (Ltd.) administered by WB Music Corp. for all British Reversionary Territories; New World Music Company (Ltd.), administered by WB Music Corp. for all other countries.

BLUE, BLUE, BLUE (Music and Lyrics by George Gershwin and Ira Gershwin)
© 1933 (Renewed) WB Music Corp. for the United States; Chappell & Co. and New World Music Company (Ltd.) administered by WB Music Corp. for all British Reversionary Territories; New World Music Company (Ltd.), administered by WB Music Corp. for all other countries.

BOY WANTED (Music and Lyrics by George Gershwin, Ira Gershwin, and Desmond Carter)
© 1921, 1924 (Renewed) WB Music Corp. for the United States; Chappell & Co. and New World Music Company (Ltd.) administered by WB Music Corp. for all British Reversionary Territories; New World Music Company (Ltd.), administered by WB Music Corp. for all other countries.

BOY! WHAT LOVE HAS DONE TO ME (Music and Lyrics by George Gershwin and Ira Gershwin)
© 1930 (Renewed) WB Music Corp. for the United States; Chappell & Co. and New World Music Company (Ltd.) administered by WB Music Corp. for all British Reversionary Territories; New World Music Company (Ltd.), administered by WB Music Corp. for all other countries.

BUT NOT FOR ME (Music and Lyrics by George Gershwin and Ira Gershwin)
© 1930 (Renewed) WB Music Corp. for the United States; Chappell & Co. and New World Music Company (Ltd.) administered by WB Music Corp. for all British Reversionary Territories; New World Music Company (Ltd.), administered by WB Music Corp. for all other countries.

BY STRAUSS (Music and Lyrics by George Gershwin and Ira Gershwin)
© 1936 (Renewed) George Gershwin Music and Ira Gershwin Music both administered by WB Music Corp. for the United States; Chappell & Co. for all other countries.

C'EST LA VIE (Music by Harold Arlen, Lyrics by Ira Gershwin and E. Y. Harburg)
Lyric © 1993 Ira Gershwin Music administered by WB Music Corp. and Glocca Morra Music for the United States and all other countries.

CHANGING MY TUNE (Music and Lyrics by George Gershwin and Ira Gershwin)
© 1946 (Renewed) Chappell & Co. for the United States and all other countries.

COULD YOU USE ME? (Music and Lyrics by George Gershwin and Ira Gershwin)
© 1930 (Renewed) WB Music Corp. for the United States; Chappell & Co. and New World Music Company (Ltd.), administered by WB Music Corp. for all British Reversionary Territories; New World Music Company (Ltd.), administered by WB Music Corp. for all other countries.

COZY NOOK TRIO (Music by Kurt Weill, Lyrics by Ira Gershwin)
Lyric © 1959 (Renewed), 1993 Ira Gershwin Music administered by WB Music Corp. for the United States and all other countries.

DISSERTATION ON THE STATE OF BLISS (LOVE AND LEARN BLUES) (Music by Harold Arlen, Lyrics by Ira Gershwin)
© 1954 (Renewed) Harwin Music Co. administered by MPL Communications and New World Music Company (Ltd.) administered by WB Music Corp. for the United States; Harwin Music Co. administered by MPL Communications for all other countries.

DO, DO, DO (Music and Lyrics by George Gershwin and Ira Gershwin)
© 1926 (Renewed) WB Music Corp. for the United States; Chappell & Co. and New World Music Company (Ltd.) administered by WB Music Corp. for all British Reversionary Territories; New World Music Company (Ltd.), administered by WB Music Corp. for all other countries.

DON'T BE A WOMAN IF YOU CAN (Music by Arthur Schwartz, Lyrics by Ira Gershwin)
© 1950 (Renewed) Putnam Music, Inc., administered by PolyGram International Publishing, Inc., as successor-in-interest for the United States and all other countries.

DOWN WITH EVERYONE WHO'S UP (UNION SQUARE) (Music and Lyrics by George Gershwin and Ira Gershwin)
© 1933 (Renewed) WB Music Corp. for the United States; Chappell & Co. and New World Music Company (Ltd.) administered by WB Music Corp. for all British Reversionary Territories; New World Music Company (Ltd.), administered by WB Music Corp. for all other countries. Additional material © 1987 George Gershwin Music and Ira Gershwin Music both administered by Warner Bros. Music for the United States and all other countries.

THE ECONOMIC SITUATION (Music by Vernon Duke, Lyrics by Ira Gershwin)
Lyric © 1993 Ira Gershwin Music administered by WB Music Corp. for the United States and all other countries.

EMBRACEABLE YOU (Music and Lyrics by George Gershwin and Ira Gershwin)
© 1930 (Renewed) WB Music Corp. for the United States; Chappell & Co. and New World Music Company (Ltd.) administered by WB Music Corp. for all British Reversionary Territories; New World Music Company (Ltd.), administered by WB Music Corp. for all other countries.

FASCINATING RHYTHM (Music and Lyrics by George Gershwin and Ira Gershwin)
© 1924 (Renewed) WB Music Corp. for the United States; Chappell & Co. and New World Music Company (Ltd.) administered by WB Music Corp. for all British Reversionary Territories; New World Music Company (Ltd.), administered by WB Music Corp. for all other countries.

A FOGGY DAY (IN LONDON TOWN) (Music and Lyrics by George Gershwin and Ira Gershwin)
© 1937 (Renewed) George Gershwin Music and Ira Gershwin Music both administered by WB Music Corp. for the United States; Chappell & Co. for all other countries.

FOR YOU, FOR ME, FOR EVERMORE (Music and Lyrics by George Gershwin and Ira Gershwin)
© 1946 (Renewed) Chappell & Co. for the United States and all other countries.

FREUD AND JUNG AND ADLER (Music and Lyrics by George Gershwin and Ira Gershwin)
© 1993 George Gershwin Music and Ira Gershwin Music administered by WB Music Corp. for the United States and all other countries.

FUN TO BE FOOLED (Music by Harold Arlen, Lyrics by Ira Gershwin and E. Y. Harburg)
© 1934 (Renewed) S. A. Music, WB Music Corp., and Glocca Morra Music for the United States; Warner Bros. Inc. and New World Music Company (Ltd.) administered by WB Music Corp. for all other countries.

GARCON, S'IL VOUS PLAIT (Music and Lyrics by George Gershwin and Ira Gershwin)
© 1932 (Renewed) WB Music Corp. assigned to WB Music Corp. for the United States; Chappell & Co. and New World Music Company (Ltd.) administered by WB Music Corp. for all British Reversionary Territories; New World Music Company (Ltd.), administered by WB Music Corp. for all other countries.

THE GAZOOKA (Music by Vernon Duke, Lyrics by Ira Gershwin)
© 1936 (Renewed) Chappell & Co. and Ira Gershwin Music administered by WB Music Corp. for the United States; Chappell & Co. for all other countries.

GIRL OF THE MOMENT (Music by Kurt Weill, Lyrics by Ira Gershwin)
© 1941 (Renewed) Chappell & Co. and Hampshire House Publishing Corp. for the United States; Chappell & Co. for all other countries.

GIVE A GIRL A BREAK (Music by Burton Lane, Lyrics by Ira Gershwin)
© 1951 (Renewed) Ira Gershwin Music administered by WB Music Corp. and Chappell & Co. for the United States and all other countries.

GOTTA HAVE ME GO WITH YOU (Music by Harold Arlen, Lyrics by Ira Gershwin)
© 1954 (Renewed) Harwin Music Co. administered by MPL Communications and New World Music Company (Ltd.) administered by WB Music Corp. for the United States; Harwin Music Co. administered by MPL Communications for all other countries.

THE GREATEST SHOW ON EARTH (Music by Kurt Weill, Lyrics by Ira Gershwin)
© 1941 (Renewed) Chappell & Co. and Hampshire House Publishing Corp. for the United States; Chappell & Co. for all other countries.

THE HALF OF IT, DEARIE, BLUES (Music and Lyrics by George Gershwin and Ira Gershwin)
© 1924 (Renewed) WB Music Corp. for the United States; Chappell & Co. and New World Music Company (Ltd.) administered by WB Music Corp. for all British Reversionary Territories; New World Music Company (Ltd.), administered by WB Music Corp. for all other countries.

HAPPY ENDING (Music by Paul Lanin, Lyrics by Arthur Francis)
Lyric © 1993 Ira Gershwin Music administered by WB Music Corp. for the United States and all other countries.

HE HASN'T A THING EXCEPT ME (Music by Vernon Duke, Lyrics by Ira Gershwin)
© 1971 Chappell & Co. and Ira Gershwin Music administered by WB Music Corp. for the United States and all other countries.

HE KNOWS MILK (Music and Lyrics by George Gershwin and Ira Gershwin)
© 1930 (Renewed) WB Music Corp. for the United States; Chappell & Co. and New World Music Company (Ltd.) administered by WB Music Corp. for all British Reversionary Territories; New World Music Company (Ltd.), administered by WB Music Corp. for all other countries.

HIGH HAT (Music and Lyrics by George Gershwin and Ira Gershwin)
© 1927 (Renewed) WB Music Corp. for the United States; Chappell & Co. and New World Music Company (Ltd.) administered by WB Music Corp. for all British Reversionary Territories; New World Music Company (Ltd.), administered by WB Music Corp. for all other countries.

HOW LONG HAS THIS BEEN GOING ON? (Music and Lyrics by George Gershwin and Ira Gershwin)
© 1927 (Renewed) WB Music Corp. for the United States; Chappell & Co. and New World Music Company (Ltd.) administered by WB Music Corp. for all British Reversionary Territories; New World Music Company (Ltd.), administered by WB Music Corp. for all other countries.

HUXLEY (Music by Kurt Weill, Lyrics by Ira Gershwin)
© 1941 (Renewed) Chappell & Co. and Hampshire House Publishing Corp. for the United States; Chappell & Co. for all other countries.

I CAN'T GET STARTED (Music by Vernon Duke, Lyrics by Ira Gershwin)
© 1935 (Renewed) Chappell & Co. and Ira Gershwin Music administered by WB Music Corp. for the United States; Chappell & Co. for all other countries.

I COULDN'T HOLD MY MAN (Music by Harold Arlen, Lyrics by Ira Gershwin and E. Y. Harburg)
Lyric © 1993 Ira Gershwin Music administered by WB Music Corp. and Glocca Morra Music for the United States and all other countries.

I DON'T THINK I'LL FALL IN LOVE TODAY (Music and Lyrics by George Gershwin and Ira Gershwin)
© 1928 (Renewed) WB Music Corp. for the United States; Chappell & Co. and New World Music Company (Ltd.) administered by WB Music Corp. for all British Reversionary Territories; New World Music Company (Ltd.), administered by WB Music Corp. for all other countries.

I GOT PLENTY O' NUTHIN' (from *Porgy and Bess* by George Gershwin, DuBose and Dorothy Heyward, and Ira Gershwin)
© 1935 (Renewed) George Gershwin Music, Ira Gershwin Music, and DuBose and Dorothy Heyward Memorial Fund (all administered by WB Music Corp.) for the United States; Chappell & Co. for all other countries.

I GOT RHYTHM (Music and Lyrics by George Gershwin and Ira Gershwin)
© 1930 (Renewed) WB Music Corp. for the United States; Chappell & Co. and New World Music Company (Ltd.) administered by WB Music Corp. for all British Reversionary Territories; New World Music Company (Ltd.), administered by WB Music Corp. for all other countries.

I KNOW A FOUL BALL (Music and Lyrics by George Gershwin and Ira Gershwin)
© 1987 George Gershwin Music and Ira Gershwin Music administered by WB Music Corp. for the United States and all other countries.

I WAS DOING ALL RIGHT (Music and Lyrics by George Gershwin and Ira Gershwin)
© 1937 (Renewed) George Gershwin Music and Ira Gershwin Music both administered by WB Music Corp. for the United States; Chappell & Co. for all other countries.

IF I BECAME THE PRESIDENT (Music and Lyrics by George Gershwin and Ira Gershwin)
© 1930 (Renewed) WB Music Corp. for the United States; Chappell & Co. and New World Music Company (Ltd.) administered by WB Music Corp. for all British Reversionary Territories; New World Music Company (Ltd.), administered by WB Music Corp. for all other countries.

THE ILLEGITIMATE DAUGHTER (Music and Lyrics by George Gershwin and Ira Gershwin)
© 1932 (Renewed) WB Music Corp. for the United States; Chappell & Co. and New World Music Company (Ltd.) administered by WB Music Corp. for all British Reversionary Territories; New World Music Company (Ltd.), administered by WB Music Corp. for all other countries.

I'M A POACHED EGG (Music and Lyrics by George Gershwin and Ira Gershwin)
© 1964 (Renewed) Chappell & Co. for the United States and all other countries.

I'M TICKLED SILLY (Music by Paul Lanin, Lyrics by Arthur Francis)
Lyric © 1993 Ira Gershwin administered by WB Music Corp. for the United States and all other countries.

IMAGINE ME WITHOUT MY YOU (Music by Lewis E. Gensler, Lyrics by Ira Gershwin)
© 1924 (Renewed) WB Music Corp. and Warner Bros. Inc. for the United States; Warner Bros. Inc. and New World Music Company (Ltd.), administered by WB Music Corp. for all other countries.

IN OUR UNITED STATE (Music by Burton Lane, Lyrics by Ira Gershwin)
© 1951, 1953 (Renewed) EMI Feist Catalog, Inc. as successor-in-interest for the United States and all other countries.

ISN'T IT A PITY? (Music and Lyrics by George Gershwin and Ira Gershwin)
© 1932 (Renewed) WB Music Corp. for the United States; Chappell & Co. and New World Music Company (Ltd.) administered by WB Music Corp. for all British Reversionary Territories; New World Music Company (Ltd.), administered by WB Music Corp. for all other countries.

IT AIN'T NECESSARILY SO (from *Porgy and Bess* by George Gershwin, DuBose and Dorothy Heyward, and Ira Gershwin)
© 1935 (Renewed) Geroge Gershwin Music, Ira Gershwin Music, and DuBose and Dorothy Heyward Memorial Fund (all administered by WB Music Corp.) for the United States; Chappell & Co. for all other countries.

IT LOOKS LIKE LIZA (Music by Kurt Weill, Lyrics by Ira Gershwin)
© 1941 (Renewed) Chappell & Co. and Hampshire House Publishing Corp. for the United States; Chappell & Co. for all other countries.

IT'S A NEW WORLD (Music by Harold Arlen, Lyrics by Ira Gershwin)
© (Renewed) Harwin Music Co. administered by MPL Communications and New World Music Company (Ltd.) administered by WB Music Corp. for the United States; Harwin Music Co. administered by MPL Communications for all other countries.

I'VE GOT A CRUSH ON YOU (Music and Lyrics by George Gershwin and Ira Gershwin)
© 1930 (Renewed) WB Music Corp. for the United States; Chappell & Co. and New World Music Company (Ltd.) administered by WB Music Corp. for all British Reversionary Territories; New World Music Company (Ltd.), administered by WB Music Corp. for all other countries.

JIM, CONSIDER WHAT YOU ARE DOING! (Music and Lyrics by George Gershwin and Ira Gershwin)
© 1930 (Renewed) WB Music Corp. for the United States; Chappell & Co. and New World Music Company (Ltd.) administered by WB Music Corp. for all British Reversionary Territories; New World Music Company (Ltd.), administered by WB Music Corp. for all other countries.

JUST ANOTHER RHUMBA (Music and Lyrics by George Gershwin and Ira Gershwin)
© 1937 (Renewed) George Gershwin Music and Ira Gershwin Music both administered by WB Corp. for the United States; Chappell & Co. for all other countries.

LET'S CALL THE WHOLE THING OFF (Music and Lyrics by George Gershwin and Ira Gershwin)
© 1936 (Renewed) George Gershwin Music and Ira Gershwin Music both administered by WB Corp. for the United States; Chappell & Co. for all other countries.

LET'S TAKE A WALK AROUND THE BLOCK (Music by Harold Arlen, Lyrics by Ira Gershwin and E. Y. Harburg)
© 1934 (Renewed) S. A. Music, WB Music Corp., and Glocca Morra Music for the United States; Warner Bros. Inc. and New World Music Company (Ltd.) administered by WB Music Corp. for all other countries.

LIZA (Music and Lyrics by George Gershwin and Ira Gershwin and Gus Kahn)
© 1929 (Renewed) WB Music Corp. and Gilbert Keyes Music for the United States; Chappell & Co. and New World Music Company (Ltd.) administered by WB Music Corp. for all British Reversionary Territories; New World Music Company (Ltd.), administered by WB Music Corp. for all other countries.

LONG AGO AND FAR AWAY (Music by Jerome Kern, Lyrics by Ira Gershwin)
© 1944 (Renewed) PolyGram International Publishing, Inc. for the United States and all other countries.

LOOKING FOR A BOY (Music and Lyrics by George Gershwin and Ira Gershwin)
© 1925 (Renewed) WB Music Corp. for the United States; Chappell & Co. and New World Music Company (Ltd.) administered by WB Music Corp. for all British Reversionary Territories; New World Music Company (Ltd.), administered by WB Music Corp. for all other countries.

THE LORELEI (Music and Lyrics by George Gershwin and Ira Gershwin)
© 1932 (Renewed) WB Music Corp. for the United States; Chappell & Co. and New World Music Company (Ltd.) administered by WB Music Corp. for all British Reversionary Territories; New World Music Company (Ltd.), administered by WB Music Corp. for all other countries.

LOSE THAT LONG FACE (Music by Harold Arlen, Lyrics by Ira Gershwin)
© 1954 (Renewed) Harwin Music Co. administered by MPL Communications and New World Music Company (Ltd.) administered by WB Music Corp. for the United States; Harwin Music Co. administered by MPL Communications for all other countries.

LOVE IS HERE TO STAY (Music and Lyrics by George Gershwin and Ira Gershwin)
© 1937, 1938 (Renewed) George Gershwin Music and Ira Gershwin Music both administered by WB Music Corp. for the United States; Chappell & Co. for all other countries.

LOVE IS SWEEPING THE COUNTRY (Music and Lyrics by George Gershwin and Ira Gershwin)
© 1931 (Renewed) WB Music Corp. for the United States; Chappell & Co. and New World Music Company (Ltd.) administered by WB Music Corp. for all British Reversionary Territories; New World Music Company (Ltd.), administered by WB Music Corp. for all other countries.

LOVE WALKED IN (Music and Lyrics by George Gershwin and Ira Gershwin)
© 1937 (Renewed) George Gershwin Music and Ira Gershwin Music both administered by WB Music Corp. for the United States; Chappell & Co. for all other countries.

THE MAN I LOVE (Music and Lyrics by George Gershwin and Ira Gershwin)
© 1924 (Renewed) WB Music Corp. for the United States; Chappell & Co. and New World Music Company (Ltd.) administered by WB Music Corp. for all British Reversionary Territories; New World Music Company (Ltd.), administered by WB Music Corp. for all other countries.

THE MAN THAT GOT AWAY (Music by Harold Arlen, Lyrics by Ira Gershwin)
© 1954 (Renewed) Harwin Music Co. administered by MPL Communications and New World Music Company (Ltd.) administered by WB Music Corp. for the United States; Harwin Music Co. administered by MPL Communications for all other countries.

MIDNIGHT MUSIC (Music by Jerome Kern, Lyrics by Ira Gershwin)
© 1943 (Renewed) Betty Kern Miller and Ira and Leonore Gershwin Trusts for the United States and all other countries.

MINE (Music and Lyrics by George Gershwin and Ira Gershwin)
© 1933 (Renewed) WB Music Corp. for the United States; Chappell & Co. and New World Music Company (Ltd.) administered by WB Music Corp. for all British Reversionary Territories; New World Music Company (Ltd.), administered by WB Music Corp. for all other countries.

MODERNISTIC MOE (Music by Vernon Duke, Lyrics by Ira Gershwin and Billy Rose)
Lyric © 1993 Ira Gershwin Music administered by WB Music Corp. for the United States and all other countries.

MY COUSIN IN MILWAUKEE (Music and Lyrics by George Gershwin and Ira Gershwin)
© 1932 (Renewed) WB Music Corp. for the United States; Chappell & Co. and New World Music Company (Ltd.) administered by WB Music Corp. for all British Reversionary Territories; New World Music Company (Ltd.), administered by WB Music Corp. for all other countries.

MY ONE AND ONLY HIGHLAND FLING (Music by Harry Warren, Lyrics by Ira Gershwin)
© 1948, 1949 (Renewed) Chappell & Co. and Four Jays Music Company for the United States and all other countries.

MY PARAMOUNT-PUBLIX-ROXY ROSE (Music by Harold Arlen, Lyrics by Ira Gershwin and E. Y. Harburg)
Lyric © 1993 Ira Gershwin Music administered by WB Music Corp. and Glocca Morra Music for the United States and all other countries.

MY SHIP (Music by Kurt Weill, Lyrics by Ira Gershwin)
© 1941 (Renewed) Chappell & Co. and Hampshire House Publishing Corp. for the United States; Chappell & Co. for all other countries.

NICE WORK IF YOU CAN GET IT (Music and Lyrics by George Gershwin and Ira Gershwin)
© 1937 (Renewed) George Gershwin Music and Ira Gershwin Music both administered by WB Music Corp. for the United States; Chappell & Co. for all other countries.

THE *NINA*, THE *PINTA*, THE *SANTA MARIA* (Music by Kurt Weill, Lyrics by Ira Gershwin)
© 1945 (Renewed) Chappell & Co. and Hampshire House Publishing Corp. for the United States; Chappell & Co. for all other countries.

NO *COMPRENEZ*, NO *CAPISH*, NO *VERSTEH*! (Music and Lyrics by George Gershwin and Ira Gershwin)
© 1987 (Renewed) George Gershwin Music and Ira Gershwin Music both administered by WB Music Corp. for the United States and for all other countries.

OH, BESS, OH WHERE'S MY BESS? (From *Porgy and Bess* by George Gershwin, DuBose and Dorothy Heyward, and Ira Gershwin)
© 1935 (Renewed) George Gershwin Music, Ira Gershwin Music, and DuBose and Dorothy Heyward Memorial Fund (all administered by WB Music Corp.) for the United States; Chappell & Co. for all other countries.

OH, FABULOUS ONE (Music by Kurt Weill, Lyrics by Ira Gershwin)
© 1941 (Renewed) Chappell & Co. and Hampshire House Publishing Corp. for the United States; Chappell & Co. for all other countries.

OH, LADY BE GOOD (Music and Lyrics by George Gershwin and Ira Gershwin)
© 1924 (Renewed) WB Music Corp. for the United States; Chappell & Co. and New World Music Company (Ltd.) administered by WB Music Corp. for all British Reversionary Territories; New World Music Company (Ltd.), administered by WB Music Corp. for all other countries.

OH ME! OH MY! (Music by Vincent Youmans, Lyrics by Arthur Francis)
© 1921 (Renewed) WB Music Corp. © (Renewed) Harms, Inc. assigned to WB Music Corp. for the United States and all British Reversionary Territories; New World Music Company (Ltd.), administered by WB Music Corp. and Warner Bros. Inc. for all other countries.

ONE LIFE TO LIVE (Music by Kurt Weill, Lyrics by Ira Gershwin)
© 1941 (Renewed) Chappell & Co. and Hampshire House Publishing Corp. for the United States; Chappell & Co. for all other countries.

PARDON MY ENGLISH (Music and Lyrics by George Gershwin and Ira Gershwin)
© 1993 [Ira Gershwin Music administered by] WB Music Corp. for the United States and all other countries.

PHOEBE (Music and Lyrics by George Gershwin and Ira Gershwin)
© 1993 [Ira Gershwin Music administered by] WB Music Corp., for the United States and all other countries.

PLEASE SEND MY DADDY BACK TO MY MOTHER (Music by Vernon Duke, Lyrics by Ira Gershwin)
Lyric © 1993 Ira Gershwin Music administered by WB Music Corp. for the United States and all other countries.

QUARTET EROTICA (Music by Harold Arlen, Lyrics by Ira Gershwin and E. Y. Harburg)
   Lyric © 1993 Ira Gershwin Music administered by WB Music Corp. and Glocca Morra Music for
   the United States and all other countries.

THE REAL AMERICAN FOLK SONG (IS A RAG) (Music and Lyrics by George Gershwin and Ira
   Gershwin)
   © 1959 (Renewed) Chappell & Co. for the United States and all other countries.

A RHYME FOR ANGELA (Music by Kurt Weill, Lyrics by Ira Gershwin)
   © 1945 (Renewed) Chappell & Co. and Hampshire House Publishing Corp. for the United States;
   Chappell & Co. for all other countries.

THE SAGA OF JENNY (Music by Kurt Weill, Lyrics by Ira Gershwin)
   © 1941 (Renewed) Chappell & Co. and Hampshire House Publishing Corp. for the United States;
   Chappell & Co. for all other countries.

SAM AND DELILAH (Music and Lyrics by George Gershwin and Ira Gershwin)
   © 1930 (Renewed) WB Music Corp. for the United States; Chappell & Co. and New World Music
   Company (Ltd.) administered by WB Music Corp. for all British Reversionary Territories; New
   World Music Company (Ltd.), administered by WB Music Corp. for all other countries.

THE SEARCH IS THROUGH (Music by Harold Arlen, Lyrics by Ira Gershwin)
   © 1954 (Renewed) Harwin Music Co. administered by MPL Communications and New World
   Music Company (Ltd.) administered by WB Music Corp. for the United States; Harwin Music Co.
   administered by MPL Communications for all other countries.

SHALL WE DANCE (Music and Lyrics by George Gershwin and Ira Gershwin)
   © 1937 (Renewed) George Gershwin Music and Ira Gershwin Music both administered by WB
   Music Corp. for the United States; Chappell & Co. for all other countries.

SHOES WITH WINGS ON (Music by Harry Warren, Lyrics by Ira Gershwin)
   © 1948, 1949 (Renewed) Chappell & Co. and Four Jays Music Company for the United States and
   all other countries.

THE SIMPLE LIFE (Music and Lyrics by George Gershwin and Arthur Francis)
   © 1921 (Renewed) WB Music Corp. for the United States; Chappell & Co. and New World Music
   Company (Ltd.) administered by WB Music Corp. for all British Reversionary Territories; New
   World Music Company (Ltd.), administered by WB Music Corp. for all other countries.

SING ME NOT A BALLAD (Music by Kurt Weill, Lyrics by Ira Gershwin)
   © 1945 (Renewed) Chappell & Co. and Hampshire House Publishing Corp. for the United States;
   Chappell & Co. for all other countries.

SOME GIRLS CAN BAKE A PIE (Music and Lyrics by George Gershwin and Ira Gershwin)
   © 1931 (Renewed) WB Music Corp. for the United States; Chappell & Co. and New World Music
   Company (Ltd.) administered by WB Music Corp. for all British Reversionary Territories; New
   World Music Company (Ltd.), administered by WB Music Corp. for all other countries.

SOMEONE TO WATCH OVER ME (Music and Lyrics by George Gershwin and Ira Gershwin)
   © 1926 (Renewed) WB Music Corp. for the United States; Chappell & Co. and New World Music
   Company (Ltd.) administered by WB Music Corp. for all British Reversionary Territories; New
   World Music Company (Ltd.), administered by WB Music Corp. for all other countries.

SONG OF THE RHINELAND (Music by Kurt Weill, Lyrics by Ira Gershwin)
   © 1945 (Renewed) Chappell & Co. and Hampshire House Publishing Corp. for the United States;
   Chappell & Co. for all other countries.

SONG OF THE ZODIAC (Music by Kurt Weill, Lyrics by Ira Gershwin)
   Lyric © 1993 Ira Gershwin Music administered by WB Music Corp. for the United States and all
   other countries.

SOON (Music and Lyrics by George Gershwin and Ira Gershwin)
   © 1929 (Renewed) WB Music Corp. for the United States; Chappell & Co. and New World Music
   Company (Ltd.) administered by WB Music Corp. for all British Reversionary Territories; New
   World Music Company (Ltd.), administered by WB Music Corp. for all other countries.

SOPHIA (Music and Lyrics by George Gershwin and Ira Gershwin)
© 1964 (Renewed) Chappell & Co. for the United States and all other countries.

STIFF UPPER LIP (Music and Lyrics by George Gershwin and Ira Gershwin)
© 1937 (Renewed) George Gershwin Music and Ira Gershwin Music both administered by WB Music Corp. for the United States; Chappell & Co. for all other countries.

STRIKE UP THE BAND (Music and Lyrics by George Gershwin and Ira Gershwin)
© 1927 (Renewed) WB Music Corp. for the United States; Chappell & Co. and New World Music Company (Ltd.) administered by WB Music Corp. for all British Reversionary Territories; New World Music Company (Ltd.), administered by WB Music Corp. for all other countries.

SURE THING (Music by Jerome Kern, Lyrics by Ira Gershwin)
© 1943, 1944 (Renewed) PolyGram International Publishing, Inc. for the United States and all other countries.

SWEET NEVADA (Music by Arthur Schwartz, Lyrics by Ira Gershwin)
Lyric © 1993 Ira Gershwin Music for the United States and all other countries.

SWING TROT (Music by Harry Warren, Lyrics by Ira Gershwin)
© 1948, 1949 (Renewed) Chappell & Co. and Four Jays Music Company for the United States and all other countries.

'S WONDERFUL (Music and Lyrics by George Gershwin and Ira Gershwin)
© 1927 (Renewed) WB Music Corp. for the United States; Chappell & Co. and New World Music Company (Ltd.) administered by WB Music Corp. for all British Reversionary Territories; New World Music Company (Ltd.), administered by WB Music Corp. for all other countries.

TCHAIKOWSKY (AND OTHER RUSSIANS) (Music by Kurt Weill, Lyrics by Ira Gershwin)
© 1941 (Renewed) Chappell & Co. and Hampshire House Publishing Corp. for the United States; Chappell & Co. for all other countries.

THAT CERTAIN FEELING (Music and Lyrics by George Gershwin and Ira Gershwin)
© 1925 (Renewed) WB Music Corp. for the United States; Chappell & Co. and New World Music Company (Ltd.) administered by WB Music Corp. for all British Reversionary Territories; New World Music Company (Ltd.), administered by WB Music Corp. for all other countries.

THERE'S A BOAT DAT'S LEAVIN' SOON FOR NEW YORK (from *Porgy and Bess* by George Gershwin, DuBose and Dorothy Heyward, and Ira Gershwin)
© 1935 (Renewed) Geroge Gershwin Music, Ira Gershwin Music, and DuBose and Dorothy Heyward Memorial Fund (all administered by WB Music Corp.) for the United States; Chappell & Co. for all other countries.

THESE CHARMING PEOPLE (Music and Lyrics by George Gershwin and Ira Gershwin)
© 1925 (Renewed) WB Music Corp. for the United States; Chappell & Co. and New World Music Company (Ltd.) administered by WB Music Corp. for all British Reversionary Territories; New World Music Company (Ltd.), administered by WB Music Corp. for all other countries.

THEY ALL LAUGHED (Music and Lyrics by George Gershwin and Ira Gershwin)
© 1936 (Renewed) George Gershwin Music and Ira Gershwin Music both administered by WB Music Corp. for the United States; Chappell & Co. for all other countries.

THEY CAN'T TAKE THAT AWAY FROM ME (Music and Lyrics by George Gershwin and Ira Gershwin)
© 1936 (Renewed) George Gershwin Music and Ira Gershwin Music both administered by WB Music Corp. for the United States; Chappell & Co. for all other countries.

THINGS! (Music by Harold Arlen, Lyrics by Ira Gershwin and E. Y. Harburg)
© 1937 (Renewed) S. A. Music, Ira Gershwin Music administered by WB Music Corp. and Glocca Morra Music for the United States; Warner Bros. Inc. and Ira Gershwin Music administered by WB Music Corp. for all other countries.

THINGS ARE LOOKING UP (Music and Lyrics by George Gershwin and Ira Gershwin)
© 1937 (Renewed) George Gershwin Music and Ira Gershwin Music both administered by WB Music Corp. for the United States; Chappell & Co. for all other countries.

THIS IS NEW (Music by Kurt Weill, Lyrics by Ira Gershwin)
© 1941 (Renewed) Chappell & Co. and Hampshire House Publishing Corp. for the United States; Chappell & Co. for all other countries.

UH-UH (Music by Milton Schwarzwald, Lyrics by Marc Connelly, George S. Kaufman and Ira Gershwin)
© 1924 (Renewed) WB Music Corp. and Warner Bros. Inc. for the United States; Warner Bros. Inc. and New World Music Company (Ltd.), administered by WB Music Corp. for all other countries.

UNION SQUARE (Music and Lyrics by George Gershwin and Ira Gershwin)
© 1933 (Renewed) WB Music Corp. for the United States; Chappell & Co. and New World Music Company (Ltd.) administered by WB Music Corp. for all British Reversionary Territories; New World Music Company (Ltd.), administered by WB Music Corp. for all other countries. Additional material © 1987 George Gershwin Music and Ira Gershwin Music both administered by Warner Bros. Music for the United States and all other countries.

THE UNOFFICIAL SPOKESMAN (Music and Lyrics by George Gershwin and Ira Gershwin)
© 1930 (Renewed) WB Music Corp. for the United States; Chappell & Co. and New World Music Company (Ltd.) administered by WB Music Corp. for all British Reversionary Territories; New World Music Company (Ltd.), administered by WB Music Corp. for all other countries.

WAITING FOR THE SUN TO COME OUT (Music and Lyrics by George Gershwin and Arthur Francis)
© 1920 (Renewed) WB Music Corp. for the United States; Chappell & Co. and New World Music Company (Ltd.) administered by WB Music Corp. for all British Reversionary Territories; New World Music Company (Ltd.), administered by WB Music Corp. for all other countries.

WHAT CAN YOU SAY IN A LOVE SONG? (Music by Harold Arlen, Lyrics by Ira Gershwin and E. Y. Harburg)
© 1934 (Renewed) S. A. Music, WB Music Corp., and Glocca Morra Music for the United States; Warner Bros. Inc. and New World Music Company (Ltd.) for all other countries.

WHAT CAUSES THAT? (Music and Lyrics by George Gershwin and Ira Gershwin)
© 1987 George Gershwin Music and Ira Gershwin Music both administered by WB Music Corp. for the United States and all other countries.

WHILE WE'RE WAITING FOR THE BABY (Music and Lyrics by George Gershwin and Ira Gershwin)
© 1993 administered by WB Music Corp. for the United States and all other countries.

WHO CARES? (Music and Lyrics by George Gershwin and Ira Gershwin)
© 1931 (Renewed) WB Music Corp. for the United States; Chappell & Co. and New World Music Company (Ltd.) administered by WB Music Corp. for all British Reversionary Territories; New World Music Company (Ltd.), administered by WB Music Corp. for all other countries.

WINTERGREEN FOR PRESIDENT (Music and Lyrics by George Gershwin and Ira Gershwin)
© 1933 (Renewed) New World Music for the United States; Chappell & Co. and New World Music Company (Ltd.) administered by WB Music Corp. for all British Reversionary Territories; New World Music Company (Ltd.), administered by WB Music Corp. for all other countries.

WORDS WITHOUT MUSIC (Music by Vernon Duke, Lyrics by Ira Gershwin)
© 1935 (Renewed) Chappell & Co. and Ira Gershwin Music administered by WB Music Corp. for the United States; Chappell & Co. for all other countries.

YOU KNOW HOW IT IS (Music and Lyrics by George Gershwin and Ira Gershwin)
© 1993 administered by WB Music Corp. for the United States and all other countries.

YOU MAY THROW ALL THE RICE YOU DESIRE (Lyric by Ira Gershwin)
© 1973, 1993 Ira Gershwin Music administered by WB Music Corp. for the United States and all other countries.

YOU'RE A BUILDER-UPPER (Music by Harold Arlen, Lyrics by Ira Gershwin and E. Y. Harburg)
© 1934 (Renewed) S. A. Music, WB Music Corp., and Glocca Morra Music for the United States; Warner Bros. Inc. and New World Company (Ltd.) Administered by WB Music Corp. for all other countries.

Lyrics On Several Occasions by Ira Gershwin © 1959 (Renewed) Ira and Leonore Gershwin Trusts.

Index